Teen Finance Series

College Financing Information For Teens, Third Edition

Teen Finance Series

College Financing Information For Teens, Third Edition

Tips For A Successful Financial Life

Including Facts About Planning, Saving, And Paying For Postsecondary Education. With Information About College Savings Plans, Grants, Loans, Scholarships, Community And Military Service, And More

OMNIGRAPHICS
615 Griswold, Ste. 901
Detroit, MI 48226

Bibliographic Note

Because this page cannot legibly accommodate all the copyright notices, the Bibliographic Note portion of the Preface constitutes an extension of the copyright notice.

* * *

Omnigraphics
a part of Relevant Information
Keith Jones, *Managing Editor*

* * *

Library of Congress Cataloging-in-Publication Data

Title: College financing information for teens: tips for a successful financial life: including facts about planning, saving, and paying for postsecondary education, with information about college savings plans, grants, loans, scholarships, community and military service, and more.

Description: Third edition. | Detroit, MI: Omnigraphics, [2017] | Series: Teen finance series | Includes bibliographical references and index.

Identifiers: LCCN 2017000513 (print) | LCCN 2017009330 (ebook) | ISBN 9780780815476 (hardcover: alk. paper) | ISBN 9780780815483 (ebook) | ISBN 9780780815483 (eBook)

Subjects: LCSH: College costs--United States. | Student aid--United States. | Finance, Personal--United States.

Classification: LCC LB2342 .C63316 2017 (print) | LCC LB2342 (ebook) | DDC 378.3/8--dc23

LC record available at https://lccn.loc.gov/2017000513

Table Of Contents

Preface

Part One: Preparing For College

Chapter 1——Assessing Yourself And Your Future 3

Chapter 2——Deciding On Postsecondary Educational
Options 9

Chapter 3——Getting Ready For College.. 17

Chapter 4——Taking College Preparatory Courses 25

Chapter 5——Importance Of Extracurricular Activities 29

Chapter 6——Taking Standardized Tests 33

Part Two: Your Role As An Education Consumer

Chapter 7——The Value Of Education.. 39

Chapter 8——Understanding College Costs.. 43

Chapter 9——Traditional College Options 49

Chapter 10—Online Education And MOOCs (Massive
Open Online Course) 57

Chapter 11—Searching For A College... 61

Chapter 12—Choosing A College.. 67

Chapter 13—Study Abroad.. 79

Part Three: Saving For College

Chapter 14—Reasons To Save For College 91

Chapter 15—Ways To Save For College 95

Chapter 16—Budgeting 101

Chapter 17—Section 529 Plans 113

Chapter 18—Coverdell Education Savings Accounts....................... 121

Chapter 19—Custodial Accounts.. 129

Chapter 20—Working During College 133

Part Four: Financial Aid And The Federal Government

Chapter 21—An Overview Of Federal Aid For Students................. 139

Chapter 22—Applying For Federal Student Aid........................... 143

Chapter 23—Estimating And Calculating Aid 149

Chapter 24—Understanding The Expected Family
Contribution (EFC) 153

Chapter 25—Accepting And Receiving Aid 163

Chapter 26—Federal Education Grants 167

Chapter 27—Federal Pell Grants And Federal
Supplemental Educational Opportunity
Grant (FSEOG) 175

Chapter 28—TEACH Grant... 179

Chapter 29—Federal Versus Private Loans 185

Chapter 30—Federal Student Loans... 189

Chapter 31—Subsidized And Unsubsidized Loans
And Entrance Counseling 195

Chapter 32—Repaying Federal Student Loans............................. 199

Chapter 33—Deferring (Postponing) Repayment Of
Federal Student Loans... 203

Chapter 34—Loan Cancellation (Forgiveness) Of Federal
Student Loans... 209

Chapter 35—Loan Servicers 215

Chapter 36—Federal Work-Study And Education For
         Unemployed Workers Programs.....................221

Chapter 37—Education Tax Credits 225

Part Five: Other Sources Of Financial Aid

Chapter 38—Finding And Applying For A Scholarship 237

Chapter 39—Avoiding Scholarship Scams...........................241

Chapter 40—The Nursing Scholarship Program......................247

Chapter 41—The National Health Service Corps
         Scholarship 257

Chapter 42—College-Bound Athletes 264

Chapter 43—College Funding For Disadvantaged
         Students And Students With Disabilities.................268

Chapter 44—Institutional Education Grants........................272

Chapter 45—Private Education Loans 275

Chapter 46—AmeriCorps Education Awards 279

Chapter 47—The Peace Corps And Leadership
         Experience 286

Chapter 48—Military Service And Education Benefits..................299

Part Six: If You Need More Information

Chapter 49—Directory Of Financial Aid Resources.........................307

Chapter 50—Directory Of State Higher Education
         Agencies...313

Index 331

Preface

About This Book

The costs associated with pursuing a college degree continues to put increasing financial strain on middle-class families across the country. According to figures from the federal government's National Center for Education Statistics, between 2004–05 and 2014–15, prices for undergraduate tuition, fees, room, and board at public institutions rose 33 percent, and prices at private nonprofit institutions rose 26 percent, after adjustment for inflation. As a result, parents and students alike are experiencing sticker shock like never before when adding up all of the costs associated with higher education. And while there are any number of financial options now available to prospective students such as grants, private and public loans, and scholarships many teens are feeling overwhelmed by the idea of going to college. The entire process, from taking the right tests in high school to making sure one gets enough financial aid, can be confusing. Many teens find themselves in a state of bewilderment when considering the vast amount of information they need to absorb in order to plan, pay for, and attend college.

College Financing Information For Teens, Third Edition, provides information about planning, paying and option available for a postsecondary education. It explains college costs and describes practical steps middle and high school students can take to begin to prepare themselves for meeting future challenges. It discusses the process of choosing among different types of colleges and vocational schools and describes the procedures involved in applying for and receiving federal financial aid. A separate section discusses alternative sources of aid, including scholarships, institutional grants, private loans, and aid associated with community service, military service, athletic pursuits, and careers in healthcare. The book concludes with directories of resources for additional information.

How To Use This Book

This book is divided into parts and chapters. Parts focus on broad areas of interest; chapters are devoted to single topics within a part.

Part One: Preparing for College addresses middle and high school students who may be wondering about postsecondary education. It explains the benefits of self-assessment in helping decide on postsecondary educational options. Key steps for getting ready for college such as college preparatory courses and extracurricular activities are discussed. The part concludes with a discussions of the various types of standardized tests a student needs to take when applying for college admission.

Part Two: Your Role As An Education Consumer begins by making a case for the value of education. It provides information to help students understand the vast array of choices they will face when making decisions about higher education, and explains the various costs involved in pursuing a college education. It talks about traditional college options as well as online education options such as Massive Open Online Courses (MOOCs). Searching for and choosing a college is also discussed. The part concludes with information on studying abroad.

Part Three: Saving For College talks about reasons to save for college, and answers questions about various tools and plans available to help families budget and save for future college expenses. It provides information on various college saving plans such as Section 529, and Coverdale Educations Savings Accounts. It also considers the advantages and disadvantages of working during college.

Part Four: Financial Aid And The Federal Government discusses the process of applying for federal financial aid and explores the three types of federal aid: grants, loans, and work-study. It discusses the process of estimating and calculating aid, accepting and receiving aid, the student's options for repaying federal loans, and the circumstances under which a loan can be deferred (postponed) or cancelled (forgiven). It provides information about loan servicers, and concludes with a discussion of federal tax credits for postsecondary education.

Part Five: Other Sources Of Financial Aid discusses aid that is available from private sources (such as scholarships and institutional loans) and government service (such as the military, the Peace Corps, and AmeriCorps). It also talks about finding and applying for scholarships and avoiding scholarship scams. The part concludes with information on other sources of financial aid specifically for students with specialized interests or needs, athletes, nurses, and those with disabilities.

Part Six: If You Need More Information offers a directory of financial aid resources, including federal and national student aid organizations, online scholarship search services, and other resources for information about planning for higher education. A separate directory of state higher education agencies will help students seeking to locate additional resources within their state of residence or the state in which they plan to attend college.

Bibliographic Note

This volume contains documents and excerpts from publications issued by the following government agencies: Corporation for National and Community Service (CNCS); EducationUSA; Federal Student Aid; Federal Trade Commission (FTC); Health Resources and Services Administration (HRSA); Internal Revenue Service (IRS); National Center For Education Statistics (NCES); Office of Management and Budget (OMB); Peace Corps; U.S. Department of Education (ED); U.S. Department of Homeland Security (DHS); U.S. Department of State (DOS); U.S. Department of Veterans Affairs (VA); and U.S. Securities and Exchange Commission (SEC).

It may also contain original material produced by Omnigraphics.

The photograph on the front cover is © elenaleonova/iStock.

Part One
Preparing For College

Chapter 1
Assessing Yourself And Your Future

If someone were to ask you how a well a friend would handle a particular situation, you'd probably be able to use what you know about the person to give an opinion on their future behavior. But humans aren't really very good at assessing themselves. So, often, when we need to make decisions about our own futures we have trouble following that same process.

But we're often faced with the need to make important, potentially life-altering decisions, such as what college to attend, what major to choose, and what career to pursue. And in those cases, the best way to proceed is to conduct an honest assessment of our talents, past performance, values and interests in order to make informed choices. Fortunately, you don't have to go it alone. There are numerous avenues of assistance available, both formal and informal, to help you conduct a meaningful self-assessment.

How Assessment Can Help

It's important to realize that self-assessment can't make decisions for you. Rather, it's a guide that provides insight and gives you some things to think about as you plan for the future.

Among other benefits, assessment can:

- help identify your skills and areas of interest

- highlight your learning style and the way you do your best work

- point out areas where you need more training or experience

- help you learn about educational or occupational opportunities that will suit you best

- get you to consider new courses of study or career paths

> Self-assessment can not only help identify educational programs and careers that align with your talents and interests, it can also pinpoint areas for improvement and guide you toward programs and occupations that you might want to pursue.

On the other hand, don't expect assessment to:

- guarantee that a given educational or career path will be open to you

- ensure that you'll like any given program or occupation

- predict how well you'll succeed

Getting Started

To begin a self-assessment there are a few questions you can ask yourself that might help get you into the process:

- **What am I good at?**

  Often we think we know what we can do, but sometimes we overlook skills we've developed through the years. To help jog your memory, ask yourself such questions as:

  - In which classes do I get the best grades?

  - In what parts of specific classes (such as labs or team projects) do I do best?

  - At what extracurricular activities do I think I excel?

  - How good am I at tasks that require manual dexterity?

  - How well do I envision and implement solutions to problems?

  - Have I gotten good responses to oral presentations?

- **What do I enjoy?**

  To help determine your areas of interest, ask yourself questions such as:

  - What classes do I like?

  - What do I do well?

- When I'm reading or watching TV, what topics draw my attention?

- What types of things am I doing when you lose track of time?

- How do I spend my spare time?

- Among people I know, who do I think has the most interesting job?

- **What is important to me?**

In addition to areas where you excel or those you enjoy, don't forget to take into account things that you feel strongly about. Some items to consider:

- Do I feel best when I work alone or with a group?

- Do I prefer difficult challenges or more frequent accomplishments?

- How much time do I invest in physical activity?

- Am I a risk-taker, or do I prefer security?

- Does competition drive me or discourage me?

- Is it important for me to be a leader?

To begin a self-assessment there are a few questions you can ask yourself that might help get you into the process:

- **What am I good at?**

Often we think we know what we can do, but sometimes we overlook skills we've developed through the years. To help jog your memory, ask yourself such questions as:

- In which classes do I get the best grades?

- In what parts of specific classes (such as labs or team projects) do I do best?

- At what extracurricular activities do I think I excel?

- How good am I at tasks that require manual dexterity?

- How well do I envision and implement solutions to problems?

- Have I gotten good responses to oral presentations?

- **What do I enjoy?**

To help determine your areas of interest, ask yourself questions such as:

- What classes do I like?

- What do I do well?

- When I'm reading or watching TV, what topics draw my attention?

- What types of things am I doing when you lose track of time?

- How do I spend my spare time?

- Among people I know, who do I think has the most interesting job?

- **What is important to me?**

  In addition to areas where you excel or those you enjoy, don't forget to take into account things that you feel strongly about. Some items to consider:

  - Do I feel best when I work alone or with a group?

  - Do I prefer difficult challenges or more frequent accomplishments?

  - How much time do I invest in physical activity?

  - Am I a risk-taker, or do I prefer security?

  - Does competition drive me or discourage me?

  - Is it important for me to be a leader?

Assessment Tools

The above series of questions is just a way of beginning to think about the assessment process. The best way to proceed is to complete a series of questionnaires and exercises specifically developed by experts to identify skills, personality types, values, areas of interest, and other factors that go into decision-making. Some of these include:

- **Myers–Briggs Type Indicator.** This well-known 93-question test, which has been around for many years, helps identify your basic personality type, which can be useful in choosing an educational or career path.

- **Strong Interest Inventory.** Developed by a psychologist named Strong, this inventory consists of almost 300 items, to which you indicate the strength of your reaction. The results are then compared to those of people happily employed in various occupations, giving you an idea of areas to investigate further.

- **Strengths Quest.** This 30-minute online assessment helps identify your current strengths in a variety of areas—and the personal characteristics behind them—and relates them to the development of educational and career strategies.

Today most schools have computerized assessment programs available that can help point you to information about degree programs, financial aid, and career paths. Check with your guidance counselor for details.

But these tools are just some of the more well-known tips of the iceberg. There are numerous other formal assessment tools, some of which may be more appropriate for you. A school guidance counselor or career counselor can help you explore other means of conducting an effective self-assessment. There are also a large number of online resources available to students planning their future educational or vocational paths, many of which can be found on college and university websites. Exploring some of these may provide some extra insight and trigger some ideas.

References

1. "Assessing Yourself And Exploring Career And Educational Options," University of Minnesota Duluth, 2007.

2. "Career Choice Requires Self-Assessment," School Guides, n.d.

3. Pelusi, Nando, Ph.D. "Assessing Yourself, Honestly," *Psychology Today*, June 9, 2016.

4. "Researching Occupations," College of the Rockies, n.d.

Chapter 2

Deciding On Postsecondary Educational Options

First Steps Toward College

Are you thinking about college or a career school? (a school, such as a vocational or trade school, that offers programs of study that take two years or less to complete.) Don't wait any longer. Start asking questions now. Talk to your teachers, your parents, your older siblings, or to other mentors. After all, it's your future.

When Should I Begin Thinking About College?

It is never too early to plan for college. You may want to start thinking about the possibilities now, but you definitely should begin seriously thinking about college when you enter the middle school grades (6th through 8th grade).

"College" means

- public and private four-year colleges and universities,
- two-year community colleges or junior colleges, and
- career schools.

What Type Of School Would Be Just Right For You?

Answer the following questions to help you create your dream school.

1. Where would this college be located (state, city)?

_____

About This Chapter: This chapter includes text excerpted from "My Future, My Way," Federal Student Aid, U.S. Department of Education (ED), April 2014.

2. What size would the school be?

3. What classes would you take (computer, theater)?

4. What types of social activities would be offered (sports, clubs)?

About Four-Year Colleges

Many students attend a four-year college after graduating from high school. They earn a degree once they have completed a program of study. A four-year college usually offers a bachelor's degree in the arts (e.g., English, history, drama) or sciences (e.g., biology, computer science, engineering). Some four-year colleges offer advanced degrees such as a master's or other graduate degree.

About Two-Year Colleges

A two-year community college or junior college awards an associate degree once a student has completed a two-year course of study. Some two-year colleges grant diplomas or certificates to students who have met course requirements and are ready to practice in their career fields.

You can start at a two-year college then transfer to a four-year college if, for example, you're concerned about college costs (community or public junior colleges usually cost less than four-year colleges). A two-year college is also a good option if you want to boost your grades before going to a four-year college.

About Career Schools

Career schools typically offer programs that take two years or less to complete. These schools provide students with formal classes and hands-on experiences related to their future career interests. Students may earn a diploma or a certificate, prepare for a licensing exam, or study to begin work as an apprentice or a journeyman in a skilled trade.

Why Think About College Now?

As a middle-school student, you probably have a lot on your mind: Will I get my school project finished on time? What's for dinner? What should I do this weekend? Will mom or dad notice that I went over my text messaging limit (yikes!!)?

But Have You Seriously Thought About College?

Here are some reasons why you should start thinking about college now.

1. The steps you take now (such as developing good study habits; reading to develop your verbal, writing, and critical thinking skills; and developing an interest in extra-curricular/community based activities) will help determine your college options later. Start planning now!

2. If no one in your family ever went to college—Be the first! Set a good example for others to follow by learning new and interesting things, and talking to other students and faculty members about career goals and opportunities.

3. The U.S. Department of Education (ED), Federal Student Aid (FSA) and others, can help meet the cost! Almost two-thirds of college students get some type of financial aid.

Myths Vs. Reality

Myth: Only students with good grades go to college.

Reality: Good grades and high test scores can definitely help when applying to college. But college admissions staff also take into account other things, such as your interests, hobbies, and school- and community-based extracurricular activities.

Myth: College will be the same as middle or high school.

Reality: College is much different from middle or high school. Making new friends, choosing your own classes and program of study, and possibly living away from home are all a part of the college experience.

Myth: I need to get a job as soon as I graduate from high school.

Reality: Sure, you can get a job with decent pay after your high school graduation. Or you can invest in your education to have a great career with better pay later!

Myth: I can't go to college because I don't know what I want to do with my life.

Reality: Most students decide what they want to do during or after college.

What Can A College Education Do For Me?

A college education will offer you more money, more job opportunities, and more freedom than a high school education.

More Money

On average, a person who goes to college earns more money than a person who doesn't. Over a lifetime, a college graduate can earn over $1.5 million more than a high school graduate!

Real-Life Examples

People with a college education typically earn more money during a shorter span of time.

Buying Groceries

- Terry is a dental hygienist (two years of college). Terry generally will earn enough money to buy groceries for a week after working only one day.
- Sam is a high school graduate and works as a salesperson in a department store. To buy the same groceries, it generally takes Sam three days' pay.

Buying a TV

- Jamie is a college graduate and works as an accountant. Based on his salary, Jamie could buy a large screen TV using less than two weeks' pay.
- Chris never went to college and works as a waiter. Based on his salary, Chris will have to work five weeks to buy the same TV.

More Job Opportunities

A major benefit of a college degree is having more jobs to choose from Table 2.1 shows just some of the possibilities available to college graduates.

Table 2.1. List Of Careers

Career School	Two-Year College	Four-Year College	More Than Four Years
Barber or Hairstylist	Book-keeper	Accountant	Archaeologist
Carpenter	Childcare worker	Athletic trainer	Architect
Disc Jockey (deejay)	Computer and office equipment repairer	Computer Programmer	Astronaut or aerospace engineer
Electrician	Dental hygienist	Conservation Scientist	College Professor
Plumber	Firefighter*	Engineer	Dentist
	Mechanic	FBI agent	Doctor
	Nurse*	Graphic Designer	Judge
	Paralegal	High School Coach	Lawyer
	Physical therapist assistant	Insurance Agent	Minister, Priest, or Rabbi
	Restaurant manager**	Pilot	Pharmacist

Table 2.1. Continued

Career School	Two-Year College	Four-Year College	More Than Four Years
	Zookeeper*	Police Officer	Principal
		Reporter	Psychologist
		Social Worker	Scientist
		Sportcaster/news reporter	Urban Planner
		Teacher***	Veterinarian
		Writer	

*Note: You can also train for these jobs at a four-year college. Why do that? Because more education usually means more earnings!

**Note: You don't need a two-year degree to be a manager, but managers with a degree may get hired faster and earn more money during their careers.

***Note: Teaching in K–12 often requires certification and thus more than a bachelor's degree; teaching college usually requires a master's and/or doctoral degree.

More Freedom

As a college student, you'll experience freedom as you never have before, by

- studying more on your own instead of in a classroom;

- meeting people from all over the country and world;

- studying abroad (it pays to learn a foreign language); and

- choosing your own unique courses, such as Biology of Extinct Animals, Music and Your Brain, Television in American Culture, forensic science, or computer graphics.

Where Do I Start?

Part of preparing for college is taking the right classes in middle school. Courses such as English, algebra, foreign language, and technology will better prepare you for more challenging courses in high school. But college preparation is about more than just classes and grades. It's also about developing the skills (such as good study habits, paying attention in class, and reading) that will help you succeed in college and life.

Who Can Help Me Go To College?

College Support Team

Getting ready for college may seem like a lot to handle, but you don't have to do it alone! Parents, teachers, counselors, coaches, and friendly folks from your community or place of worship are all good people to go to if you have questions. Think of them as your college support team. Any adult with whom you have a connection is a good addition to your college support team. If they don't have the answers themselves, they may know where to look.

Talk To Your Team: Tell Someone You Know That You Want to Go!

Start discussing your plans for college today with your family and with people at school. They will not know you need support and encouragement unless you let them in on your plans. Once everyone knows the plan, you can work together to reach your college goals.

How Will I Pay For College?

College Costs

When it comes to college costs, remember

- Some colleges cost less than other colleges.

- Lots of financial aid is available—there are more opportunities now than ever before!

- You and your family have time to start saving for college. So start looking into college savings plans, if you have not already done so.

The bottom line is that if you want to go to college and are willing to work at it, you can find the money to pay for it. While it's very important that your family prepare financially for college (save, save, save!), don't forget—you don't have to pay for college all by yourself!

What Is Financial Aid?

Financial aid is money to help pay for college or career school. This money can come from the U.S. government, the state where you live, or the college you attend. But, remember, you have to apply for it!

Types Of Aid

There are two basic types of financial aid:

1. "Gift" aid: money that does not have to be paid back (for example, grants and scholarships)

2. "Self-help" aid: money that you work for or that you will need to pay back later (for example, work-study or loans)

More About Scholarships

Scholarships may pay for all or part of your education. Unlike most federal student aid, many scholarships are not "need-based" (i.e., aid awarded to a student on the basis of financial need) and are available for all kinds of students based on

- good grades;

- certain religious, ethnic, or cultural backgrounds; or

- athletic, artistic, or creative abilities.

A number of businesses and community organizations offer scholarships. Some colleges also have special scholarships for incoming students. Students who receive scholarships generally have to maintain a certain grade point average or GPA. There are tons of scholarships out there. The most important thing is to find out what your options are. Keep in mind that no scholarship is too small!

Another Way To Pay For College: Serving Our Country

When you serve our country—during or after college—there are opportunities for aid that will cover either some or all of your educational costs:

- AmeriCorps—this nonmilitary community-service program provides help with college costs and student loans to members who successfully complete service.

- U.S. service academies—the U.S. Air Force, U.S. Army, U.S. Coast Guard, U.S. Merchant Marine, and U.S. Navy provide free education for students who commit to serve in the military upon completion of their education.

- Reserve Officer Training Corps (ROTC)—this campus-based program offers scholarships in varying sizes to students interested in serving in the military after college.

- GI Bill—men and women who enlist and serve in the armed forces may apply for and receive financial support for college.

Next Steps

Take the next steps in learning about education beyond high school and learning how to pay for it!

- Start saving a portion of your allowance, birthday money, and any other money you receive for college. No matter how much or how little you save, every cent makes a difference in affording your higher education!

- Stay in touch with members of your college support team. Routinely discuss with them your college and career plans.

- Visit StudentAid.gov/early for additional information and resources.

- If you have an older brother or sister either already in college or getting ready to attend, talk with them about their experiences and expectations. Don't be afraid to ask questions. You can gain from their knowledge.

- Check out StudentAid.gov/resources to find our latest fact sheets, infographics, and other publications about financial aid.

Five Important Questions About Paying For College

Please discuss the following questions related to funding your education beyond high school with your guidance counselor.

1. What scholarships are available in my state or school district?

2. How can my grades affect my financial aid opportunities?

3. Why should I fill out a FAFSA® when I'm a high school senior?

4. What else can I do to learn about financial aid opportunities?

5. How can I discuss paying for college with my family or college support team?

Chapter 3
Getting Ready For College

Preparing For College

Thinking about college, career, technical, or trade school, or graduate school? There's so much to consider when it comes to getting ready for college: where to go, what to study, how to apply, how to pay for it all, and more.

It's never too early—or too late—to explore your options for college or career school. The chapter explains some key steps in preparing for college and provide resources that can help you along the way.

Why Go To College?

Here's a simple equation: a college or career school education = more money, more job options, and more freedom. As you'll see from the figure below, as you get more education, you'll make more money and have more job opportunities. A college education is a long-term investment. With careful planning you can find the school and funding options that work best for your situation and put you on the path to success.

Exploring Your Career Options

A college or career school education can give you the skills needed to pursue a career that really interests you. Love working with animals? Or how about computers?

About This Chapter: Text beginning with the heading "Preparing For College" is excerpted from "Prepare For College," Federal Student Aid, U.S. Department of Education (ED), January 20, 2017; Text under the heading "Your To-Do List" is excerpted from "College Preparation Checklist," Federal Student Aid, U.S. Department of Education (ED), July 2016.

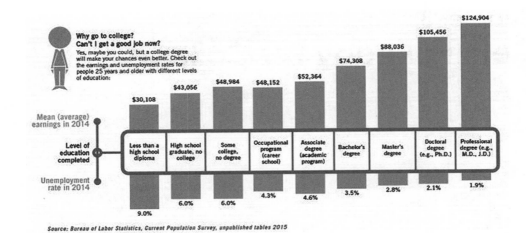

Figure 3.1. Levels Of Education And Mean Earnings And Unemployment Rate

Checklists To Help You Get Ready Financially And Academically

Whether you're in highschool now, in elementary or middle school, out of school, or perhaps never finished school, there are a number of steps you can take to get "college ready." The checklists in the chapter will explain steps you can take to find and get into the college or career school that's right for you and to get ready to pay.

Choosing A school

You have a variety of college options, from two-year community and junior colleges, to four-year colleges and universities, to technical, vocational, and trade schools. Get tips on things to consider when you're choosing a school, and use college search tools to find a school that matches your interests, career goals, and financial situation.

Taking Required Tests

You may be required to take certain tests when you apply to college or graduate school.

Applying To Schools

Each college, career school, or graduate school has its own admission requirements. We provide some tips and information as you get ready to apply to school.

Learning About Budgeting

Learn what a budget is and how it can help you stay on track with your goals during and after college.

Your To-Do List

Elementary School

- Do your best in school.
- Read a lot.
- Have fun learning!

Junior High Or Middle School

- Think about college as an important part of your future. Discuss your thoughts and ideas with your family and with people at school.
- Start saving for college if you haven't already.
- Take challenging and interesting classes to prepare for high school.
- Ask your parent or guardian to help you research which high schools or special programs will most benefit your interests.
- Develop strong study habits.
- Do your best in school and on standardized tests. If you are having difficulty, don't give up—get help from a teacher, tutor, or mentor.
- Become involved in school- or community-based activities that let you explore your interests and learn new things.
- Speak with adults, such as your teacher, school counselor or librarian, relatives, or family friends, who you think have interesting jobs. Ask them what they like about their job and what education they needed for it.

- Begin taking advanced courses such as Algebra I and a beginning foreign language class. (But, remember, take only the most difficult courses you can handle.)
- Start reading magazines or newspaper articles.
- Keep a journal to develop good writing skills.

(Source: "My Future, My Way," Federal Student Aid, U.S. Department of Education (ED).)

High School

- Work with a parent to estimate your potential financial aid using *FAFSA4caster* at fafsa. gov, and continue to save for college.

- Take challenging classes in core academic subjects. Most colleges require four years of English, at least three years of social studies (history, civics, geography, economics, etc.), three years of math, and three years of science. Many require two years of a foreign language. Round out your course load with classes in computer science and the arts.

- Stay involved in school- or community-based activities that interest you or let you explore career interests. Consider working or volunteering. Remember that it's quality—not quantity—that counts.

- Talk to your school counselor and other mentors about education after high school. Your counselor can answer questions about what classes to take in high school, how to sign up for standardized tests, and where to get money for college.

- Keep doing your best in school—study hard, earn good grades, and participate in class.
- Ask your counselor about challenging and interesting courses you can take in high school.

(Source: "My Future, My Way," Federal Student Aid, U.S. Department of Education (ED).)

9th Grade

- Talk to your school counselor or teachers about Advanced Placement courses. Find out what courses are available, whether you are eligible, and how to enroll in them.

- Use the career search at StudentAid.gov/careersearch to research your career options.

- Make a list of your awards, honors, extracurricular activities, and paid and volunteer work. Consider participating in academic enrichment programs, summer workshops, and camps with specialty focuses such as music, arts, or science.

10th Grade

- Meet with your school counselor or mentor to discuss colleges and their admissions requirements.

- Consider taking a practice Preliminary Scholastic Assessment Test (PSAT)/National Merit Scholarship Qualifying Test (PSAT/NMSQT®) or PSAT™ 10, or the PreACT™.

- Plan to use your summer wisely: Work, volunteer, or take a summer course (away from home or at a local college).

- Go to career information events.

- Research majors that might be a good match with your interests and goals. Consider what fits well with your results from the career search at StudentAid.gov/careersearch.

11th Grade

...All Year

- Explore careers and their earning potential with the *Occupational Outlook Handbook* search tool at www.bls.gov/oco.

- Learn about choosing a college (and find a link to our free college search tool) at StudentAid.gov/prepare-for-college/choosing-schools.

- Go to college fairs and college-preparation presentations hosted by college representatives

...Fall

- Take the PSAT/NMSQT.* You must take the test in 11th grade to qualify for scholarships and programs associated with the National Merit Scholarship Program.

...Spring

- Register for and take exams for college admission.* The tests that many colleges require are the Scholastic Assessment Test (SAT), the SAT Subject Tests, and the American College Testing (ACT). Check with the colleges you are interested in to see what tests they require.

- Use the free scholarship search tool at StudentAid.gov/scholarships to find scholarships for which you might want to apply. Some deadlines fall as early as the summer between 11th and 12th grades, so prepare now to submit applications soon.

REMEMBER: Register for all tests in advance, and be sure to give yourself time to prepare appropriately! If you have difficulty paying a registration fee, ask your school counselor about getting the fee waived.

Summer Before 12th Grade

- Create a username and password called an FSA ID that you'll use to confirm your identity when accessing your government financial aid information and electronically signing your federal student aid documents. You and your parent will each need your own unique FSA ID. Learn about the FSA ID, and create yours, at StudentAid.gov /fsaid. Note: You must create your own FSA ID; if your parent creates it for you, that'll cause confusion later and will slow down the financial aid application process.

- Narrow down the list of colleges you are considering attending. If you can, visit the schools that interest you.

- Contact colleges to request information and applications for admission. Ask about financial aid, admission requirements, and deadlines.

- Decide whether you are going to apply under a particular college's early decision or early action program. Be sure to learn about the program's deadlines and requirements.

- Apply for scholarships. Your goal is to minimize the amount of loan funds you borrow so you have less to pay back later.

12th Grade

...All Year

- Work hard all the way to graduation—second-semester grades can affect scholarship eligibility.

- Stay involved in after-school activities, and seek leadership roles if possible.

...Fall

- As soon as possible after its October 1 release, complete and submit your *Free Application for Federal Student Aid* (FAFSA®) at fafsa.gov, along with any other financial aid applications your chosen school(s) may require. You should submit your FAFSA® by the earliest financial aid deadline of the schools to which you are applying, usually by early February.

- After you submit the FAFSA®, you should receive your *Student Aid Report* (SAR) within three days to three weeks. This document lists your answers to the questions on your FAFSA® and gives you some basic information about your aid eligibility. Quickly make any necessary corrections and submit them to the FAFSA® processor.

- If you haven't done so already, register for and take such exams as the SAT, SAT Subject Tests, or ACT for college admission. Check with the colleges you are interested in to see what tests they require.

- Apply to the colleges you have chosen. Prepare your applications carefully. Follow the instructions, and PAY CLOSE ATTENTION TO DEADLINES!

- Well before your college application deadlines, ask your counselor and teachers to submit the required documents (e.g., transcript, letters of recommendation) to the colleges to which you're applying.

- Complete any last scholarship applications.

...Spring

- Visit colleges that have invited you to enroll.

- Review your college acceptances and compare the colleges' financial aid offers. Use the "Compare Financial Aid Offers" tool at www.consumerfinance.gov/paying-for-college to analyze aid offers side by side.

- Contact a school's financial aid office if you have questions about the aid that school has offered you. In fact, getting to know your financial aid staff early is a good idea no matter what—they can tell you about deadlines, paperwork you might need to submit, and other aid for which you might wish to apply.

- When you decide which school you want to attend, notify that school of your commitment and submit any required financial deposit. Many schools require this notification and deposit by May 1.

Chapter 4
Taking College Preparatory Courses

For teens who are interested in going to college, it is a good idea to begin planning while you are in high school. You can improve your chances of getting into the school of your choice by taking high-school courses that build a solid academic foundation for college success. College admissions officers evaluate applicants based on their performance in college preparatory courses. They not only look at your grade point average (GPA), but also consider whether you took at least five solid academic classes each semester in high school. They often give preference to applicants who have challenged themselves by taking honors or advanced placement (AP) classes, even if their GPA is lower than applicants who have taken only basic classes.

The College Prep Curriculum

Although the term "college preparatory" (or "college prep") can have several different meanings, it is most often used to refer to the standard, required courses in the core high-school curriculum. Since one of the main goals of high school is to prepare students for college, all high-school classes can technically be considered college prep. In this context, college prep can also be used to differentiate the standard courses that most students take from remedial or advanced courses.

Although the core college prep classes can vary depending on the state and the individual school, the requirements for high-school graduation typically include the following:

- 4 years of English or language arts to develop your reading comprehension, vocabulary, and written communication skills;

"Taking College Preparatory Courses," © 2017 Omnigraphics.

- 3–4 years of mathematics, including some combination of algebra, geometry, trigonometry, and calculus;

- 3–4 years of laboratory science classes—usually including biology or earth science, chemistry, and physics—to improve your ability to think analytically, make observations, and apply theories;

- 2–3 years of social studies classes, including both U.S. and world history, to improve your understanding of politics, government, cultures, and world events;

- 2 years of study in a second language; and

- 1 year of study in the fine or applied arts—such as music, dance, drama, painting, pottery, or graphic arts—to develop your creativity, flexibility, and problem solving skills.

As you plan which courses to take in high school, an important factor to consider is how much to challenge yourself with honors, AP, International Baccalaureate (IB), or dual-enrollment college courses. These classes tend to be more academically rigorous, which can affect your performance and lower your GPA. As a result, some students decide to stick with the standard high-school college prep curriculum in hopes of maintaining the highest possible GPA. But college admissions officers often look beyond the GPA for evidence that applicants will be up to the challenge of college-level academic work. Admissions data show that elite universities prefer students who are willing to push themselves by taking more advanced high-school classes.

To improve your chances of being admitted to your preferred college, experts suggest taking 1–2 advanced courses per year in high school. They recommend choosing courses in subject areas that interest you and play to your strengths, so that you feel confident that you can earn a letter grade of B or higher. Most colleges would prefer to see a B in an advanced class than an A in a standard-level course. On the other hand, experts discourage students from taking too many honors classes at one time or taking advanced courses in weaker subject areas. If you end up with Cs and Ds, they will assume that you either did not apply yourself or made poor decisions regarding your schedule.

Your teachers or guidance counselor can help you research the academic requirements and admission standards of the colleges you are interested in attending. You can use this information to help you decide which classes to take and stay on track academically.

College Prep Schools And Programs

The term "college prep" is also used to describe a type of high school that focuses on securing college admission for its students. These schools can be found throughout the United States.

Some are public schools, while others are private, parochial, charter, or boarding schools. To help students prepare to succeed in college, they offer assistance with researching schools, making campus visits, submitting applications, and earning college credit for coursework completed in high school. Some prep schools require students to be admitted to a college before they are allowed to graduate.

Another usage of the term "college prep" describes various government, community, and nonprofit programs whose mission is to increase access to college for teens who might otherwise be unlikely to pursue higher education. Such programs target low-income and minority students, first-generation college students, and students with disabilities. They vary as to their size, funding, and the student populations they serve. Some try to catch and engage academically promising students as early as elementary school, while others offer financial and other assistance to students near the end of high school. In general, these programs are designed to prepare deserving students for college by increasing academic skills, assisting with college and financial aid applications, and incorporating community service projects.

The U.S. government offers a number of programs aimed at helping low-income, minority, and disabled teens access higher education. These federal efforts are known collectively as the TRIO programs because they originated with three programs in the 1960s. Some examples include the following:

- **Upward Bound,** which provides tutoring, counseling, individualized instruction, and motivational support to help people from underrepresented groups get ready for college;

- **Talent Search,** which identifies students with potential from low-income backgrounds and offers a range of counseling and support services to help them apply to college, prepare for entrance exams, access financial aid, select courses, improve study skills, and find a career;

- **Student Support Services (SSS),** which provides financial aid, academic advising, career counseling, tutoring, and mentoring to help low-income and first-generation students earn a college degree; and

- **Gaining Early Awareness and Readiness for Undergraduate Programs (GEAR UP),** which partners with state governments to fund and administer early outreach programs that provide mentoring, tutoring, and career planning to students from seventh through twelfth grades.

In addition to the various federal programs, states such as New York, New Jersey, California, and Florida offer programs to help ensure that all promising students have an opportunity to go to college, regardless of their personal background or economic circumstances. Some of these state programs work in partnership with colleges, high schools, businesses, community organizations, and parent groups to help students increase their academic achievement and develop the skills they need to succeed in college. Various state universities also provide academic enrichment programs to prepare and motivate underrepresented students in middle and high school to pursue higher education.

Finally, nonprofit organizations and community-based groups also offer college prep programs aimed at helping low-income, minority, and disabled teens attend college. Some examples of successful programs include the following:

- **Advancement Via Individual Determination (AVID),** which helps close the achievement gap between high- and mid-rank students in fifth through twelfth grades to help more kids become eligible for college;

- **I Have a Dream,** which adopts an entire elementary classroom or age group from a public housing development and provides long-term tutoring, mentoring, and academic enrichment to increase student achievement; and

- **ENLACE,** which works to strengthen K-through-12 education for Latino students in order to increase opportunities for them to attend college.

Did You Know...

"A strong college-prep curriculum is by far the best predictor of initial college success," according to Peterson's educational service. "Careful college planning will not only help you get into college, but will also help you do well on campus."

(Source: "College Prep: Choosing Your High School Classes," Peterson's.)

References

1. "College Preparatory Programs," National Council of State Legislatures (NCSL), 2017.

2. "High School Classes Colleges Look For," *Big Future,* The College Board, 2017.

3. Wulick, Anna. "What Are College Prep Courses And Classes?" *PrepScholar,* September 6, 2015.

Chapter 5
Importance Of Extracurricular Activities

There is more to education than the time you spend in the classroom or doing homework. While academics are important, getting involved in extracurricular activities—such as sports, clubs, the performing arts, student government, or service organizations—can be a valuable part of your school experience as well. Participating in extracurricular activities is not only fun, but it can help you develop skills you need to succeed in school and become a responsible, productive adult. Extracurricular activities also look good on your college applications. They provide admissions officers with insight into your abilities and interests, which may improve your chances of getting into your dream school.

Benefits Of Extracurricular Activities

Extracurricular activities benefit students in many ways. Since most students choose clubs or activities based on their interests, you are likely to make friends with people who share your passions. Participating in group discussions and working together to achieve a goal can also help improve your social skills and teamwork. Clubs, teams, and student organizations also provide leadership opportunities. By holding an office in a student organization or serving as a team captain, you gain valuable experience in managing and motivating people.

Even though extracurricular activities require a time commitment, studies have shown that participating can actually improve your academic performance. It helps you learn to manage your time wisely, prioritize tasks, and balance competing demands. These skills become increasingly valuable as you move on to college and the world of employment. In addition, you need to maintain a minimum grade point average (GPA) to take part in many extracurricular activities, which provides extra motivation to keep up with your studies. The National Federation of State High School Associations (NFHS) reports that students who participate in extracurricular activities generally have higher grades, better attendance, fewer disciplinary issues, and lower dropout rates than other students.

Having a solid list of extracurricular activities can also improve your prospects for being accepted into college or graduate school. Many admissions officers view participation in extracurriculars as evidence that you can take responsibility, follow through on commitments, and manage your time wisely. Your accomplishments outside of school also provide information about your skills, interests, leadership potential, and other qualities that are valued by colleges.

Types Of Extracurricular Activities

Many different types of extracurricular activities are available to match virtually any student's interests. Most high schools offer a wide variety of academic, athletic, and special-interest clubs. In addition, most communities have local theater and music groups, service organizations, and volunteer opportunities for students. Finally, students can gain experience and skills by working part-time in local businesses, pursuing internships or job-shadowing opportunities, or tutoring.

Within the school environment, some of the most popular types of extracurricular activities include the following:

- **Academic clubs**

  These clubs are based around students' interest in a particular academic subject, such as reading, chemistry, or a foreign language. They often provide opportunities to supplement classroom learning through discussion groups, guest speakers, field trips, or cultural experiences.

- **Academic competitions**

  Many schools organize teams to compete in interscholastic intellectual contests, from academic decathlons and science fairs to robotics and graphic design competitions. These events help students develop their problem-solving and teamwork skills.

- **Debate or forensics teams**

  Preparing for debate competitions requires students to research a topic, organize an argument, and present a persuasive case according to established rules. Debaters develop skills in research, communication, analytical and logical reasoning, thinking quickly, and performing under pressure. All of these skills are highly valued by colleges and employers, and they are particularly important for students who are interested in careers in law or politics.

- **Student government**

  Most schools allow students to elect representatives who serve as liaisons between the student body and school administrators. Holding an office in student government gives you an opportunity to exercise your leadership and communication skills. You may also be involved in planning school events and organizing fundraisers.

- **Student publications**

  Students with strong writing and editing skills may be interested in working on a student newspaper, yearbook, or literary magazine. These activities allow you to learn about publishing, provide a source of information for classmates, and build a portfolio of published articles to submit when applying for college or jobs.

- **Athletics**

  Sports are a very popular form of extracurricular activity. Participating in athletic competition requires dedication, commitment, and effort. Student-athletes develop self-confidence, strength, and fitness as well as teamwork, leadership, and time-management skills.

- **Performing arts**

  Many high schools offer students the opportunity to participate in the performing arts, such as marching band, orchestra, choir, theater, and dance. Student performers dedicate significant amounts of time and energy to practices, performances, and judged competitions. They gain valuable skills in communication, teamwork, and time management.

- **Service organizations**

  A variety of service organizations give socially conscious students opportunities to do charitable work within a structured environment. Many large national and international

Did You Know...

According to the U.S. Census Bureau, 57 percent of school-aged kids participated in at least one extracurricular activity in 2014. Sports was the most popular activity, attracting 37 percent of participants, followed by clubs and lessons (such as music, dance, or a second language), each at 29 percent.

organizations have student branches, while many community-based nonprofit groups welcome teen volunteers.

Finding An Extracurricular Activity

There are extracurricular clubs, teams, and organizations to fit most students' interests. The key to choosing the right activity for you is to figure out where your interests lie. Although some types of activities may seem like they would add more value to a college application, experts recommend basing your choice on genuine interest. Otherwise, participating will seem like a chore and you will be less likely to follow through on your commitment. It is also important to consider the amount of time you have available and avoid activities that would interfere with your studies. Finally, it helps to remember that the main idea of getting involved in extracurricular activities is to have fun.

To find suitable activities, groups, and clubs, talking to your friends, teachers, or guidance counselor is a good place to start. Your school's website may also provide information about clubs and activities, while community or national groups often list volunteer and service opportunities on their websites. If you are unable to find a group that caters to the issue or interest you feel most strongly about, consider forming your own club. You will not only be able to devote time and energy to your favorite cause, but you will also impress potential colleges by taking the initiative.

References

1. "The Case For High School Activities," National Federation of State High School Associations, 2015.

2. "Extracurriculars Matter—To You And To Colleges," *Big Future*, The College Board, 2017.

3. Lawhorn, Bill. "Extracurricular Activities: The Afterschool Connection," *Occupational Outlook Quarterly*, Winter 2008–2009.

Chapter 6
Taking Standardized Tests

The first step to studying in the United States is researching your options to find a college or university that best fits your needs. You shouldn't try to match yourself to the school, but rather find the school that matches you and your priorities and long-term goals.

Remember that no official ranking system exists for colleges and universities in the United States. The best college or university is the one that is best for you and meets your requirements—academic, financial, and personal.

At least 12 to 18 months prior to the academic year in which you hope to attend a U.S. college or university, you should begin your research.

> Application and financial aid deadlines affect when you take standardized tests because test results must reach admissions offices no later than their application deadlines.

Prepare For U.S. Standardized Tests, Community College

Prepare For Standardized Tests

As part of the application process, most undergraduate programs require one or more U.S. standardized test score(s). Your test scores, academic record, and other factors are used to

---

About This Chapter: This chapter includes text excerpted from "Research Your Options," EducationUSA, U.S. Department of State (DOS), March 24, 2015.

predict how well you will do as a college student. Test scores are one way to compare students from the United States and international students from different educational systems.

Community colleges typically have more flexible admissions processes than four-year institutions and often don't require standardized test scores for admission. Check the website of the community college that you plan to attend for specific testing requirements of that institution.

English Language Ability Tests

If English is not your native language, most U.S. colleges and universities will ask you to take an English language proficiency test before admission.

The most common tests for English language ability are the Test of English as a Foreign Language (TOEFL), the International English Language Testing System (IELTS), the Michigan English Language Assessment Battery (MELAB) and the Pearson Test of English (PTE).

Because community colleges provide their own assessments and frequently offer Intensive English Programs (IEPs) to students who require additional English proficiency, English language test scores are not always required for the admissions process.

Admissions Tests

Most four-year colleges and universities require the SAT or ACT (see definitions below) for admissions. Community colleges typically do not require these standardized tests, but might offer a placement test in your area of study upon arrival. Check the website of the community college that you plan to attend for that institution's specific testing requirements.

Scholastic Assessment Test (SAT): a primarily multiple-choice test of mathematics and English that is used for admission into an undergraduate program. The SAT Subject Tests is a multiple-choice test that measures your knowledge in specific subject areas.

American College Testing (ACT): a multiple-choice test of English, mathematics, reading, and science reasoning (plus an optional writing component) used for admission into undergraduate programs.

Prepare For U.S. Standardized Tests, Undergraduate

Prepare For Standardized Tests

As part of the application process, most undergraduate programs require one or more U.S. standardized test scores. Your test scores, academic record, and other factors are used to predict how well you will do as a university student. The test scores are one way to compare students from the United States and international students from different educational systems.

In the United States, there is no national college entrance examination administered by the government that students must pass to gain admission to higher education. Rather, different universities or schools establish their own admission requirements, including which third-party standardized test they accept.

Standardized tests should be taken a year to 18 months before you plan on studying. Many students take the exams more than once to achieve higher scores. There are many websites, books, and tutors available to help you prepare.

English Language Ability Tests

Being able to communicate in English is a basic requirement for successful undergraduate study in the United States. If English is not your native language, U.S. colleges and universities will ask you to take an English Language proficiency test before admission.

The most common tests for English language ability are the Test of English as a Foreign Language (TOEFL), the International English Language Testing System (IELTS), the Michigan English Language Assessment Battery (MELAB), and the Pearson Test of English (PTE).

Admissions Tests

Most colleges and universities in the United States require the SAT or ACT for undergraduate admissions. Admissions requirements vary, so be sure to confirm which test(s) you need with the institutions that interest you.

SAT: a test that measures critical reading, writing, and mathematical abilities. The SAT Subject Tests measure knowledge in specific subject areas. Please note that an updated SAT made its debut in March 2016 and impacts students in the class of 2017 and younger.

ACT: a curriculum-based multiple-choice test that measures knowledge on subjects.

Prepare For U.S. Standardized Tests, Graduate

As part of the application process, most graduate programs require one or more standardized test scores. In the United States, universities or schools establish their own admission requirements, including which third-party standardized tests they accept.

Take these exams a year to 18 months before the date you plan to study in the United States since you may want to take them more than once to improve your scores. There are many websites, books, and tutors available for test preparation.

English Language Ability Tests

Being able to communicate in English is a basic requirement for successful graduate study in the United States. If English is not your native language, U.S. colleges and universities will ask you to take an English language proficiency test.

The most common tests of English language ability are the Test of English as a Foreign Language (TOEFL), the International English Language Testing System (IELTS), the Michigan English Language Assessment Battery (MELAB), and the Pearson Test of English (PTE).

Admissions Tests

Testing requirements vary among graduate programs, so be sure to confirm requirements with institutions. Some of the specialized graduate-level examinations:

Graduate Record Examination (GRE): a standardized test of verbal reasoning, quantitative reasoning, and analytical writing that measures readiness for graduate-level study.

Graduate Management Admission Test (GMAT): a standardized test for MBA applicants that measures basic verbal, mathematical, and analytical writing skills that have been developed over time through education and work.

Medical College Admission Test (MCAT): a standardized, multiple-choice examination that assesses problem solving, critical thinking, writing skills, and knowledge of science concepts and principles prerequisite to the study of medicine.

Law School Admission Test (LSAT): a standardized test that measures acquired reading and verbal reasoning skills that law schools use as one assessment factor for admission.

Dental Admission Test (DAT): a multiple-choice test to measure general academic ability, comprehension of scientific information, and perceptual ability, used for admission to Dental schools.

Part Two
Your Role As An Education Consumer

Chapter 7
The Value Of Education

Parents, teachers, guidance counselors, politicians, and even celebrities like to talk about the importance of education. If you are a teenager weighing your options for what to do after high school, it may be helpful to learn some facts about the costs and benefits of higher education. College is expensive, and the costs keep getting higher. According to the U.S. Department of Treasury, in-state tuition at public four-year colleges and universities across the country increased by two-thirds from 2000 to 2012. But education also offers many benefits for individuals, as well as for the nation and society as a whole.

Benefits Of Higher Education

One of the ways education improves society is by helping you become an informed citizen, so you can participate in the democratic process or even become a future leader. It also provides you with valuable knowledge and skills so that you can get a good job and be a productive member of the workforce. Advanced education prepares you for highly skilled positions that help businesses compete in a fast-paced, technology-based global economy. A better-prepared workforce, in turn, helps the nation's economy advance and create more opportunities for citizens.

Education also provides many benefits to you as an individual. The rigorous academic environment in college helps you gain skills in communication, time management, critical analysis, and problem solving. Studies have shown that people who develop these skills generally enjoy a better quality of life than those who do not.

Pursuing higher education also provides you with many exciting opportunities that you might not otherwise have. You can get involved in sports, clubs, and other activities, meet new people who share your interests, and be exposed to new ideas and ways of thinking. Many colleges and universities offer students the opportunity to study abroad for a semester. By taking advantage of these programs, you can live in a different country, learn about the language and culture, and expand your life experiences and worldview.

Education As An Investment

Getting a college education also holds significant financial value. Studies have consistently shown that people with higher levels of education earn more money, on average, than those with only a high-school diploma. The more education you receive, the higher your income is likely to be. In addition, people with higher levels of education are less likely to face unemployment during economic downturns.

In 2011, the average worker with a bachelor's degree earned two-thirds more per week than the average worker with a high-school diploma, and the unemployment rate among college graduates was half that of high-school graduates. People with graduate and professional degrees earned even higher salaries and experienced even lower unemployment rates.

Did You Know...

According to the National Center for Education Statistics (NCES), in 2015 Americans between the ages of 25 and 34 with a college degree earned 66 percent more per year, on average, than those with only a high school diploma.

People who obtain a college education tend to pass along these socioeconomic benefits to their children. Research shows that the children of college graduates are more likely to go to college themselves, which makes them 75 percent more likely to advance to a higher income bracket than children whose parents did not go to college.

Comparing Costs And Benefits

There is no doubt that college is expensive. Tuition at public four-year colleges and universities has increased much faster than the rate of inflation. Meanwhile, the amount of funding provided by state and local governments has fallen, so students and their families must bear a larger proportion of college costs than ever before. Many students must take out loans to help pay for their college education. Coupled with the time involved in completing college, which delays their entry into the workforce, these debts can create financial hardships for students.

Despite the high costs, however, studies have shown that the rewards of higher education typically outweigh the costs. Experts recommend viewing a college education as an investment in your future. The return that you get by investing in your education—in the form of a better job, a higher income, and an improved quality of life—is greater than you would receive by investing your college funds in other alternatives, like the stock market.

In addition, the federal government has launched a number of programs designed to make college more affordable and accessible for all Americans. Some of these programs include Pell grants, the American Opportunity Tax Credit (AOTC), low-interest Stafford loans, and income-based repayment plans that cap monthly student loan payments at a certain percentage of the borrower's income. Despite the high costs, more young people are pursuing college degrees than ever before. As more employers require a bachelor's degree for entry-level jobs, getting a college education will become increasingly important in the future.

Did You Know...

American colleges awarded 1.9 million bachelor's degrees in 2014, an increase of 46 percent over the 1.3 million degrees awarded in 2000.

References

1. Bidwell, Allie. "Is College Worth It? That Depends On A Lot of Things," National Association of Student Financial Aid Administrators (NASFAA), October 2, 2015.

2. Cassidy, John. "College Calculus: What's The Real Value Of Higher Education?" *New Yorker*, September 7, 2015.

3. Eberly, Jan, and Carmel Martin. "The Economic Case For Higher Education," *Treasury Notes*, December 13, 2012.

Chapter 8
Understanding College Costs

The cost of college can include a variety of items including some you might not expect. By understanding college costs, you can compare schools and explore options for how to lower your costs.

What Is Included In The Cost Of College?

College costs include more than tuition and room and board. Here are common costs:

Table 8.1. Common Costs

Item	Description
Tuition	The cost of taking courses. Course costs vary by school.
Room and board	Lodging and food costs vary by school.
Books and school supplies	Books can be expensive. School supplies include • book bags; • notebooks; • pens and pencils; • paper and computer paper; • and desk accessories such as folders, trays, and pen holders.
Fees	Fees depend upon your school. Examples include activity fees and parking decal fees. Schools can provide a list of fees.

About This Chapter: This chapter includes text excerpted from "Understanding College Costs," Federal Student Aid, U.S. Department of Education (ED), January 20, 2017.

Table 8.1. Continued

Item	Description
Equipment and room materials	This category might include • a computer and printer; • reading lamps; • a microwave and refrigerator; and • sheets, towels, etc.
Travel and miscellaneous expenses	• If you commute to school, include transportation costs. • If you live on campus, include travel during school breaks. • You may also want to include clothing and mobile phone costs.

Make sure colleges and career schools give you a clear statement of their tuition and fees.

How Can I Lower The Cost Of College?

Here are some suggestions on how you might be able to lower the cost of college. For many of these suggestions, you'll want to follow up with the colleges or career schools you are interested in to get additional details.

- Set a budget and stick to it! Having a budget will help you compare anticipated college or career school expenses against your potential available income and financial aid. You also can use a budget to compare costs between different schools.

- College or career school costs can vary significantly and there are many schools with affordable tuition and generous financial assistance. Make sure to research all schools that may meet your academic and financial needs.

- You may be able to get school credit based on your knowledge or life experiences, and you can manage your course work to reduce costs.

  - Ask your school whether it's possible to "test out of" any classes. If you don't take a class, you may not have to pay for the credits.

  - Some colleges give credit for life experiences, thereby reducing the number of credits needed for graduation.

  - Most schools charge a set price for a specific number of credits taken in a semester. If academically possible, take the maximum number of credits allowed. This strategy reduces the amount of time needed to graduate.

- Some schools offer combined degree programs or three-year programs that allow you to take all of the courses needed for graduation in three years, instead of four, thereby eliminating one year's educational expenses.

- Colleges and career schools may offer discounts on tuition if
  - you are a child of an alumnus or alumna (i.e., if your parent went to the school);
  - more than one family member is enrolled at the school;
  - you are a student government leader or the editor of the college newspaper or yearbook;
  - you are an older student;
  - your family's main wage earner is unemployed; or
  - you or a member of your family works at the school.

- Housing costs can add up. Here are some tips for reducing your housing costs:
  - If you go to a college or career school near home, consider living with your parents or other family.
  - If you live off-campus, consider sharing a house or apartment with multiple house-mates to cut down the cost of rent, and carpool to save on gas and parking.
  - Most colleges and universities sponsor resident advisor programs that offer reduced tuition or reduced room and board costs if you work in a residence hall.

- You may be eligible for important new healthcare benefits through the Affordable Care Act (ACA). Examples of these benefits include the following:
  - Most young adults can stay on their parents' family plan until they turn 26, even if they are married or still living with their parents.
  - If you have been uninsured because of a pre-existing condition, you may be eligible to join the Pre-Existing Condition Insurance Plan (PCIP).
  - If you are in a new insurance plan, insurance companies cannot charge you a deductible or copays for recommended or preventive services such as flu shots or other immunizations.

- You can work part-time to pay part of your costs. Be sure your work and school schedules don't conflict and that you have enough time for studying. Here are a couple of options:
  - The Federal Work-Study Program (FWS) provides an opportunity to earn money while going to school. Ask schools if they participate in the program.

- Cooperative education programs allow students to alternate between working full time and studying full time.

- Most schools have placement offices that help students find employment and personnel offices that hire students to work on campus.

- Taking small steps can add up. For example, you can lower the cost of textbooks if you buy used books or rent textbooks (if you won't need the books once you finish the class).

A credit card can help you build a credit history, if you use it wisely. But use it for emergencies only and don't spend more than you can afford to pay. If you decide to get a credit card, make sure you understand the terms.

> Between 2004–05 and 2014–15, prices for undergraduate tuition, fees, room, and board at public institutions rose 33 percent, and prices at private nonprofit institutions rose 26 percent, after adjustment for inflation. The price for undergraduate tuition, fees, room, and board at private for-profit institutions decreased 18 percent between 2004–05 and 2014–15, after adjustment for inflation.
>
> *(Source: "Fast Facts: Tuition Costs Of Colleges And Universities," U.S. Department of Education (ED), National Center for Education Statistics (NCES).)*

How Can I Compare The Costs Of Colleges?

You can find information about whether the cost of a college is low, medium, or high by using the College Scorecard (collegescorecard.ed.gov). Keep in mind that a higher-priced school might have more financial aid available to help you pay for your education, so take a look at the school's net price if you want an idea of how much it might cost you after financial aid is taken into account.

Table 8.2. Past And Current Tuition Costs Of Colleges And Universities

Constant 2014–15 Dollars				Current Dollars		
Year And Control Of Institution	All Institutions	4-Year Institutions	2-Year Institutions	All Institutions	4-Year Institutions	2-Year Institutions
All Institutions						
2013–14	21,148	24,878	9,959	20,995	24,699	9,887
2014–15	21,728	25,409	10,153	21,728	25,409	10,153

Table 8.2. Continued

Constant 2014–15 Dollars			Current Dollars		
Year And Control Of Institution	**All Institutions**	**4-Year Institutions**	**2-Year Institutions**	**All Institutions**	**4-Year Institutions**	**2-Year Institutions**
Public Institutions						
2013–14	15,743	18,231	9,349	15,630	18,100	9,281
2014–15	16,188	18,632	9,586	16,188	18,632	9,586
Private Nonprofit And For-Profit Institutions						
2013–14	36,247	36,854	24,033	35,985	36,587	23,859
2014–15	37,424	37,990	24,317	37,424	37,990	24,317

(Source: "Fast Facts: Tuition Costs Of Colleges And Universities," U.S. Department of Education (ED), National Center for Education Statistics (NCES).)

Chapter 9
Traditional College Options

Public Or Private?[1]

Public schools are operated or funded by state and local governments. Private schools are not affiliated with a government organization. They may be nonprofit colleges, such as those run by private foundations or religious denominations. Or, they may be for-profit businesses, such as many career, online, or technical schools.

Since private schools receive less (or no) money from state and local governments, they usually cost the same whether you live in or outside of the state. This cost is often higher than the cost of attending a public school in your state.

Because costs can vary significantly from school to school, you should make sure to research the schools you are interested in. Any school that participates in the federal student aid programs is required to provide information on its cost of attendance on its website. The school is also required to provide a net price calculator which will give you an idea of how much a program may cost after subtracting any financial aid.

Four-Year Colleges And Universities[1]

Students who attend a four-year college or university typically earn a bachelor's degree once they have successfully completed a program of study, which usually takes about four years.

About This Chapter: This chapter includes text excerpted from documents published by three public domain sources. Text under headings marked 1 are excerpted from "Types Of Schools," U.S. Department of Education (ED), January 20, 2017; text under headings marked 2 are excerpted from "What Is Community College?" U.S. Department of Homeland Security (DHS), March 13, 2012; text under headings marked 3 are excerpted from "How To Go To College," U.S. Department of Education (ED), October 28, 2014.

A college usually offers a four-year bachelor's degree in the arts (such as English, history, drama) or sciences (such as biology, computer science, engineering). Some colleges also offer advanced degrees, such as master's or other graduate degrees, after you've earned your bachelor's degree.

Universities offer bachelor's, master's, and doctorate degrees, and sometimes have professional schools such as a law school or medical school. Universities tend to be larger than colleges, may have larger class sizes, and often focus on scholarly or scientific research.

Community College[2]

The United States offers many types of postsecondary education. One type of note, once unique to the United States but becoming known and established in other countries, is the community college. Community colleges, sometimes called junior colleges, are two-year schools that provide affordable postsecondary education as a pathway to a four-year degree.

According to the American Association of Community Colleges (AACC), 1,167 community colleges in the United States enroll more than 12.4 million students and serve almost half of all undergraduate students in the United States. Many of these community colleges are Student and Exchange Visitor Program (SEVP)-certified, and all have nationally-recognized accreditation. These community colleges offer a wide variety of options to postsecondary students:

- Open access to postsecondary education

- Preparation for transfer to four-year college or university

- Workforce development and skills training

- A range of noncredit programs, such as English as a second language, skills retraining, community enrichment programs and cultural activities

Community colleges offer a distinct learning environment, and are recognized for smaller class sizes, more individualized attention and a supportive atmosphere. Community colleges also offer the following:

- A Pathway to a Four-Year Degree—Because community colleges are accredited, students can easily transfer between a community college and a four-year college or university.

- Affordability—Attending a community college can offer savings of thousands of dollars. The average cost of attending public community college is $2,713 per year. By comparison, the average cost of attending a public four-year college or university is $7,605 per year.

- Relevance—New businesses, such as emerging green technologies, will require workers trained in new ways. Technology is central to supporting much of this change. Many community colleges provide technical or vocational training for international students.

- Partnership with Industry—To ensure students have adequate preparation for jobs that require higher education or workforce training, community college officials are working with employers to develop flexible, affordable and relevant training programs that meet business and regional economic needs. The partnership between businesses and community colleges can maximize workforce development strategies, job training programs, and ultimately, job placement. International students can take advantage of these opportunities through optional practical training, a one-year authorization to work.

With the opportunity for more individualized attention and services, getting a two-year postsecondary degree and advancing to university is a more reachable goal.

Two-Year Colleges (Community And Junior Colleges)

Community colleges and junior colleges award associate degrees once students have successfully completed a two-year course of study. Some two-year colleges grant diplomas or certificates of completion to students who have met course requirements and are ready to practice in their career fields, such as nursing. Community and junior colleges are similar, except that a junior college is usually a private school.

Because costs are often lower and admission is more open at two-year colleges, many students begin their college careers here. If you plan to start at a community or junior college and later transfer to a four-year college, you should make sure your community college courses will transfer to those colleges you are interested in and that your courses will count toward your bachelor's degree. Many community colleges have "articulation agreements" with four-year colleges under which the course work taken at the community college transfers into the four-year degree program. Be sure to ask about the types of articulation agreements the community college has, with whom, and for what programs of study.

(Source:"Types Of Schools," U.S. Department of Education (ED).)

Career Schools[1]

Career schools, also known as technical, vocational, or trade schools

- may be public or private, although many are for-profit businesses;

- typically offer programs that are two years or less; and

- provide students with formal classes and hands-on experience related to their future career interests, from welding to cosmetology to medical imaging.

Technical schools teach the science behind the occupation, while vocational schools focus on hands-on application of skills needed to do the job. You may earn a diploma or a certificate, prepare for a licensing exam, or study to begin work as an apprentice or journeyman in a skilled trade.

Some schools offer distance learning, which allows you to access lectures or course materials online or through other electronic media. Since not every distance learning course or online degree is accredited and/or eligible for federal student aid, check with the school's financial aid office to find out whether you can receive federal aid.

Table 9.1. Graduation Time By Program Or Degree And Type Of School

Program Or Degree	Schools Where Offered	Typical Time To Graduate
Career, technical, trade, or vocational courses	Career, technical, vocational, and trade schools Community and junior colleges	1–2 years
Associate Degree	Community and junior colleges	2 years
Bachelor's Degree	Four-year colleges and universities	4 years
Master's Degree	Four-year colleges and universities	Bachelor's degree + 1–2 years of additional study
Doctorate Degree	Four-year colleges and universities	Bachelor's degree + Master's degree + 2–3 years of additional study

International Schools

Are you considering going to college outside the United States? Make sure you do your research, whether you plan to spend one semester abroad or get your entire degree from an international school.

Explore Your Options[3]

What's the best job in the world?

The one that's right for you!

It might sound crazy, but with hard work and advance planning, it's possible to earn a living doing exactly what you like. Someone has to create video games, design roller coasters, become the vice president, or tap dance on Broadway. Why not you?

One step in finding a career that you'll love is matching your personal profile (abilities, interests, and needs) with different career clusters and jobs.

If you haven't yet talked to your school's career or guidance counselor, now would be a good time. Meet with your guidance counselor to take an interest inventory. These short quizzes ask you questions like: Do you like to build things? Do you like to analyze things? Or, do you like to help people? There is no right or wrong answer to the questions, and in the end, your interest inventory results will suggest career clusters that you might like.

Career Clusters

Career clusters are groups of jobs or professions that require similar interests, skills, and abilities. Check out Table 9.2 on career cluster chart to see the jobs and professions that match each cluster. Interest inventories help you focus on a few career clusters, but their results are only suggestions. Your likes and dislikes change over time. Research all career clusters and jobs that interest you, not just those suggested by your interest inventory.

Also, jobs can fit into more than one career cluster. Web designers, for example, mix business, technology, and graphic design. Consider jobs that combine all of your interests.

Researching Careers

Find out what jobs and career clusters are like in the real world, and what opportunities will be available in the future. You certainly don't want to study a long time to become a VCR repairman if everyone knows that DVD's are the wave of the future. Get information about job growth trends, wages, benefits, and working conditions before you decide on a career. There are several ways you can get this kind of career information. The U.S. Department of Labor (DOL), U.S. Bureau of Labor Statistics (BLS) Online (www.bls.gov) offers information about career clusters in the *Career Guide to Industries*. The career guide tells you which skills, abilities, and interests are important for each career cluster, what jobs are available in each cluster, and what earnings and benefits are available in each cluster. The Bureau of Labor Statistics Online also has information about specific jobs. Every two years, the bureau publishes the *Occupational Outlook Handbook*. This tells you what workers do on the job, how much training and education is needed for the job, and how many jobs will be available in the future. All of these things can help you decide if a career cluster or job is the right one for you. If you don't have Internet access, many public libraries have hard copies of the *Career Guide to Industries* and the *Occupational Handbook* for you to review. And talk to your school or guidance counselor. They can usually give you information about careers in your city or town.

Table 9.2. Career Clusters

Career Cluster	Agriculture And Natural Resources	Art, Media, Design, And Communications	Manufacturing, Construction, And Transportation	Business, Management, And Finance	Education, Social, And Health Services	Services And Hospitality	Engineering, Science, And Technology	Machine Repair And Operations
Jobs	Farmer/Rancher Veterinarian Timber Harvester Forest Ranger Geologist Surveyor	Actor Graphic Designer Spokesperson Librarian Director Journalist	General Contractor Millwright Plumber Truck Driver Electrician Line Worker	Accountant Stock Broker Business Owner Manager Marketing Specialist Secretary	Teacher Social Worker Police Officer Firefighter Doctor Physical Therapist	Hotel Clerk Cosmetologist Travel Agent Hostess Flight Attendant Cashier	Engineer Programmer Scientist Architect Computer Systems Analyst	HVAC Technician Air Traffic Controller Cable Technician Data Entry Clerk Auto Mechanic TV/VCR Repairman
Career Focus	Working with and managing resources in the natural world.	Using ideas and information to communicate with people.	Working with objects to create, move, change, or build things.	Working with data, numbers, and people in the business world.	Working to help people and solve social problems.	Working to meet the comfort and recreational needs of people.	Using ideas to develop, change, or understand things.	Using data and information to operate or repair things.
Other Information	Agriculture and natural resources work is often done in open outdoor spaces. Many people work 50 hours or more each week. Educational requirements vary widely.	Communications professions are very competitive. Creativity, reading, writing, and critical thinking are very important. Educational requirements vary widely.	Industrial careers usually require onthe-job or apprenticeship training that can last up to five years. Generally, workers must be in good physical condition.	Management professionals usually work in offices with computers, budgets, and accounts. These jobs often require a two- or four-year degree.	Human services workers need excellent communication skills. Most jobs in this cluster require at least two years of college and many require more.	This is the largest cluster of jobs in the United States. Many require on-the-job training only. However, some positions do require a college degree, license, or certificate.	Workers in this cluster design structures, improve technology, and develop new medicines. These jobs typically require a four-year degree.	Equipment operators and repairers work in offices, homes, businesses, construction areas, and more. Most jobs require on-thejob or apprenticeship training.

Case Study

Cindy loves to spend hours working in the garage with her uncle. She likes to take things apart and put them back together again. Her algebra teacher is impressed by her math skills and always tells her that she is a future engineer. But Cindy is starting to worry because her friends don't act or think like her anymore, and some kids at school are starting to tease her.

- Which career clusters match Cindy's personal profile?

- Where could Cindy look to find information on careers?

- What are some of Cindy's special challenges?

- What advice would you give Cindy to help her find the right path?

Activity Ideas

- List 10–15 activities and subjects that you enjoy (or use your list from a previous exercise). Decide whether each activity involves people, things, ideas, or data (numbers and figures) and write down your answers. Based on your answers, what do you most like to work with: people, things, ideas, or data? Which career clusters match your interests?

- Identify five jobs that interest you and research them using the *Occupational Outlook Handbook* and *Career Guide to Industries*. Talk to a school counselor, parent, or friend about those jobs.

Chapter 10
Online Education And MOOCs (Massive Open Online Course)

Online education, also known as distance learning, involves taking classes without physically going to a school and sitting in a classroom. Instead, the classes are conducted electronically using the Internet, email, mobile apps, telephones, or other technologies. To be considered online education, at least 80 percent of the course content must be delivered to students online. Most distance-learning options do not involve any in-person, face-to-face interactions between students and instructors.

> **Did You Know...**
> A survey of academic leaders found that 68 percent believe distance learning requires more self-discipline than traditional, face-to-face courses. Students should keep this factor in mind when considering whether to enroll in online courses.

More than 70 percent of all public colleges and universities in the United States offer some sort of online education. Students generally must register with the institution and pay tuition to access these courses, and they receive credit toward a degree for successfully completing a class.

A Massive Open Online Course (MOOC) is a type of distance learning that provides instructional materials online, free of charge, for large numbers of students. MOOCs are open to anyone who wants to participate, and students are not expected to pay tuition or meet qualifications for admission. The only requirement for entry is that students have access to the Internet. In some cases, hundreds or even thousands of students may be enrolled in a single MOOC. They typically have little or no direct contact with the instructors. Although MOOCs offer a full course of study in various subject areas, students do not receive college credit for successfully completing a class.

In addition to courses that are offered exclusively online, some colleges and universities offer blended or hybrid courses. In this alternative, between 30 percent and 80 percent of the course content is delivered online, but students also physically attend classes or meetings on campus on an occasional or part-time basis. When an instructor makes some use of the Internet but delivers less than 30 percent of course content online, it is known as a Web-facilitated face-to-face course. When 100 percent of course content is delivered in person, whether orally or in writing, it is known as a traditional face-to-face course.

Prevalence Of Online Education

The popularity of online education has grown rapidly among both students and institutions of higher education. Surveys conducted by the Integrated Postsecondary Education Data System (IPEDS) in 2015 showed that more than 70 percent of all public, degree-granting institutions in the United States offered at least some distance-learning options. Some institutions offer individual courses online, while others offer full-time degree programs at both the undergraduate and graduate levels.

Large colleges and universities, with total enrollment of more than 5,000 students, are the main providers of online education in the United States. More than 95 percent of such institutions offered online education in 2015, compared to 83 percent of mid-sized colleges (with enrollment between 1,000 and 5,000 students) and 47 percent of small colleges (with enrollment of less than 1,000 students). According to the IPEDS surveys, around 75 percent of academic leaders felt that online education produced the same or better learning outcomes for students as face-to-face classroom instruction.

MOOCs make up a much smaller, yet growing, part of the online education landscape. Around 8 percent of all institutions of higher learning in the United States offered a MOOC in 2015, up from 5 percent in 2013. Nearly half of the institutions surveyed said they had no plans to offer a MOOC, however, while 40 percent said they were undecided.

As of 2013, the total number of students enrolled in at least one online course was estimated at 5.25 million, or about one-quarter of the overall higher education student body of 25.9 million. Enrollment in online education increased at a rate of 20 percent per year during most of the 2000s before starting to slow down in 2010.

Benefits Of Online Education

Distance learning courses and MOOCs hold a great deal of appeal for certain types of students, including:

- high-school students seeking dual enrollment options for college credit;

- people who are employed full-time but want to earn a degree or continue their education;

- people who cannot attend classes in person due to childcare or eldercare obligations;

- people who want to pursue a specific degree or course of study that is only offered at a distant location;

- people who want to test their aptitude for a certain area of study before committing to a full-time, residential degree program;

- people who are seeking personal enrichment or self-improvement rather than a degree;

- international students who wish to experience a foreign education system without relocating.

International students who take advantage of distance-learning offerings from American colleges and universities must be aware of certain limitations. Those who enroll in online-only courses—even full-time online degree programs—are not eligible for U.S. student visas. If these students are required to attend in person, however, they must obtain a student visa. Depending on the type of student visa, online courses and MOOCs may or may not count toward the requirement that international students maintain a full course of study for each academic term while they reside in the United States.

Choosing Online Courses

If you are interested in taking online courses, you should look for proven programs offered by accredited colleges and universities. The curriculum should be reviewed and updated on a regular basis, and the school should provide access to student evaluations of the program. If you are hoping to earn credit toward a degree, you should check the requirements carefully and make sure online credits will transfer if you decide to enroll at a different school. If you are mainly looking to expand your subject knowledge or increase your job qualifications, then a MOOC might be an affordable option. You should also understand the time commitment involved in distance learning and make sure it fits with your existing academic or work schedule. Your teachers or guidance counselor can provide more information to help you find reputable, manageable online education options.

References

1. Allen, I. Elaine, and Jeff Seaman. "Grade Level: Tracking Online Learning In The United States," Babson Survey Research Group, February 2015.

2. "Definition: Massive Open Online Courses (MOOCs)," OpenUpEd, March 12, 2015.

3. "Online Learning," Education USA, 2017.

4. "What You Need To Know About MOOCs," Study in the States, U.S. Department of Homeland Security, January 9, 2015.

Chapter 11
Searching For A College

There are more than 3,000 institutions of higher learning in the United States that offer four-year degrees. Each college or university is different in terms of its location, size, facilities, academic programs, and cost. With so many options to choose from, finding the school that best fits your individual needs and interests may seem like an overwhelming task. Yet there is a great deal of information available to help you focus your college search. Experts recommend starting early—as soon as your sophomore year of high school—and following a step-by-step process that includes:

- figuring out what is important to you,
- identifying colleges that match your priorities,
- narrowing down your list of choices, and
- selecting the schools to which you will apply.

Figuring Out What You Want

There is no doubt that selecting the right college is an important decision. After all, college is very expensive, and earning a degree occupies several years of your life. In addition, the education you receive will play a role in determining your future career path. To ensure that you find a good fit, the first step in the college search process is to think carefully about what factors are most important to you. Once you identify your "must-have" qualities, you will be better equipped to find schools that offer what you want.

"Searching For A College," © 2017 Omnigraphics.

Based on surveys of prospective college students, here are some characteristics that are important to consider:

- **Location**

  For many students, location is among the primary factors affecting their choice of college. Some teens want to stay close to home so they have the option of commuting to school or visiting friends and family on the weekends. Other teens view college as an opportunity to expand their horizons and experience a different region of the country. Other factors to consider relating to location include whether you prefer a rural, suburban, or urban setting; whether you want to be near a major city, convenient airport, or outdoor recreation opportunities; and whether you prefer a certain type of weather or climate.

- **Size**

  Institutions of higher learning range in size from small, private colleges with a few hundred students to large, public universities with tens of thousands of students. Smaller schools tend to offer a more personalized education experience, with lower student-to-faculty ratios and more one-on-one attention. But large universities can also offer advantages, including a broader range of course offerings, a wider variety of extracurricular activities, a more diverse student body, and a larger alumni network.

- **Cost**

  Although cost is an important factor in choosing a college, many students do not end up paying the full price of tuition, room and board, and other expenses listed on college websites. Before rejecting a potential school of interest as too expensive, you should look into the percentage of students who receive scholarships, grants, or other forms of financial aid, as well as the average amount awarded. In many cases, more expensive schools also have more funds available to help students afford to go there. Another cost-related factor to consider is the graduation rate. Schools with a high percentage of first-year students who earn a bachelor's degree in four years may turn out to be less expensive in the long run than schools where most students require additional years of study in order to graduate.

- **Academic programs or majors**

  If you have a good idea about what you would like to study in college, the courses and majors offered by various schools should factor into your decision. You want to be sure that your school of choice gives you access to the curriculum you intend to study. But you should avoid selecting a school solely because it offers a specific major, because most students change their majors several times before they graduate from college. In addition, many students enter college without a clear idea of what type of degree they want to pursue, and it is fine to postpone that decision until later in your college career.

- **Academic reputation**

  A school's academic reputation—or how the education it provides is regarded by employers, educators, and alumni—is another factor to consider when choosing a college. While some students thrive in a challenging, rigorous, competitive academic environment, others find the pressure overwhelming and prefer a more supportive, team-oriented approach. You are most likely to be satisfied if you choose a school that provides the level of intellectual challenge that you are prepared and willing to undertake.

- **Facilities and housing**

  Another important factor to consider in choosing a college is whether the campus facilities—including classrooms, libraries, laboratories, and dormitories—are well maintained, up to date, and equipped with the latest technologies. If first-year students are required to live on campus, you should check to see if the housing is safe, comfortable, and offers the amenities you want. If most students have campus meal plans, you should make sure the dining options are appealing and offer good food.

- **Special programs**

  If you are interested in special programs—such as honors, study abroad, or Reserve Officers' Training Corps (ROTC)—it is important to look for schools that offer those options.

- **Support services**

  Colleges also differ greatly in the support services they offer to students, such as counseling, academic advising, tutoring, career planning, recruiting, and mentoring. If you have a disability, you should look for schools with strong disability-support programs, services, and housing options.

- **Extracurricular activities**

  Another important factor to consider is whether you plan to get involved in extracurricular activities during your college years. Many schools offer students the opportunity to participate in athletics, clubs, fraternities and sororities, and other activities.

- **Demographic factors**

  In addition to location, cost, facilities, and programs, you should also look for colleges that match your personal preferences as far as being public or private, religious or secular, and politically liberal or conservative.

Something To Consider...

Be sure to keep your own individual preferences and educational interests front and center during the search process. You should never choose a college because your best friend goes there, or your parents went there, or you've always been a fan of its sports teams. Selecting a college is a highly personal decision, so investigate all your options and make the best choice for *you*.

Identifying Colleges That Match Your Interests

Once you have identified the "must-have" characteristics of the college you want to attend, the next step is gathering information in order to find schools that match your preferences. There are many resources available to help you in this part of the college search process, including the following:

- **High-school guidance counselors**

  The counseling office at your high school has lots of information about colleges. Make an appointment and talk to your counselor about the factors that are most important to you. Based on this information and your academic record, the counselor will be able to suggest some schools for you to consider.

- **Parents, family, and friends**

  People who are close to you and know your personality and interests may have some ideas about where you would be happy going to school.

- **Online college search tools**

  A number of free, online tools are available to help you find colleges that match your interests. Sites like MyCollegeOptions and CollegeView allow you to create a personal profile, rank the factors that are most important to you, and search for colleges that fit your criteria. You will receive a list of schools in order of compatibility, with links to more information about them.

- **College guides**

  Your school or public library will have books and other resources that provide information about various college options.

- **College websites, brochures, and admission packets**

  You can also visit the websites of different colleges or request brochures or admission packets in order to gather information. Although these materials can give you an idea about a school's emphasis and personality, you should keep in mind that they are designed to present the school in the best possible light.

Narrowing Your Choices

After researching your college options, you will have enough information to develop a list of contenders. The next step in the process involves narrowing down your list of choices and deciding where to apply. Although some students may apply to as many as a dozen schools, most only apply to a handful. Completing college applications is time consuming, after all, and most colleges require an application fee of around $50. Narrowing your list involves taking a hard look at your academic record, your financial situation, and the campus atmosphere at your top schools.

- **Academic qualifications**

  The first thing to consider is your likelihood of being accepted to a particular school based on its admission standards and your academic qualifications. It may be helpful to divide your top choices into three categories, based on your realistic chances of admission: reach schools, where your grades and test scores put you at the low end of the range for admission; mid-range schools, where your qualifications fall in the middle of the admission standards; and safety schools, where your qualifications rank near the top of applicants. You should apply to between one and three schools in each category. Keep in mind that the most selective schools do not necessarily provide the highest quality education, or the best fit for you.

- **Financial considerations**

  The next thing to consider when narrowing down your choices is whether you can realistically afford to go to each school. Submit the *Free Application for Federal Student Aid* (FAFSA®) to see whether you qualify for grants, loans, or other forms of financial aid. Talk to your parents about how much they are willing to contribute to your higher education. Investigate the scholarships and assistance that each school on your list typically offers to students in your financial situation.

- **Campus atmosphere**

    One of the most helpful ways to narrow down your list and choose a college is to visit campuses, tour the facilities, and meet with admissions officers, instructors, and students. The best way to learn whether a certain school feels welcoming, comfortable, and right for you is by experiencing the campus atmosphere in person.

References

1. "Beginning Your College Search Process," MyCollegeOptions, 2017.

2. "Essential Steps To Selecting A College," MyCollegeOptions, 2017.

3. McGuire, Jeff. "College Selection Guide," CollegeView, n.d.

Chapter 12
Choosing A College

Basic Factors In Choosing A College

As you research colleges and career schools, consider such factors as cost, location, accreditation, and more. There are a number of factors that can help you figure out what schools are right for you.

School Costs And Net Price

School costs can be one of the most important factors in choosing potential colleges or career schools—and costs can vary significantly from school to school. While the cost of college includes tuition and fees, it also includes equipment, travel, and more. Learn about what is included in the cost of college and ways to reduce college costs.

You'll want to make sure that the cost of your school is reasonable compared to your earning potential in your future career. In other words, you want to make sure that you can earn enough money to cover any student loan payments you may need to make, along with living expenses, after you graduate.

Any school that participates in the federal student aid (FSA) programs is required to provide information on its cost of attendance and to offer a net price calculator on its website.

About This Chapter: Text under the heading "Basic Factors In Choosing A College," is excerpted from "Things To Consider," Federal Student Aid, U.S. Department of Education (ED), January 20, 2017; Text under the heading "Using A College Scorecard" is excerpted from "Choose A College More Easily With The College Scorecard," U.S. Department of Education (ED), September 14, 2016; Text under the heading "Choosing A College: Questions To Ask" is excerpted from "Choosing A College: Questions To Ask," Federal Trade Commission (FTC), May 26, 2015; Text under the heading "Four Things You Should Consider When Choosing A College" is excerpted from "4 Things You Should Consider When Choosing A College," U.S. Department of Education (ED), March 7, 2016.

This calculator will give you an idea of how much a program may cost after subtracting any financial aid. The average net price to attend the school is determined by subtracting the average amount of federal, state/local government, or institutional grant or scholarship aid from the total cost of attendance for the institution's largest program.

You can look up the cost and assess the value of colleges using the College Scorecard (collegescorecard.ed.gov).

Financial Aid

Many students worry that tuition and the other costs of continuing their education will be out of reach. But don't let the potential costs stop you. Cost is only part of the picture. Most students receive some kind of financial aid; and a few students even get a "free ride," with all their costs covered.

There are many sources of financial aid to help you cover the cost of college or career school. You should

- learn about financial aid including grants, scholarships, work-study, and loans;

- find out whether the school (and the major/program) you're considering participates in the federal student aid programs (the biggest source of aid for college and career school);

- apply for all types of aid for which you might qualify; and

- meet all deadlines!

The Internal Revenue Service (IRS) also provides tax benefits for education.

To help you see the total annual costs of schools you're interested in and to find out if the schools participate in the federal student aid programs, explore the college search tool.

As you head off to college, you should create and manage your own budget. Keep track of your income and expenses, save for your goals, and adjust your budget as your life changes.

Academics

Does the school offer the major or program you'd like to pursue? Does the program have a good reputation? Talk to professionals in the field you'd like to pursue, do a web search, and talk to students who are enrolled in that program.

If you aren't sure what you want to do, does the school give you plenty of options? You can also use the U.S. Department of Labor's (DOL) career search to find careers that might match your interests.

Accreditation

An accredited school meets certain standards set by an independent agency. It helps ensure the training or education you get meets employer standards in a specific field.

If you attend a school that isn't accredited, you might not be able to get any financial aid. The U.S. Department of Education (ED) requires that schools participating in the federal student aid programs be accredited. Also, your state education agency's aid programs may not offer financial aid at unaccredited schools.

In addition, attending an unaccredited school poses the following risks:

- You might not be able to transfer your credits to another school. For example, if you attend an unaccredited two-year school and then transfer to a four-year school to earn a bachelor's degree, you might have to start over again at the four-year school if it doesn't recognize the classes you took.

- It may be difficult to get a job. Some employers may not hire someone with a certificate from a school that is unaccredited.

A diploma mill is an unaccredited school (or a business claiming to be a school) that awards a degree without requiring classwork that meets college-level standards. Some will send a "diploma" without you doing any work at all if you pay a fee. Others assign classwork that is so easy that your resulting degree is worthless, compared to a degree from an accredited school, and it won't help you get a good job.

Admission Requirements

Admission requirements vary from school to school, so check the websites of all the colleges you're interested in. Learn about applying to schools and taking required tests.

School Location, Size, And Campus Life

Give consideration to a school's location, size, and activities when researching colleges and career schools. Some students want to stay close to their families and others like the opportunity to go away to school to live on their own. Do you want to go to school in a big city or a small town? Do you want a small, intimate setting? A school that's big enough to be a city by itself? Or something in between? Keep in mind that the location of a school and your housing options can impact your overall cost.

Does the school offer activities and social opportunities you like? Does it offer services you need? Does it have a good campus security system?

While the school's website and the college search tool can help you determine some of these factors, a campus visit will help the most. Or, see if the school offers virtual tours of its campus.

Work Flexibility

If you need to work full-time while you're in school, does the school have night courses or other options to accommodate you? Will they let you attend part-time? Do they offer summer courses? Check the school's website or talk to the admissions staff at the college or career school that you're interested in to see what are your options.

Statistics That Count

Some numbers can help you evaluate schools.

Table 12.1. Statistics That Count

Statistic	Description	Where to Find the Info
Graduation Rate	The percentage of a school's first-time, first-year undergraduate students who complete their program within 150 percent of the standard time for the program. For example, for a four-year degree program, entering students who complete within six years are counted as graduates.	U.S. Department of Education's College Navigator website
Retention Rate	The percentage of a school's first-time, first-year undergraduate students who continue at that school the next year. For example, a student who studies full-time in the fall semester and continues studying in the program in the next fall semester is counted in this rate.	U.S. Department of Education's College Navigator website
Job Placement Rate	The percentage of students who are placed in jobs relevant to their courses of study within a set amount of time. You may also want to contact a school's career center and find out what kind of job placement services it offers students and graduates.	The college's or career school's website or career center

Table 12.1. Continued

Statistic	Description	Where to Find the Info
Loan Default Rate	The percentage of a school's federal student loan borrowers who enter repayment during a particular federal fiscal year, October 1 to September 30, and default within a certain timeframe. You might not be able to get aid from some of our programs at a school that has a high default rate.	U.S. Department of Education's College Navigator website

Enrollment Contracts

Read any school enrollment contract carefully before you sign it. The contract explains what the school will give you for your money. If a school representative promises you something (such as help finding a job) that's not in the contract, ask the representative to write that promise into the contract and have it signed and dated. A promise is usually not enforceable unless it's in writing.

Refund Policies

Find out the school's tuition refund policy. If you enroll but never begin classes, you should get most of your money back. If you begin attending classes but leave before completing your course work, you might be able to get some of your money back.

Also find out the school's return-of-aid policy. If you receive federal student aid (except for Federal Work-Study) and you withdraw from school, some of that money might have to be given back to the source by you or by your school.

Even if you don't finish your coursework, you'll have to repay the loan funds you received, minus any student loan funds your school has returned to the U.S. Department of Education (ED).

Distance Learning Or Online Degrees

Lots of schools have begun to offer distance learning, which allows you to access lectures or course materials online or through other electronic media. Whether a distance learning course or degree is right for you is a matter of personal preference.

Be aware that not every distance learning course or online degree is accredited and/or eligible for federal student aid. To find out whether you can receive federal student aid for your program, check with your school's financial aid office.

Past Complaints And Reputation

Just because a school participates in the federal student aid programs doesn't mean the U.S. Department of Education (ED) endorsed the quality of education the school offers. The U.S. Department of Education (ED) doesn't approve a school's curriculum, policies, or administrative practices, except as they relate to the administration of the federal student aid programs.

To find out whether there have been any complaints about the school, contact your local Better Business Bureau (BBB), state higher education agency, or the consumer protection division of your state attorney general's office.

Ask employers what they think about the school. Ask recent graduates about their experience at the school. Check with the agency that licenses or accredits the school to see whether it meets required standards.

Using A College Scorecard

Choosing a college is an overwhelming process. There were few independent reviews of colleges and no real way of knowing if the information found is accurate. The College Scorecard, solves this challenge by giving everyone—students, families, guidance counselors and non-profits—access to a whole host of data verified by the U.S. Department of Education (ED) on thousands of institutions across the nation in an easy-to-use online tool. College is still the best investment a person can make in them self—bachelor's degree-holders earn roughly $1 million more over their lifetimes than high school graduates. The College Scorecard makes choosing between thousands of institutions easier by providing simple to understand information on institutions' incoming students and the graduating students' outcomes.

Choosing A College: Questions To Ask

Some schools may take your money and leave you without the training and qualifications to get into the career you want. They tell you to sign up for courses that don't suit your needs, or press you to take out loans that will be hard to pay off. Before committing to any program, do some research, know exactly what you're paying for, and determine if you'll end up with the credentials you want.

Ask some key questions to help you avoid pitfalls as you pick the college that's right for you.

What's The Total Cost?

Will you pay by the course, semester, or program? Are there fees for dropping or adding a class? How much will you pay for books, equipment, uniforms, lab fees, or graduation fees?

How Will I Pay For It? Will Federal Loans Cover The Cost?

You may be eligible for federal financial student aid that may offer more favorable terms than a private loan. ED administers several major student aid programs—grants, loans, and work-study programs. Get details at ED's StudentAid.gov. There is a lifetime cap on the total amount of federal loans a student can take out and you might hit the cap before you've finished your education. Some research and planning can help you avoid getting stuck in a private loan with less favorable terms. Consider different options, too. For example, community colleges often offer similar programs for a fraction of the price of for-profit colleges.

Will This School Get Me Where I Want To Go? Will I Earn The Credentials I Want?

Some schools may try to hide the number of classes or amount of time it will take to complete a program. Some might change course requirements after you enroll. Don't commit to any program unless you understand what you'll have to do to complete it. Get details about each required course, including when it is offered, how long it takes to complete, and other requirements for the degree or certificate. Ask the school whether degree or program requirements have changed in the past. If so, ask how often and why. If you're pursuing a profession that requires a license, contact your state licensing organization to find out what training and credentials they require to grant one. Ask if the school's program meets the state's licensing requirements. If it does not, you won't be qualified to get a license—or a job—in that field.

Can I Transfer Credit I Earn At This School To Other Schools?

If you may transfer in the future, find out whether the school you might transfer to would accept the credits you earned at the first school. If you attend a community college, ask about their articulation agreement: that's a formal statement of what community college courses and credits you can transfer to a particular four-year college. Your ability to transfer credits depends a lot on the type of accreditation held by the school where you earned the credits.

What Percentage Of Students Graduate?

Use ED's College Navigator to check loan default rates, average debt at the school, tuition and expenses, and accreditation. Ask the schools you're considering to give you information in writing about job placement and average salaries for their graduates in the program you want to study. They may paint a glowing picture of student success and try to convince you that credentials from their institution will lead to a high-paying career in your chosen field. But some schools manipulate the data or lie about how well their graduates fare. Do some research using the U.S. Department of Labor's (DOL) site, MyNextMove (www.mynextmove.org), which can help you figure out what careers you might like to pursue. DOL's *Occupational Outlook Handbook* has information about the average salary workers in a particular field are earning, the education or training needed, and the careers with the most new jobs, so you can evaluate whether the results the school claims are realistic. College Navigator also can help you compare schools based on their graduation rates which can help you assess students' successful completion of a program at that institution.

What Percentage Of Recent Graduates Is Late In Paying Back Their Loans?

A high default rate among graduates who borrowed money could be a tip-off that students are burdened by too much debt or having trouble finding jobs in their field. Get information about student borrowers' default rates at College Navigator (for the colleges you're considering) and ED's StudentAid.gov (default rate by type of school—public, private non-profit, or private for-profit.)

Is There Pressure To Enroll?

Is a recruiter or advisor for the school rushing you to commit? Are they leaning on you to decide before you have a chance to research the program and confirm the details of financial aid? Recruiters, whom some schools also might refer to as "counselors" or "academic advisors," may be paid based on how many students they bring in. Before you decide on a program, read the materials, including the contract. Can you cancel within a few days of signing up and, if so, do the materials tell you how to cancel? If the school refuses to give you documents to review before you commit, don't enroll. Period.

Four Things You Should Consider When Choosing A College

A college or career school education = more money, more job options, and more freedom. Yet, with more than 7,000 colleges and universities nationwide, deciding which college is right for you can be difficult. Maybe you want to find a school with the best nursing program, or study abroad options, or the best college basketball team; every person values different things. However, it's also important to remember that college is one of the biggest financial investments you will make in yourself. Just as important as academics and extracurricular activities are the financial factors: how much a college costs, whether students are likely to graduate on time, and, if alumni are able to find good jobs and pay off their loans. That is why the U.S. Department of Education developed the College Scorecard. It provides clear information to answer all of your questions regarding college costs, graduation, debt, and postcollege earnings.

As you're comparing colleges, use the College Scorecard to compare these four things:

Net Cost

For starters, you should consider how much you'll actually be paying on an annual basis. That's not necessarily the sticker price, but it's the sticker price minus all of the scholarships and grants that you will receive when enrolling in an institution. This is called the net price, and it's important because it's the average amount students actually pay out of pocket. The College Scorecard can show you the average net price of each school compared to the national average. It can also give you a net price estimate for each school broken down by family income. Here's an example:

Average Annual Cost ⓘ

$16,574

$16,541
✔ ABOUT AVERAGE

By Family Income

Depending on the federal, state, or institutional grant aid available, students in your income bracket may pay more or less than the overall average costs.

FAMILY INCOME	AVERAGE COST
$0-$30,000	$10,159
$30,001-$48,000	$12,613
$48,001-$75,000	$18,324
$75,001-$110,000	$20,879
$110,001+	$21,655

Figure 12.1. Costs

Graduation Rate

Next, you should consider a school's graduation rate as a factor when choosing a college. College graduation rates refer to the percentage of undergraduate students who complete their program within 150 percent of the standard time for the program. For example, for a four-year degree program, entering students who complete their degrees within six years are counted in that school's graduation rate. You want to attend a college that has a high graduation rate. A college's graduation rate gives a good indication if students who attend that institution are likely to end up with a degree. Retention rate is the percentage of a school's first-time, first-year undergraduate students who continue at that school the next year. For example, a student who studies full-time in the fall semester and keeps on studying in the program in the next fall semester is counted in this rate. The College Scorecard can help you find schools that have a high rate of success among their students from a particular college. Here's an example:

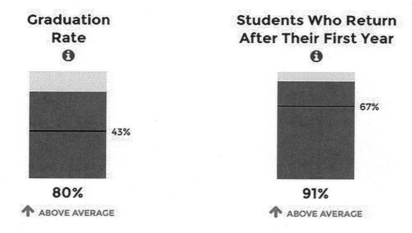

Figure 12.2. Graduation And Retention

Students Paying Down Their Debt

In addition to costs, you may consider if students are able to repay their loans after attending a college or career school. The Scorecard can help you find out the amount of debt that you can expect to take on at an institution and the percentage of students who are able to repay that debt upon leaving. This is one of the most important factors to consider, as you may not want to attend an institution where you are expected to take out lots of loans and have little chance of repaying them in the future.

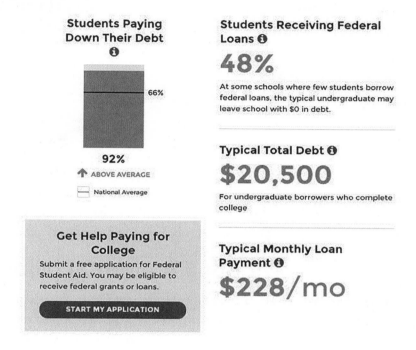

Figure 12.3. Financial Aid And Debt

Postcollege Earnings

With the cost of college continuing to increase, salary has become a critical factor students and families take into account when considering college choices. Knowing how much students typically earn after attending an institution will help you find out if students were able to find a good paying job, pay off their student loans, and have a financially secure future. Luckily, the Scorecard contains comprehensive and reliable data on postcollege earnings for students who attended all types of undergraduate institutions. The new Scorecard includes:

1. The proportion of former students earning over $25,000, which is the average earnings of high school graduates; and

2. The median earnings of students 10 years after they enroll in a particular college.

Here's an example of what the Scorecard will show you:

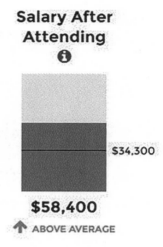

Percentage Earning Above High School Grad ⓘ

74% of students

who attend this school earned, on average, more than those with only a high school diploma.

Salary After Attending ⓘ

$34,300

$58,400

⬆ ABOVE AVERAGE

Figure 12.4. Earnings After School

A college degree is the best investment you can make for your future. It's important that you choose a school that will give you the skills and a degree that employers value, while allowing you to earn a comfortable living.

Chapter 13
Study Abroad

Advantages Of Studying Abroad

The importance of study abroad experience for students, colleges and universities, and our nation can be summarized with four widely recognized benefits:

- Study abroad programs provide young citizens with cognitive and affective competencies necessary for them to thrive in a global economy, while concurrently providing the nation with a citizenry that is economically competitive and politically savvy; necessary skills for the maintenance of national interests, security, and the ability to effectively respond to political instability, including threats of terrorism.

- International experience and competency contributes to a comprehensive liberal arts education. There is a substantive research literature that demonstrates that some of the core values and skills of a liberal arts education are enhanced by participation in study abroad programs. These values and skills include:

- Critical thinking skills;

- Ability to communicate in more than one language;

- Ability to communicate across cultural and national boundaries; and the

- Ability to make informed judgments on major personal and social issues based on the analysis of various perspectives.

About This Chapter: Text under the heading "Advantages Of Studying Abroad" is excerpted from "International Education Programs Service," U.S. Department of Education (ED), January 21, 2011; Text under the heading "U.S. Government Resources" is excerpted from "U.S. Government Resources," U.S. Department of State (DOS), November 17, 2015; Text beginning with the heading "International Schools" is excerpted from "International Schools," Federal Student Aid, U.S. Department of Education (ED), November 30, 2016.

- Study abroad programs can provide specialized training not available at home institutions such as:

- Advanced level foreign language competency courses;

- Specialized courses in disciplines such as archeology, art, international business, development studies, education, engineering, nursing/allied health, performance, and world music.

- Study abroad experiences promote personal growth, development and maturity among participating students.

U.S. Government Resources

The U.S. Department of State (DOS) is committed to supporting the next generation of diverse American leaders to gain the knowledge and skills they need to succeed in a globalizing world. Study abroad is a time of great discovery—young Americans experience the world and begin to form networks that will enhance their prospects in the world's marketplace and their potential as global problem-solvers. Americans who study abroad build understanding as unofficial ambassadors for our country, defining American values and debunking stereotypes.

Chart your future as a global leader today!

Programs

The federal government supports study and research abroad for individuals and institutions. The U.S. Department of State (DOS) and other federal agencies fund a number of programs that enable K-12 students, university students, educators, and scholars to conduct research, work, or study abroad. In addition, the Department of State provides funds and other programming to help both U.S. and foreign institutions improve their capacity to host study abroad programs.

For U.S. K-12 School Students

Programs conducted during the academic year for Kindergarten through 12th grade students, including language learning programs, exchanges, and foreign study.

Information For U.S. High School Students

- **Kennedy-Lugar Youth Exchange and Study Abroad (YES Abroad)** provides merit-based scholarships to study abroad for an academic year.

- **The Congress Bundestag Youth Exchange (CBYX)** provides merit-based scholarships to high school students, recent vocational graduates and young professionals for an academic year of study in Germany.

- **National Security Language Initiative for Youth (NSLI-Y)** provides merit-based scholarships to learn less-commonly studied foreign languages in summer and academic year immersion programs.

- **American Youth Leadership Program (AYLP)** provides opportunities for students and educators to travel abroad on a three- to four-week exchange program.

For U.S. Undergraduate And Graduate Students

Are you pursuing an undergraduate or graduate degree? Interested in research? Enhance your education by studying abroad. You can learn how to communicate across cultures and work with diverse teams while working toward your degree. Find a program that's right for you.

Information For U.S. Undergraduate And Graduate Students

- **Benjamin A. Gilman International Scholarship Program** provides need-based scholarships of up to $5000 for students of limited financial means to study or intern abroad.

- **Critical Language Scholarship (CLS) Program** provides fully funded intensive summer language institutes overseas in fourteen critical languages.

- **Fulbright U.S. Student Program** sends recent college graduates and early career professionals to live, study and conduct research abroad in 140 countries.

- **Fulbright English Teaching Assistant (ETA) Program** places recent college graduates in classrooms in 75 countries to help teach English and serve as cultural ambassadors.

- **The Boren Award for International Study** is an initiative of the National Security Education Program (NSEP) that provides funding for U.S. undergraduate students to study less commonly taught languages in world regions critical to U.S. interests and underrepresented in study abroad.

- **The Language Flagship** offers programs at 22 universities and colleges across the United States combined with overseas study opportunities at ten Flagship Overseas Centers.

- **Project GO (Global Officers)** provides scholarships to Reserve Officers'Training Corps (ROTC) students in three services for critical language study domestically and abroad.

- **Fulbright-Hays Doctoral Dissertation Research Abroad (DDRA) Fellowship Program** provides opportunities to doctoral candidates to engage in full-time dissertation research abroad in modern foreign languages and area studies. Grants are given in all world areas except Western Europe as the program aims to encourage the study of regions and cultures that are not commonly explored.

- **Foreign Language and Area Studies (FLAS) Fellowships** provide opportunities for outstanding undergraduate and graduate students to engage in area studies and world language training at schools that have established a FLAS fellowship program. FLAS provides allocations of fellowships to institutions of higher education, which then make awards directly to meritorious undergraduate students and graduate students. Students must be enrolled at and apply through a FLAS-recipient institution.

Below are additional programs that provide funding for education and research. While not exclusively for international programs, they do allow for study and research abroad.

- **Barry Goldwater Scholarship and Excellence in Education Program** provides a continuing source of highly qualified scientists, mathematicians, and engineers by awarding scholarships to college students who intend to pursue research careers in these fields.

- **Central Intelligence Agency (CIA) Student Scholarships** are available to both undergraduate and graduate students.

- **Dr. Nancy Foster Scholarship Program** recognizes outstanding scholarship and encourages independent graduate level research—particularly by female and minority students—in The National Oceanic and Atmospheric Administration (NOAA) mission-related sciences of oceanography, marine biology and maritime archaeology, including all science, engineering and resource management of ocean and coastal areas.

- **Ernest F. Hollings Scholarship** seeks to increase undergraduate training in oceanic and atmospheric science, research, technology, and education and foster multidisciplinary training opportunities.

- **Export.gov** provides internship opportunities with the U.S. Commercial Service (CS) in U.S. embassies abroad.

- **Cobell Scholarship** is annual, non-renewable, and available to any full-time and degree-seeking American Indian or Alaska Native postsecondary student attending any nationally, regionally and industry accredited non-profit, public and private, institution while pursuing a vocational certificate or diploma, associate's, bachelor's, master's, doctoral, professional degree or certificate.

- **Greater Research Opportunities (GRO) Undergraduate Fellowships** The Environmental Protection Agency (EPA) offers fellowships for undergraduate students in environmentally related fields of study.

- **Harry S. Truman Scholarship Foundation** awards merit-based scholarships to college students who plan to pursue careers in government or elsewhere in public service. Truman Scholars receive up to $30,000 for graduate or professional school, participate in leadership development activities, and have special opportunities for internships and employment with the federal government.

- **Hubert Global Health Fellowship** provides third- and fourth-year medical and veterinary students with public health experience in a developing country.

- **National Science Foundation (NSF)** supports international research and education through a variety of programs, including fellowships, travel grants, summer institutes, workshops, and research and education projects.

- **National Institutes of Health (NIH) Fogarty International Center** supports and facilitates global health research conducted by U.S. and international investigators. Fogarty seeks partnerships between health research institutions in the United States and abroad who will train the next generation of scientists to address global health needs.

- **National Oceanic and Atmospheric Administration (NOAA) Educational Partnership Program Undergraduate Scholarship** provides scholarships for two years of undergraduate study to students majoring in Science, Technology, Engineering, and Mathematics (STEM) fields that directly support NOAA's mission. Participants conduct research at a NOAA facility during two paid summer internships.

- **Registered Apprenticeship Program** provides the opportunity for workers seeking high-skilled, high-paying jobs and for employers seeking to build a qualified workforce. In this regard, the Registered Apprenticeship system effectively meets the needs of both employers and workers. Registered Apprenticeship is highly active in traditional industries such as construction and manufacturing, but it is also instrumental in the training and development of emerging industries such as healthcare, energy, and homeland security.

- **Saul T. Wilson Jr., Scholarship Program** is offered through the U.S. Department of Agriculture Animal and Plant Health Inspection Service (APHIS). Students interested in a career in veterinarian services are encouraged to apply.

- **Science, Mathematics and Research for Transformation (SMART) Scholarship for Service Program** is an opportunity for students pursuing an undergraduate or graduate degree in Science, Technology, Engineering, and Mathematics (STEM) disciplines to receive a full scholarship and be gainfully employed upon degree completion.

- **Science To Achieve Results (STAR)** supports masters and doctoral candidates in environmental studies. Students can pursue degrees in traditionally recognized environmental disciplines as well as other fields such as social anthropology, urban and regional planning, and decision sciences.

- **Stokes Scholarship Program** develops students for future permanent employment while they pursue a degree relevant to NGA's (National Geospatial-Intelligence Agency) mission. The intent of the Stokes Scholarship Program is to recruit high-caliber undergraduate students who have demonstrated financial need and provide them with financial assistance to complete their undergraduate degrees.

- **Thomas R. Pickering Foreign Affairs Fellowship** provides undergraduate and graduate students with financial support, mentoring and professional development to prepare them academically and professionally for a career in the U.S. Department of State Foreign Service.

- **Udall Undergraduate Scholarship** awards scholarships to college sophomores and juniors for leadership, public service, and commitment to issues related to American Indian nations or to the environment.

- **United States Agency for International Development (USAID)** is the lead U.S. Government agency that works to end extreme global poverty and enable resilient, democratic societies to realize their potential. Funding opportunities are available to universities and research scholars.

- **USDA/1994 Tribal Scholars Program** provides scholarships for applicants attending 1994 Land Grant Tribal Colleges and Universities seeking careers in food, agriculture, and natural resource sciences, and/or other related disciplines.

- **USDA/1890 National Scholars Program** designed to increase the number of minorities studying agriculture, food, natural resource sciences, and the related disciplines.

- **William F. Helms Internship Program** help protect U.S. agriculture and the environment while facilitating global trade of pest and disease-free agricultural goods.

For U.S. Scholars

The federal government funds many programs that will enable you to diversify your research by working overseas.

Information For U.S. Scholars:

- The Fulbright U.S. Scholar Program offers opportunities for American faculty members and scholars to conduct research, lecture, and/or consult with other scholars and institutions abroad.

- The Fulbright Specialist Program sends U.S. faculty and professionals to serve as expert consultants on curriculum, faculty development, institutional planning and related subjects at overseas academic institutions for a period of two to six weeks.

The Fulbright-Hays Faculty Research Abroad Fellowship Program, sponsored by the U.S. Department of Education (ED), offers awards to postdoctoral U.S. faculty to support research and training efforts overseas that focus on non-western foreign languages and area studies.

International Schools

Many students get federal student aid to help pay for their study at international schools, either at the undergraduate or graduate level.

Whether you plan to study abroad for a semester or get your entire degree outside the United States, you may be able to use federal student aid to pay your expenses. The type of aid you can get—and the process you must follow—will depend on the type of program (study-abroad or full degree) you plan to enter. Your status as an undergraduate or graduate student also affects the type of aid for which you're eligible, just as it does at schools in the United States.

Study Abroad For A Semester Or Year

You may receive federal student aid for a study-abroad program, if you meet the aid eligibility criteria. If you aren't already in the habit of filling out a *Free Application for Federal Student Aid* (FAFSA®) each year for college, be sure to learn about the federal student aid programs and the FAFSA® process. You'll need to fill out a FAFSA® before you can receive federal student aid to study abroad.

To determine which types of aid you'll be able to use for your study-abroad program, contact the financial aid office at your American school. (If your American school doesn't participate in the federal student aid programs, then you won't be able to get federal student aid to help pay for your study abroad.) Start early, because it's important to get all necessary paperwork done on time, both at your American school and at the international school.

Get A Degree From An International School

If you've decided to get your degree from a school outside the United States, congratulations.

How Can I Research Schools And Their Requirements?

First, don't panic. You're on your own, but if you're organized and determined, you'll be okay. In this chapter, we'll share some tips about preparing to study at an international school and some resources to help you learn about schools that participate in the American federal student aid programs.

Here are general tips:

- Start early. You've got more to do than your friends who are going to American schools, so don't think you can apply for financial aid this month and use it to pay your tuition next month.

- If you're interested in a particular school, check its website to find out about program availability (does it offer the degree you want?), cost, enrollment policies, and resources and programs for international students.

- Do your research and keep a to-do list. For instance, what paperwork needs to be done? (Visas? Housing forms? Registering with the police? Valid passport? Emergency contacts? Medical insurance?)

- Create a file to organize your documents and information from your school.

- Find out who at the school will be processing your financial aid. Get their email address, and contact them when you have questions. (If you're not sure where to start, try the school's office for international students.)

- Don't forget that you can get help filling out the FAFSA® either within the form itself at fafsa.gov (in the "Help and Hints" section on each page of the application) or by phone at 800-4-FED-AID (800-433-3243).

What Federal Student Aid Can I Receive For My Degree At An International School?

At many schools around the world, you can receive a federal student loan from the William D. Ford Federal Direct Loan (Direct Loan) Program. (Find out which international schools participate in the Direct Loan Program.) You may receive a Direct Subsidized Loan or Direct Unsubsidized Loan for your undergraduate education. Direct Unsubsidized Loans and Direct PLUS Loans are available to graduate students. Your parent also might be able to borrow on your behalf; he or she should ask about getting a Direct PLUS Loan for parents. International schools do not participate in the U.S. Department of Education's grant programs, so you will not be able to obtain a Federal Pell Grant to get your degree at an international school.

How Much Can I Receive In Federal Student Loan Funds?

The annual limit for Direct Subsidized Loans plus Direct Unsubsidized Loans varies from $5,500 to $20,500, depending on a variety of factors (year in school, status as a dependent or independent student, etc.). Direct PLUS Loan amounts are determined by subtracting any other financial aid you're receiving from your total cost of attendance at the school.

How Do I Apply For A Federal Student Loan To Use At An International School?

Apply for student loans at your international school using the same process you use to apply for aid in the United States.

1. Fill out a FAFSA® at fafsa.gov as early as possible. The FAFSA® is available on October 1 for school attendance that begins any time from July 1 of the following year through June of the year beyond that. There is no special FAFSA® for students planning to attend international schools.

2. Make sure the school you plan to attend has your FAFSA® information. International schools have the ability to access your FAFSA® information electronically. When you fill out the FAFSA®, list the school you plan to attend in the question about Federal School Codes. (The FAFSA® site has a tool to let you search for your school's Federal School Code [https://fafsa.ed.gov/FAFSA/app/schoolSearch?].) Once it's listed on your FAFSA®, your school will then download your data.

3. Find out the next steps from your chosen school. Different schools proceed differently at this stage of the process. Ask your school how you will get your loan money—what paperwork do you need to fill out, what are the deadlines, etc. Keep track of everything that is required

of you; make copies of paper documents (or scan them) and file them safely; and meet those deadlines! And if your parent plans to get a Direct PLUS Loan, he or she should keep a close eye on required documents and deadlines as well.

4. If you are a first-year student borrowing federal funds for the first time, you will have to complete entrance counseling. This means you'll be required to read text or watch a video online, or attend an in-person presentation, in order to learn about the responsibilities of taking out a loan. Your entrance counseling might happen before you leave the United States or after you arrive at your school; it depends on the school.

How Will I Get Paid?

Your loan funds will be electronically transmitted from the U.S. Department of the Treasury to the international school's designated bank. First the school will put the funds toward anything you owe them (tuition, fees, etc.). If there is any money left over after the funds are applied to your account at the school, the extra money will go to you.

Your funds might not be disbursed (paid out) before you leave the United States, so you will most likely have to come up with your travel expenses yourself.

When And How Do I Repay The Loan?

That depends on whether it's a subsidized or unsubsidized loan versus a PLUS loan. Repayment of a loan used to pay for international study works the same way as repayment of a loan used to pay for an American school.

Part Three
Saving For College

Chapter 14
Reasons To Save For College

The cost of a four-year college education has increased much faster than the rate of inflation over the past few decades. From 1995 to 2015, for instance, the average cost of tuition and fees at private colleges rose 179 percent to reach $31,200 per year. Meanwhile, the average cost of in-state tuition and fees at public universities rose 296 percent to reach $9,100 per year. For many families, the high cost of college stretches budgets to the limit and forces students to take on ever-increasing amounts of debt.

One approach to dealing with the skyrocketing costs of higher education is to begin saving for college early in your child's life. By investing a small amount of money on a regular basis, you can accumulate enough over time to make a big dent in tuition costs.

Did You Know...
Putting even $2 per day—the cost of a cup of coffee—into a college savings account that earns 1 percent interest would add up to more than $12,000 over the course of seventeen years.

Some financial planners argue that parents should focus on paying down their own debts and saving for retirement rather than setting aside money for college. After all, scholarships, grants, and loans are available to help pay for college, while you are unlikely to receive assistance toward meeting your other financial goals. But saving money for college offers you a number of important benefits, including the following:

- **You can receive tax benefits**

  Many states offer income-tax deductions for contributions to a 529 college savings plan. In addition, the money you contribute—plus any earnings on your initial

---

investment—can be withdrawn tax-free later to pay for qualified education expenses. If you put that money in a regular investment account instead, you would not receive the state income-tax deduction and any earnings would be taxable.

- **You may not qualify for financial aid**

  Although the U.S. government provides billions of dollars in financial aid to students, your eligibility is based on your family's financial need, which is determined by a complex formula. Many online tools are available to help you estimate the amount of need-based aid you would qualify to receive if your child enrolled in college at the present time. If your child will not enter college for a few years, though, you may not be able to count on that money. Either your income or the financial aid rules could change to make you ineligible by the time your child actually starts college.

- **Savings have a limited impact on financial aid**

  Some people resist saving for college because they believe it will only reduce the amount of financial aid they qualify to receive. In the formula used to calculate financial aid, however, your income affects your Expected Family Contribution (EFC) much more than your savings. The federal government puts more emphasis on income because it wants to encourage families to save for college. As a result, an average family would only reduce their calculated financial need by about $60 for every $1,000 in college savings. In other words, they would still be $940 closer to paying for college.

- **Your student will graduate with less debt**

  Many students have to borrow money in order to afford college. In fact, the average 2016 college graduate owed more than $37,000 in student loans. Repaying these debts can take many years and prevent college graduates from accomplishing other financial goals. Saving for college when your child is young can reduce your family's need for student loans in the future. In addition, it can increase your child's chances of graduating from college debt free.

- **Your student may have more college choices**

  Some of the most selective colleges base their financial awards for prospective students on merit rather than on need. If your child manages to win admission to a dream school, you want them to be able to enroll even without receiving merit-based scholarships or grants. A college savings fund might make up the difference and allow your child to attend their top choice school.

- **College savings offer flexibility**

Although college savings accounts must be used for qualified education expenses, they do offer some flexibility to adapt to changing circumstances. If your child does not end up needing the money for college, you can designate a new beneficiary for the funds. Your child can also put the money toward graduate school, professional programs, or non-traditional educational opportunities.

- **Family members can contribute as well**

Once you set up a college savings account, you can invite other family members to contribute to it instead of buying your child birthday and holiday gifts. Relatives who place a high value on education will feel good about supporting your child's future opportunities.

References

1. Becker, Matt. "Five Good Reasons To Use A College Savings Account," Mom and Dad Money, February 16, 2016.

2. Lieber, Ron. "Why It Makes Good Sense To Save For College Now," *New York Times,* October 23, 2015.

3. "Saving Early = Saving Smart," Federal Student Aid, U.S. Department of Education, 2017.

Chapter 15
Ways To Save For College

A four-year college degree is almost mandatory for most entry-level positions these days, but for something that's so important, the costs can be intimidating for students and parents alike.

> Students can get started contributing to their own future college education. Ideas include working part time, using cash gifts from relatives and friends to start a savings account, and beginning early to investigate scholarships and other forms of financial aid.

According to the College Board, the average annual outlay for tuition, books, and other fees for the 2016–17 school year at private colleges was $33,480, and at public universities the costs came to $9,650 for state residents and $24,930 for nonresidents. So, in many cases, four years of college can run into six figures.

Those are scary numbers, to be sure, but families generally don't pay college fees out-of-pocket on a yearly basis. According to the latest figures available from the College Board, 27 percent of spending on higher education came from parent income and savings and 11 percent from student income and savings. That means that just over one-third of the annual expenses were paid in family cash. The rest came from a combination of grants and scholarships (30%), parent and student loans (27%), and other sources, such as gifts from relatives.

Still, the amount of college expense that does come from family income can be mitigated by advance preparation. There are a number of ways to save for higher education in which even a small investment can pay off abundantly over a period of time.

Here are a few common ones.

529 Plans

These education-specific, tax-advantaged savings plans are named after the section of the Federal Tax Code that regulates them. Most states offer them, and there are many different types of plans available, so you'll need to do some research to determine which is best for you.

- Advantages:
  - Money earned on the account is tax-deferred, and if it's spent on education, it's tax-free.
  - They're not based on need, so 529 Plans are available to any income level.
  - 529 Plans are easy to open, sometimes for as little as $25.
  - There may be tax breaks if you invest in your own state's plan, but you aren't limited to your state.

- Disadvantages:
  - The biggest downside is that the money in a 529 Plan must be used for education. If it's withdrawn for any other reason, the tax advantages could evaporate and you may need to pay a penalty, as well.
  - 529 Plan funds count toward the student's assets when calculating financial-aid based on need, so plan money may reduce the amount of aid available.
  - Types of investments are limited to those approved by the plan.
  - There may be annual fees or other operating costs to maintain the plan.

Coverdell Education Savings Accounts

Also called simply an ESA, this type of account is similar to a 529 Plans in that funds invested are specifically earmarked for educational expenses.

- Advantages:
  - They carry many of the same tax benefits as a 529 Plan.
  - Unlike 529 Plans, funds are not able to be used only for postsecondary education but can be directed to private elementary and high-school fees, which may be a important to some families.
  - There are almost limitless investment options, unlike 529 Plans, which have restrictions on investment types.

- Disadvantages:
  - Low annual contribution limit (currently $2,000 per student).
  - Income restrictions. Although these are fairly high, they may affect some families.
  - Funds not used by the time the student reaches the age of 30 are subject to taxes.
  - Depending on investment type, there can be fees associated with it.

Prepaid College Tuition Plans

As the name implies, these plans allow you to pay for college credits in advance. They're run by individual states and each plan is different, so research will be necessary to determine whether or not your state's policies meet your needs.

- Advantages:
  - Prepaid tuition plans lock you in at the current tuition rate. So, if the cost is now $10,000 per year, that's what you'll pay when the money starts being used. The way college fees are increasing, this can be a huge advantage.
  - As with 529 Plans, there are federal and state tax advantages, although these vary by state.
  - Unlike many other college savings plans, in which investment funds are directly tied to stock market fluctuations, in most cases these plans are more secure.
- Disadvantages:
  - Although Prepaid College Tuition Plans were very popular for some years, they have fallen somewhat out of favor, so not all states offer them.
  - Funds invested in these plans must be used at in-state public colleges.
  - Although some investments are guaranteed by the states, in other cases they're not, so funds could be at risk due to budget cuts or other issues.

Custodial Accounts

These accounts are established under the Uniform Gift to Minors Act (UGMA) or the Uniform Transfer to Minors Act (UTMA) and are designed to act as a trust for the student. They can be set up at a financial institution or brokerage firm by parents, grandparents, or other adult custodian, who then makes all decisions regarding the account's investments until the student reaches the age of majority.

- Advantages:
  - Currently, for children younger than age 19 (or younger than 24 if a full-time student) the first $1,050 of unearned income is tax-free.
  - There are no income limits or contribution limits, although any contribution over $14,000 is subject to a gift tax.
  - There are no limits on types of investments.
- Disadvantages:
  - Once funds are deposited into the account, they belong to the child. Although the adult custodian retains control of the investment decisions, money can only be disbursed for expenditures that benefit the student.
  - The student will have full legal control of the funds once he or she attains the age of majority (18–21, depending on the state). And the money doesn't necessarily need to be used for educational purposes.
  - The student may need to file income-tax returns once the account reaches a certain amount (currently $1,000).
  - The account is treated as part of the student's assets, which means it could affect eligibility for need-based financial aid.
  - Earnings are subject to federal and state taxes.

Roth IRAs

A Roth IRA, or Individual Retirement Account (IRA), is another type of tax-advantaged saving plan. They're generally considered retirement savings instruments, but they can function as college saving accounts.

- Advantages:
  - As with 529 Plans, money earned on a Roth IRA can be withdrawn at a later date tax-free—usually at age 59½ for retirement purposes, but also for qualified educational expenses after five years.
  - If the student elects not to go to college, the money is still there serving as a retirement account.
  - Roth IRAs are not considered student assets when applying for need-based financial aid. (Although money disbursed for education does count toward the next year's asset calculation.)

- Disadvantages:

  - There is an annual contribution limit (currently $5,500) on Roth IRAs.

  - Using a Roth IRA for educational savings can have a negative impact on parents' overall retirement planning.

  - Although many states have income-tax benefits for 529 Plans, these benefits don't apply to Roth IRAs.

Savings Accounts

What about good old bank savings accounts? They're a good way to get young people into the saving habit early, and many parents or grandparents open one in the child's name as soon as he or she is born.

- Advantages:

  - Easy to open in minutes by anyone at any bank.

  - Deposits are already taxed, and the funds are easily accessible.

  - Money is guaranteed to be there by the federal government.

  - The account can be in the student's name, the adult's name, or both.

- Disadvantages:

  - Interest rates are generally so low that they struggle to keep up with inflation.

  - It can be tempting to use the funds for purposes other than education.

  - Interest, although it's low, is considered taxable income.

There are a number of other ways to save for a college education, including certificates of deposit (CDs), savings bonds, trusts and simple brokerage account (those not specifically directed at saving for education). And you're not locked into any one method of saving; you might choose to make use of several at the same time, or at different times. Whatever you do, make sure you understand the risks involved in investing, the tax benefits and liabilities, the fees associated with your investment, and limitations that may be placed on the use of your funds.

> The federal and state tax laws related to saving for college are extremely complicated. Before making an investment decision, be sure to consult with your financial adviser so you understand the implications.

References

1. Andriotis, AnnaMaria. "The Best Ways To Save For College," *Wall Street Journal*, February 13, 2015.

2. Fulciniti, Francesca. "A Practical Guide: The 5 Best Ways To Save For College," PrepScholar.com, November 15, 2015.

3. "How America Saves For College 2016," Sallie Mae and Ipsos, 2017.

4. Kuchar, Kristen. "How To Save For Your Child's College Education," TheSimpleDollar.com, May 3, 2016.

5. *Smart Saving For College: Better Buy Degrees*, Financial Industry Regulatory Authority, 2016.

6. "Trends In Higher Education," CollegeBoard.org, 2017.

7. Wong, Alice. "7 Reasons Why A 529 Plan Could Be The Best Savings Account For Your College Dream," Upromis.com, October 13, 2016.

Chapter 16
Budgeting

While you're in college or career school, you'll need to learn how to manage your finances, plan for changes, and prepare for the unexpected. Budgeting will help you build decision-making skills and reach your financial and academic goals.

Why Should I Create A Budget?

A budget is a guide that keeps you on the path to reach your financial goals. Budgeting keeps your finances under control, shows when you need to make adjustments to your spending, and helps you decide where your money goes instead of wondering where it all went.

Budgeting helps you answer these important questions:

- Where does all my money go?

- Is there a way to spend less?

- How will I handle unexpected expenses like replacing a broken cell phone or repairing my car?

- How can putting money into savings help me with some of my bigger financial goals?

Budgeting Helps You Achieve Academic And Financial Goals

Writing down your goals is the first step in creating a plan to make them realities. A budget will also help you prepare for unexpected expenses and obstacles. Budgeting involves challenging decision-making, but setting goals will make the tough choices a little easier.

About This Chapter: This chapter includes text excerpted from "Budgeting," Federal Student Aid, U.S. Department of Education (ED), November 30, 2016.

As you create a budget, you'll want to set short-, medium-, and long-term goals and track your progress toward achieving them.

Short-term goals:

Short-term goals might be within the next couple of months. Consider your needs, wants, and priorities. A short-term goal may be as simple as buying your textbooks (so that you don't have to use a credit card), a weekend road trip with friends, or your next cell phone bill.

Medium-term goals:

Medium-term goals involve thinking a bit farther into the future, perhaps the next one to three years. These goals could include buying a new laptop computer, saving $1,000 for an emergency fund, completing your program of study, or saving $5,000 for a down payment on a car.

Long-term goals:

What do you want to do beyond three years and into the future? Long-term goals could include paying off your student loans after graduation, saving toward a down payment on a house, or saving for retirement.

Budgeting Makes It Easier To Plan, To Save, And To Control Your Expenses

When you set up your budget, you'll be able to see whether your expenses exceed your income and, if so, then you can identify expenses that can be reduced. Once you're paying attention to your income and spending, you can make informed decisions that will help you meet your financial goals.

Plus, if you have problems keeping your spending under control, a budget will help you manage your spending. Following a budget can help you free up money for the things that really matter to you.

Budgeting Can Help You Avoid Debt And Improve Your Credit

When you stick to a budget, you avoid spending more than you earn and you can avoid or reduce your credit card debt. If you have received student loans to help with the cost of college or career school, then a budget will help you make the most of the money you've borrowed and can help you determine how long it will take to repay your debt and how much it will cost. If you do borrow, being able to pay what you owe on time each month will have a positive impact on your creditworthiness and your financial future.

How Do I Create A Budget?

Creating a budget is pretty straightforward and starts with this simple equation:

What you earn (your income) minus what you spend (your expenses).

The steps involved in creating a budget include

- determining your timeframe and setting goals,
- finding a budgeting tool that works for you,
- identifying your income and expenses,
- subtracting your expenses from your income to see if you have money left over or if you have a shortfall, and
- making any needed adjustments.

Budgeting is not just a one-time event. You'll need to track your spending over time and update your budget as needed.

How Do I Balance A Job And School?

For some students, working while in college is a necessity; for others, it is a way to build a résumé or earn extra money for luxuries. Whatever the reason, it's important to know the pros and cons of working while you're attending school.

If you have a job, determine how many hours a week you'll be able to work and still be able to stay on track with school demands. For example, if you want to earn more money and potentially reduce your need for student loans (or reduce the amount that you borrow), then you could consider working more hours. Managing a schedule with limited free time is an excellent way to prepare for your future. But remember, you may also need to take fewer classes to accommodate your work schedule. Keep in mind that part-time enrollment will delay your graduation, postpone your ability to earn a higher income, and possibly impact your eligibility for some federal aid. Tuition and fees may also be higher for part-time enrollment.

You may opt to work fewer hours and maximize the benefit of your student loans by taking a heavier class load instead of the minimum requirements. By taking extra classes, you may be able to graduate earlier. Alternatively, you may find that taking classes during the summer leaves you better able to balance work and school during the academic year and still stay on track to graduate on time. Keep in mind that the longer it takes to complete your program of study, the more you will pay in total.

What Should I Know About Budgeting After I Leave School?

Your expenses will change after you leave school. For example, if you recently graduated, you usually won't be required to begin paying off your student loans for six months, but when that payment is added to your monthly expenses, it will have a big impact on your budget. When you leave school, you'll want to update your budget to include student loan payments, as well as your new income and living costs. Leaving school can be an exciting (and stressful) time, but you don't want to stop tracking and managing your finances.

As you move through changes in your life, you'll need to constantly reevaluate your income and expenses. Your goals will change as well. You may want to buy a car, get married, have children, continue your education, or start a business, and all these activities affect your budget in some way. Think of your budget as a living document. You have the power to revise it at any time to keep track of your finances and reach your goals.

Creating Your Budget

Creating a budget may sound complicated, but all you need to do to get started is set aside some time and get organized—the benefits will make the effort worthwhile. The following steps will help you setup your budget and manage your finances by helping you track your income and expenses.

1. Determine A Time Span For Your Budget

You can create your budget for a month, academic year, or calendar year. If you are currently attending college or career school, you may want to consider creating a monthly budget for an academic term, such as your fall semester. Keep in mind that your income may vary from month to month, and not all of your expenses will be the same each month. Larger expenses (such as car insurance and books) and seasonal expenses (such as a trip home at the holidays or a higher electricity bill in summer when the air conditioning is on) need to be incorporated into your budget.

2. Choose A Tool To Help You Manage Your Budget

To create a budget, you'll want to use a tool for tracking your income and expenses. You can use pen and paper, a simple automated spreadsheet, or a budgeting app. Many banks offer budgeting tools, so see what works best for you.

The Financial Awareness Counseling Tool (FACT) is a free interactive tool (https://studentloans.gov/myDirectLoan/counselingInstructions.action) that can help you manage your finances. FACT covers topics ranging from managing your budget to avoiding default. Plus, you can access your loan information and receive personalized feedback to help you better understand your financial obligations.

3. Review Your Monthly Income

First, estimate how much money you will have coming in each month. Here are some tips for assessing your income:

- Your income may come from sources such as your pay from work, financial contributions from family members, or financial aid (scholarships, grants, work-study, and loans).

- If you're working while in school, review your records to determine how much your take-home pay is each month. If you earn most of your money over the summer, you may want to estimate your yearly income then divide it by 12.

- Include income from any financial aid credit balance refunds—money that may be left over for other expenses after your financial aid is applied toward tuition and fees.

Table 16.1. Monthly Income Tracking Example

Income Source	Monthly Income
Income from work	$1,200
Tax refund ($360 total divided by 12)	$30
Estimated financial aid credit balance refund ($2,100 total divided by 12)*	$175
Monthly support from parents and/or family member	$250
Other income	
Total Monthly Income	**$1,655**

Note: If you are getting ready to attend school, you'll want to estimate your federal aid credit balance by taking your estimated financial aid and subtracting your expected tuition and fees. If you have not yet received an aid offer from your school, you can use FAFSA4caster to get an early estimate of your eligibility for federal student aid.

4. Identify And Categorize Your Expenses

To estimate your monthly expenses, you'll want to start by recording everything you spend money on in a month. This may be a bit time-consuming but will definitely be worthwhile in helping you understand where your money is going and how to better manage it. After that, gather your bank records and credit card statements that will show you other expenditures that may be automatically paid.

If you are currently attending college or career school or getting ready to go, you'll also need to estimate your college costs. In addition to tuition and fees (unless covered by financial aid), you'll want to make sure to include books and supplies, equipment and room materials, and travel expenses.

If you are still researching your school options, keep in mind that college and career school costs can vary significantly from school to school.

Once you've identified your expenses, you should group them into two categories—fixed expenses and variable expenses.

1. Fixed expenses stay about the same each month and include items such as rent or mortgage payments, car payments, and insurance. These obligations are generally non negotiable until you realize that you are spending too much money on rent and take steps to find a cheaper place! When creating a monthly budget, divide the amount due by the number of months the bill covers. For example, take your yearly $1,200 insurance bill that's paid in two $600 installments six months apart, and divide it by 12 to know you need to set aside $100 per month.

2. Variable expenses are those that are flexible or controllable and can vary from month to month. Examples of variable expenses include groceries, clothing, eating out, and entertainment. You'll want to examine these expenses to make sure they stay under control and don't bust your budget at the end of the month.

Table 16.2. Monthly Expenses Tracking Example

Fixed Expenses	Projected Cost
Rent or dorm fee	$500
Books	$70
Electricity	$35
Gas and water	$22
Cable and Internet	$50
Car insurance ($600 divided by 12 months)	$50
Parking fee ($84 divided by 12)	$7
Car maintenance and repairs ($480 divided by 12 months)	$40
Cell phone (basic charges)	$60

Table 16.2. Continued

Fixed Expenses	Projected Cost
Car loan payment	$125
Money set aside for savings	$50
Total Fixed Expenses	**$1,009**
Variable Expenses	**Projected Cost**
Groceries	$250
Dining out	$50
Entertainment (example: concerts)	$50
Music downloads	$20
Movies (theater and downloads)	$48
Medical (including prescriptions)	$40
Hair and nails	$40
Clothing	$50
Laundry and dry cleaning	$10
Health club	$40
Credit card monthly payment	$25
Public transportation	$25
Gas for car	$60
Total Variable Expenses	**$708**
Total Expenses	**$1,717**

5. Save For Emergencies

Include "Savings" as a fixed expense in your monthly budget. Pay yourself first every month! Your savings can be used as an emergency fund to help you deal with unexpected expenses. The ideal amount of an emergency fund typically covers three to six months of your expenses.

6. Balance Your Budget

Now that you've identified your sources of income and expenses, you'll want to compare the two to balance your budget. To do so, you simply subtract your expenses from your income.

If you have a positive balance, then your income is greater than your expenses. In other words, you're earning more money than you're spending. If you have a positive balance, you shouldn't start looking at new ways to spend your money. Instead, focus on putting the extra

Table 16.3. Balance Your Budget

Total Monthly Income	$1,655
Minus Total Expenses	$1,717
= +/- Difference	-$62

money toward your savings to cover your emergency fund or to support future goals such as buying a car. Also, if you have a positive balance but you've borrowed student loan funds, pay back some of your loans and consider borrowing less in the future.

If you have a negative balance, then you are spending more money than you have. You'll want to balance your budget and make sure your expenses don't exceed your income. Balancing your budget may include monitoring your variable expenses, reducing your expenses, and/or finding ways to increase your income. Spending less can be a lot easier than earning more. Consider eating out less frequently and making your own lunch. Rent books rather than buying them, or buy books to download to your computer. Use a shopping list when grocery shopping, and buy only what you need. Ask yourself before buying anything, "Do I really need this?"

7. Maintain And Update Your Budget

Now that you've created your budget, you'll want to make sure it remains a living document and you update it over time. Here are some smart practices to keep in mind:

- **Review your budget on a monthly basis.** Regular review and maintenance of your budget will keep you on top of things and may help you avoid being blindsided by something unexpected.

- **Forgive yourself for small spending mistakes and get back on track.** Most people overspend because they buy things on impulse. The next time you're tempted to make an impulse buy, ask yourself the following questions:

- What do I need this for?

- Can I afford this item?

- If I buy this item now, will I still be happy that I bought it a month from now?

- Do I need to save this money for a financial goal?

- Will this item go on sale? Should I wait to buy it?

- Does it matter if I buy brand-name or can I get by with generic?

If you take a moment to think about what you're buying, you're more likely to make a choice that fits your budgeting goals.

Budgeting Tips

As you create and maintain your budget, you'll want to keep some important tips and suggestions in mind.

Get Started

Here are some important points to keep in mind as you build your budget and identify what goes into your income and expenses.

- **Overestimate your expenses.** It's better to overestimate your expenses and then underspend and end up with a surplus.

- **Underestimate your income.** It's better to end up with an unexpected cash surplus rather than a budget shortfall.

- **Involve your family in the budget planning process.** Determine how much income will be available from family sources such as parents or your spouse. Discuss how financial decisions will be made.

- **Prepare for the unexpected by setting saving goals to build your emergency fund.** Budgeting will help you cover unusual expenses and plan for changes that may happen while you're in school.

- Planning to move off campus? Short-term budgeting goals for the year can include saving for the rent deposit and furniture for your new apartment.

- Starting an internship next semester? Adjust your budget to save for buying new clothes to wear to work and paying increased transportation costs.

- Finishing school in the next year? Budget to include job search expenses such as résumé preparation, travel to interviews and job fairs, and professional exam fees. Also, you may need to think about how you will manage your money between leaving school and finding a job—this is a time when an emergency fund can really help out.

Differentiate Between Needs And Wants

One benefit of budgeting is that it helps you determine if you have the resources to spend on items that you want versus those you need.

- Start by making a list of things you'd like to save up for.

- Identify whether each item on the list is something you absolutely need or is really a want.

- If you decide you want something, ask yourself if you will still be happy you bought the item in a month.

- Next, prioritize each item on the list.

- Once you have set your priorities, you can then determine whether you should incorporate each item into your budget.

Table 16.4. Differentiate Between Needs And Wants

First Step My Needs and Wants	Second Step Need or Want?	Third Step Priority Importance? 1=must have 2=really want 3=would be nice
Save for a vacation	Want	3
Buy a new computer	Want	2
Go to college	Need	1
Buy a better car	Want	2
Save for an emergency fund	Need	1
Save money for a down payment on a house	Need	3
Pay off credit cards	Need	1

Pay Yourself First!

Include "Savings" as a recurring expense item in your monthly budget. Small amounts that you put away each month do add up.

Manage Your Budget

Keeping track of all your spending may seem like a lot of work. But if you're organized, keep good records, and use some of the following tips, you'll find it's easier than you may think. And, don't be too hard on yourself if you slip up.

- **Record your actual expenses.** Have you noticed how fast your cash disappears? To get a handle on where you cash is going, carry a small notebook or use a phone app to record even the smallest expenditures such as coffee, movie tickets, snacks, and parking. Some expenses that are often ignored include music downloads, charges for extra cell phone usage, and entertainment expenses. Search for an online tool to assist you—many are free!

- **Organize your records.** Decide what system you're going to use to track and organize your financial information. There are mobile apps and computer-based programs that work well, but you can also track your spending using a pencil and paper. Be sure to be consistent and organized, and designate a space to store all your financial information. Good record-keeping saves money and time!

- **Create a routine.** Manage your money on a regular basis, and record your expenses and income regularly. If you find that you can't record your expenses every day, then record them weekly. If you wait longer than two weeks to record information, you may forget some transactions and be overwhelmed by the amount of information you need to enter.

- **Include a category in your budget called "Unusual."** There will be some expenses every month that won't fall neatly into one category or that you couldn't have planned for. An "Unusual" category will help you budget for these occasional expenses.

- **Review your spending for little items that add up to big monthly expenditures.** The daily cup of coffee and soda at a vending machine will add up. Consider packing your lunch rather than eating out every day. Spending $10 a day eating out during the week translates to $50 a week and $200 a month. A $5 packed lunch translates into a savings of $1,200 a year. Save even more by looking for ways to manage and reduce your transportation and entertainment expenses.

- **Make your financial aid credit balance refund last.** If your school applies your financial aid to your tuition and fees and there's money left over, the school will refund that money to you so you can use it for other education-related expenses (textbooks, transportation, food, etc.). Remember that your financial aid is supposed to help you cover your cost of attendance for the whole semester or term, so be sure to make that refund stretch over time rather than spending it all as soon as you get it.

- **Comparison shop.** Comparison shopping is simply using common sense to compare products in an attempt to get the best prices and best value. This means doing a little research before running out to buy something, especially when it comes to more expensive items. Make the most of tools like phone apps for comparing prices and value.

- **Use credit cards wisely.** Think very carefully before you decide to get your first credit card. Is a credit card really necessary, or would another payment option work just as well? If you receive a credit card offer in the mail, don't feel obligated to accept it. Limit the number of cards you get.

- **Don't spend more on your credit card than you can afford to pay in full on a monthly basis.** Responsible use of credit cards can be a shopping convenience and help you establish a solid credit rating and avoid financial problems. Consider signing up for electronic payment reminders, balance notices, and billing statement notifications from your credit card provider.

Expect The Unexpected

Your emergency fund should be used for expenses that fall outside the categories of annual and periodic bills. Unexpected expenses are the result of life events such as job loss, illness, or car repairs. Redefine your notion of "unexpected" bills to encompass these unforeseen events rather than more common but infrequent expenses. The good news is that if you do not use your emergency fund, you will have savings—which should always be a priority when managing your finances. And, if you have to use your emergency fund, you may avoid unnecessary borrowing.

Chapter 17
Section 529 Plans

What Is A 529 Plan?

A 529 plan is a tax-advantaged savings plan designed to encourage saving for future college costs. 529 plans, legally known as "qualified tuition plans," are sponsored by states, state agencies, or educational institutions and are authorized by Section 529 of the Internal Revenue Code (IRC).

There are two types of 529 plans: prepaid tuition plans and college savings plans. All fifty states and the District of Columbia (DC) sponsor at least one type of 529 plan. In addition, a group of private colleges and universities sponsor a prepaid tuition plan.

What Are The Differences Between Prepaid Tuition Plans And College Savings Plans?

Prepaid tuition plans generally allow college savers to purchase units or credits at participating colleges and universities for future tuition and, in some cases, room and board. Most prepaid tuition plans are sponsored by state governments and have residency requirements. Many state governments guarantee investments in prepaid tuition plans that they sponsor.

College savings plans generally permit a college saver (also called the "account holder") to establish an account for a student (the "beneficiary") for the purpose of paying the beneficiary's eligible college expenses. An account holder may typically choose among several investment options for his or her contributions, which the college savings plan invests on behalf of the

About This Chapter: This chapter includes text excerpted from "An Introduction To 529 Plans," U.S. Securities and Exchange Commission (SEC), January 6, 2014.

account holder. Investment options often include stock mutual funds, bond mutual funds, and money market funds, as well as, age-based portfolios that automatically shift toward more conservative investments as the beneficiary gets closer to college age. Withdrawals from college savings plans can generally be used at any college or university. Investments in college savings plans that invest in mutual funds are not guaranteed by state governments and are not federally insured.

The following table outlines some of the major differences between prepaid tuition plans and college savings plans.

Table 17.1. Differences Between Prepaid Tuition Plans And College Savings Plans

Prepaid Tuition Plan	College Savings Plan
Locks in tuition prices at eligible public and private colleges and universities.	No lock on college costs.
All plans cover tuition and mandatory fees only. Some plans allow you to purchase a room and board option or use excess tuition credits for other qualified expenses.	Covers all "qualified higher education expenses," including: Tuition, Room and board, Mandatory fees, Books, computers (if required)
Most plans set lump sum and installment payments prior to purchase based on age of beneficiary and number of years of college tuition purchased.	Many plans have contribution limits in excess of $200,000.
Many state plans guaranteed or backed by state.	No state guarantee. Most investment options are subject to market risk. Your investment may make no profit or even decline in value.
Most plans have age/grade limit for beneficiary.	No age limits. Open to adults and children.
Most state plans require either owner or beneficiary of plan to be a state resident.	No residency requirement. However, nonresidents may only be able to purchase some plans through financial advisers or brokers.
Most plans have limited enrollment period.	Enrollment open all year.

How Does Investing In A 529 Plan Affect Federal And State Income Taxes?

Investing in a 529 plan may offer college savers special tax benefits. Earnings in 529 plans are not subject to federal tax, and in most cases, state tax, so long as you use withdrawals for eligible college expenses, such as tuition and room and board.

However, if you withdraw money from a 529 plan and do not use it on an eligible college expense, you generally will be subject to income tax and an additional 10 percent federal tax penalty on earnings. Many states offer state income tax or other benefits, such as matching grants, for investing in a 529 plan. But you may only be eligible for these benefits if you participate in a 529 plan sponsored by your state of residence. Just a few states allow residents to deduct contributions to any 529 plan from state income tax returns.

If you receive state tax benefits for investing in a 529 plan, make sure you review your plan's offering circular before you complete a transaction, such as rolling money out of your home state's plan into another state's plan. Some transactions may have state tax consequences for residents of certain states.

What Fees And Expenses Will I Pay If I Invest In A 529 Plan?

It is important to understand the fees and expenses associated with 529 plans because they lower your returns. Fees and expenses will vary based on the type of plan. Prepaid tuition plans typically charge enrollment and administrative fees. In addition to "loads" for broker-sold plans, college savings plans may charge enrollment fees, annual maintenance fees, and asset management fees. Some of these fees are collected by the state sponsor of the plan, and some are collected by the financial services firms that the state sponsor typically hires to manage its 529 program. Some college savings plans will waive or reduce some of these fees if you maintain a large account balance or participate in an automatic contribution plan, or if you are a resident of the state sponsoring the 529 plan. Your asset management fees will depend on the investment option you select. Each investment option will typically bear a portfolio-weighted average of the fees and expenses of the mutual funds and other investments in which it invests. You should carefully review the fees of the underlying investments because they are likely to be different for each investment option.

Investors that purchase a college savings plan from a broker are typically subject to additional fees. If you invest in a broker-sold plan, you may pay a "load." Broadly speaking, the load is paid to your broker as a commission for selling the college savings plan to you. Broker-sold plans also charge an annual distribution fee (similar to the "12b 1 fee" charged by some mutual funds) of between 0.25 percent and 1.00 percent of your investment. Your broker typically receives all or most of these annual distribution fees for selling your 529 plan to you.

Many broker-sold 529 plans offer more than one class of shares, which impose different fees and expenses. Here are some key characteristics of the most common 529 plan share classes sold by brokers to their customers:

- **Class A shares** typically impose a front-end sales load. Front-end sales loads reduce the amount of your investment. For example, let's say you have $1,000 and want to invest in a college savings plan with a 5 percent front-end load. The $50 sales load you must pay is deducted from your $1,000, and the remaining $950 is invested in the college savings plan. Class A shares usually have a lower annual distribution fee and lower overall annual expenses than other 529 share classes. In addition, your front-end load may be reduced if you invest above certain threshold amounts—this is known as a breakpoint discount. These discounts do not apply to investments in Class B or Class C shares.

- **Class B shares** typically do not have a front-end sales load. Instead, they may charge a fee when you withdraw money from an investment option, known as a deferred sales charge or "back-end load." A common back-end load is the "contingent deferred sales charge" or "contingent deferred sales load" (also known as a "CDSC" or "CDSL"). The amount of this load will depend on how long you hold your investment and typically decreases to zero if you hold your investment long enough. Class B shares typically impose a higher annual distribution fee and higher overall annual expenses than Class A shares. Class B shares usually convert automatically to Class A shares if you hold your shares long enough. Be careful when investing in Class B shares. If the beneficiary uses the money within a few years after purchasing Class B shares, you will almost always pay a contingent deferred sales charge or load in addition to higher annual fees and expenses.

- **Class C shares** might have an annual distribution fee, other annual expenses, and either a front- or back-end sales load. But the front- or back-end load for Class C shares tends to be lower than for Class A or Class B shares, respectively. Class C shares typically impose a higher annual distribution fee and higher overall annual expenses than Class A shares, but, unlike Class B shares, generally do not convert to another class over time. If you are a long-term investor, Class C shares may be more expensive than investing in Class A or Class B shares.

Is There Any Way To Purchase A 529 Plan But Avoid Some Of The Extra Fees?

- **Direct-Sold College Savings Plans.** States offer college savings plans through which residents and, in many cases, non-residents can invest without paying a "load," or sales fee. This type of plan, which you can buy directly from the plan's sponsor or program manager without the assistance of a broker, is generally less expensive because it waives or does not charge sales fees that may apply to broker-sold plans. You can generally find information on a direct-sold plan by contacting the plan's sponsor or program manager or visiting the plan's website. Websites such as the one maintained by the College Savings Plan Network (CSPN [www.collegesavings.org]) as well as a number of commercial websites, provide links to most 529 plan websites.

- **Broker-Sold College Savings Plans.** If you prefer to purchase a broker-sold plan, you may be able to reduce the front-end load for purchasing Class A shares if you invest or plan to invest above certain threshold amounts. Ask your broker how to qualify for these "breakpoint discounts."

What Restrictions Apply To An Investment In A 529 Plan?

Withdrawal restrictions apply to both college savings plans and prepaid tuition plans. With limited exceptions, you can only withdraw money that you invest in a 529 plan for eligible college expenses without incurring taxes and penalties. In addition, participants in college savings plans have limited investment options and are not permitted to switch freely among available investment options. Under current tax law, an account holder is only permitted to change his or her investment option one time per year. Additional limitations will likely apply to any 529 plan you may be considering. Before you invest in a 529 plan, you should read the plan's offering circular to make sure that you understand and are comfortable with any plan limitations.

Does Investing In A 529 Plan Impact Financial Aid Eligibility?

While each educational institution may treat assets held in a 529 plan differently, investing in a 529 plan will generally reduce a student's eligibility to participate in need-based financial aid. Beginning July 1, 2006, assets held in prepaid tuition plans and college savings plans will be treated similarly for federal financial aid purposes. Both will be treated as parental assets in the calculation of the expected family contribution toward college costs. Previously, benefits from prepaid tuition plans were not treated as parental assets and typically reduced need-based financial aid on a dollar for dollar basis, while assets held in college savings plans received more favorable financial aid treatment.

Is Investing In A 529 Plan Right For Me?

Before you start saving specifically for college, you should consider your overall financial situation. Instead of saving for college, you may want to focus on other financial goals like buying a home, saving for retirement, or paying off high interest credit card bills. Remember that you may face penalties or lose benefits if you do not use the money in a 529 account for higher education expenses. If you decide that saving specifically for college is right for you, then the next step is to determine whether investing in a 529 plan is your best college saving option. Investing in a 529 plan is only one of several ways to save for college. Other tax-advantaged ways to save for college include Coverdell education savings accounts, Uniform Gifts to Minors Act ("UGMA") accounts, Uniform Transfers to Minors Act ("UTMA") accounts, tax-exempt municipal securities, and savings bonds. Saving for college in a taxable account is another option. Each college saving option has advantages and disadvantages, and may have a different impact on your eligibility for financial aid, so you should evaluate each option carefully. If you need help determining which options work best for your circumstances, you should consult with your financial professional or tax advisor before you start saving.

What Questions Should I Ask Before I Invest In A 529 Plan?

Knowing the answers to these questions may help you decide which 529 plan is best for you.

- Is the plan available directly from the state or plan sponsor?

- What fees are charged by the plan? How much of my investment goes to compensating my broker? Under what circumstances does the plan waive or reduce certain fees?

- What are the plan's withdrawal restrictions? What types of college expenses are covered by the plan? Which colleges and universities participate in the plan?

- What types of investment options are offered by the plan? How long are contributions held before being invested?

- Does the plan offer special benefits for state residents? Would I be better off investing in my state's plan or another plan? Does my state's plan offer tax advantages or other benefits for investment in the plan it sponsors? If my state's plan charges higher fees than another state's plan, do the tax advantages or other benefits offered by my state outweigh the benefit of investing in another state's less expensive plan?

- What limitations apply to the plan? When can an account holder change investment options, switch beneficiaries, or transfer ownership of the account to another account holder?

- Who is the program manager? When does the program manager's current management contract expire? How has the plan performed in the past?

Chapter 18

Coverdell Education Savings Accounts

If your modified adjusted gross income (MAGI) is less than $110,000 ($220,000 if filing a joint return), you may be able to establish a Coverdell Education Savings Account (ESA) to finance the qualified education expenses of a designated beneficiary. For most taxpayers, MAGI is the adjusted gross income as figured on their federal income tax return.

There is no limit on the number of separate Coverdell ESAs that can be established for a designated beneficiary. However, total contributions for the beneficiary in any year can't be more than $2,000, no matter how many accounts have been established.

This benefit applies not only to higher education expenses, but also to elementary and secondary education expenses.

What Is The Tax Benefit Of The Coverdell ESA?

Contributions to a Coverdell ESA aren't deductible, but amounts deposited in the account grow tax free until distributed. If, for a year, distributions from an account aren't more than a designated beneficiary's qualified education expenses at an eligible educational institution, the beneficiary won't owe tax on the distributions.

What Is A Coverdell ESA?

A Coverdell ESA is a trust or custodial account created or organized in the United States only for the purpose of paying the qualified education expenses of the Designated beneficiary (defined later) of the account. When the account is established, the designated beneficiary

About This Chapter: This chapter includes text excerpted from "Coverdell Education Savings Account," Internal Revenue Service (IRS), January 18, 2017.

Table 18.1. Coverdell ESA At A Glance

Question	Answer
What is a Coverdell ESA?	A savings account that is set up to pay the qualified education expenses of a designated beneficiary.
Where can it be established?	It can be opened in the United States at any bank or other IRS-approved entity that offers Coverdell ESAs.
Who can have a Coverdell ESA?	Any beneficiary who is under age 18 or is a special needs beneficiary.
Who can contribute to a Coverdell ESA?	Generally, any individual (including the beneficiary) whose modified adjusted gross income for the year is less than $110,000 ($220,000 in the case of a joint return).
Are distributions tax free?	Yes, if the distributions aren't more than the beneficiary's adjusted qualified education expenses for the year.

must be under age 18 or a special needs beneficiary. To be treated as a Coverdell ESA, the account must be designated as a Coverdell ESA when it is created.

The document creating and governing the account must be in writing and must satisfy the following requirements.

- The trustee or custodian must be a bank or an entity approved by the IRS.

- The document must provide that the trustee or custodian can only accept a contribution that meets all of the following conditions.

- The contribution is in cash.

- The contribution is made before the beneficiary reaches age 18, unless the beneficiary is a special needs beneficiary.

- The contribution wouldn't result in total contributions for the year (not including roll-over contributions) being more than $2,000.

- Money in the account can't be invested in life insurance contracts.

- Money in the account can't be combined with other property except in a common trust fund or common investment fund.

- The balance in the account generally must be distributed within 30 days after the earlier of the following events.

- The beneficiary reaches age 30, unless the beneficiary is a special needs beneficiary.

- The beneficiary's death.

Qualified Education Expenses

Generally, these are expenses required for the enrollment or attendance of the designated beneficiary at an eligible educational institution. For purposes of Coverdell ESAs, the expenses can be either qualified higher education expenses or qualified elementary and secondary education expenses.

Designated beneficiary. This is the individual named in the document creating the trust or custodial account to receive the benefit of the funds in the account.

Contributions to a qualified tuition program (QTP). A contribution to a QTP is a qualified education expense if the contribution is on behalf of the designated beneficiary of the Coverdell ESA. In the case of a change in beneficiary, this is a qualified expense only if the new beneficiary is a family member of that designated beneficiary.

Eligible Educational Institution

For purposes of Coverdell ESAs, an eligible educational institution can be either an eligible postsecondary school or an eligible elementary or secondary school.

Eligible postsecondary school. This is any college, university, vocational school, or other postsecondary educational institution eligible to participate in a student aid program administered by the U.S. Department of Education (ED). It includes virtually all accredited public, nonprofit, and proprietary (privately owned profit-making) postsecondary institutions. The educational institution should be able to tell you if it is an eligible educational institution.

Certain educational institutions located outside the United States also participate in the U.S. Department of Education's Federal Student Aid (FSA) programs.

Eligible elementary or secondary school. This is any public, private, or religious school that provides elementary or secondary education (kindergarten through grade 12), as determined under state law.

Qualified Higher Education Expenses

These are expenses related to enrollment or attendance at an eligible postsecondary school. As shown in the following list, to be qualified, some of the expenses must be required by the school and some must be incurred by students who are enrolled at least half-time.

- The following expenses must be required for enrollment or attendance of a designated beneficiary at an eligible postsecondary school.

    - Tuition and fees.

    - Books, supplies, and equipment.

- Expenses for special needs services needed by a special needs beneficiary must be incurred in connection with enrollment or attendance at an eligible postsecondary school.

- Expenses for room and board must be incurred by students who are enrolled at least half-time. The expense for room and board qualifies only to the extent that it isn't more than the greater of the following two amounts.

    - The allowance for room and board, as determined by the school, that was included in the cost of attendance (for federal financial aid purposes) for a particular academic period and living arrangement of the student.

    - The actual amount charged if the student is residing in housing owned or operated by the school.

You may need to contact the eligible educational institution for qualified room and board costs.

- The purchase of computer or peripheral equipment, computer software, or Internet access and related services if it is to be used primarily by the beneficiary during any of the years the beneficiary is enrolled at an eligible postsecondary school. (This does not include expenses for computer software for sports, games, or hobbies unless the software is predominantly educational in nature.)

Half-time student. A student is enrolled "at least half-time" if he or she is enrolled for at least half the full-time academic workload for the course of study the student is pursuing, as determined under the standards of the school where the student is enrolled.

Qualified Elementary And Secondary Education Expenses

These are expenses related to enrollment or attendance at an eligible elementary or secondary school. As shown in the following list, to be qualified, some of the expenses must be required or provided by the school. There are special rules for computer-related expenses.

- The following expenses must be incurred by a designated beneficiary in connection with enrollment or attendance at an eligible elementary or secondary school.

- Tuition and fees.

- Books, supplies, and equipment.

- Academic tutoring.

- Special needs services for a special needs beneficiary.

- The following expenses must be required or provided by an eligible elementary or secondary school in connection with attendance or enrollment at the school.

- Room and board.

- Uniforms.

- Transportation.

- Supplementary items and services (including extended day programs).

- The purchase of computer technology, equipment, or Internet access and related services is a qualified elementary and secondary education expense if it is to be used by the beneficiary and the beneficiary's family during any of the years the beneficiary is in elementary or secondary school. (This doesn't include expenses for computer software designed for sports, games, or hobbies unless the software is predominantly educational in nature.)

Contributions

Any individual (including the designated beneficiary) can contribute to a Coverdell ESA if the individual's MAGI (defined later under Contribution Limits) for the year is less than $110,000. For individuals filing joint returns, that amount is $220,000. Organizations, such as corporations and trusts, can also contribute to Coverdell ESAs. There is no requirement that an organization's income be below a certain level.

Contributions must meet all of the following requirements.

- They must be in cash.

- They can't be made after the beneficiary reaches age 18, unless the beneficiary is a special needs beneficiary.

- They must be made by the due date of the contributor's tax return (not including extensions).

Contributions can be made to one or several Coverdell ESAs for the same designated beneficiary provided that the total contributions aren't more than the contribution limits (defined later) for a year.

Contributions can be made, without penalty, to both a Coverdell ESA and a QTP in the same year for the same beneficiary.

When contributions are considered made. Contributions made to a Coverdell ESA for the preceding tax year are considered to have been made on the last day of the preceding year. They must be made by the due date (not including extensions) for filing your return for the preceding year.

For example, if you make a contribution to a Coverdell ESA in February 2016, and you designate it as a contribution for 2015, you are considered to have made that contribution on December 31, 2015.

Contribution Limits

There are two yearly limits.

1. One on the total amount that can be contributed for each designated beneficiary in any year.

2. One on the amount that any individual can contribute for any one designated beneficiary for a year.

Limit for each designated beneficiary. For 2015, the total of all contributions to all Coverdell ESAs set up for the benefit of any one designated beneficiary can't be more than $2,000. This includes contributions (other than rollovers) to all the beneficiary's Coverdell ESAs from all sources.

Example:

When Maria Luna was born in 2014, three separate Coverdell ESAs were set up for her, one by her parents, one by her grandfather, and one by her aunt. In 2015, the total of all contributions to Maria's three Coverdell ESAs can't be more than $2,000. For example, if her grandfather contributed $2,000 to one of her Coverdell ESAs, no one else could contribute to any of her three accounts. Or, if her parents contributed $1,000 and her aunt $600, her grandfather or someone else could contribute no more than $400. These contributions could be put into any of Maria's Coverdell ESA accounts.

Limit for each contributor. Generally, you can contribute up to $2,000 for each designated beneficiary for 2015. This is the most you can contribute for the benefit of any one beneficiary for the year, regardless of the number of Coverdell ESAs set up for the beneficiary.

Example:

The facts are the same as in the previous example except that Maria Luna's older brother, Edgar, also has a Coverdell ESA. If their grandfather contributed $2,000 to Maria's Coverdell ESA in 2015, he could also contribute $2,000 to Edgar's Coverdell ESA.

Reduced limit. Your contribution limit may be reduced. If your MAGI (defined later) is between $95,000 and $110,000 (between $190,000 and $220,000 if filing a joint return), the $2,000 limit for each designated beneficiary is gradually reduced. If your MAGI is $110,000 or more ($220,000 or more if filing a joint return), you can't contribute to anyone's Coverdell ESA.

Chapter 19
Custodial Accounts

Parents, grandparents, and other adults who want to invest money for the future education of a child can do so by establishing a custodial account. A custodial account is a type of savings account in which an adult, known as the custodian, controls the funds on behalf of a child, known as the beneficiary. While the beneficiary is a minor, the custodian makes all of the investment decisions and approves any withdrawals. Once the beneficiary reaches legal adulthood (between the ages of 18 and 24, depending on state laws), however, ownership of the account transfers from the custodian to the beneficiary. The beneficiary gains full control over the funds and can decide how and when to use them.

You can set up a custodial account through a financial institution, brokerage firm, or mutual fund company. They are easy to open, like a regular bank account or investment account. There are two types of custodial accounts, which are named after the legislation that created them: Uniform Gift to Minors Act (UGMA) accounts and Uniform Transfer to Minors Act (UTMA) accounts. Deposits to UGMA accounts can take the form of cash, savings bonds, stocks, annuities, or life insurance. UTMA accounts can also hold various types of property, plus they allow custodians to postpone distribution of assets to the beneficiary up to a certain age, which varies by state. Both types of accounts offer a wide variety of investment choices. Minimum account balances, interest rates, and fees depend on the financial institution.

Advantages And Disadvantages

Custodial accounts offer several financial benefits for people who are saving money toward a child's education or other future goals, such as starting a business or buying a home. There is

---

"Custodial Accounts And Trusts," © 2017 Omnigraphics.

no limit on contributions, although any amount over $14,000 is subject to a gift tax. In addition, anyone can contribute to a custodial account, regardless of their income level. Custodial accounts also offer some limited tax advantages. The first $1,050 of unearned income is tax free for children under age 19, or for full-time students under age 24. The next $1,050 of unearned income is taxed at the child's federal tax rate, which is likely to be lower than the custodian's tax rate. Withdrawals of funds can be made without penalty and used for any purpose that directly benefits the beneficiary, not only for qualified education expenses.

Custodial accounts also have a few disadvantages. Contributions to a custodial account are irrevocable, meaning that they automatically become the property of the beneficiary. Once the beneficiary reaches legal adulthood, they take control of the account and can use the money for anything they want. Some parents and grandparents are reluctant to give up all control over how the money is spent. Another potential disadvantage is that a custodial account in your child's name might reduce your family's eligibility for student financial aid. Money in an UTMA is considered the child's asset, which is given more weight than parents' assets in the formula used to determine financial aid. In addition, you cannot change beneficiaries if your child gets a scholarship or decides not to go to college. Finally, investment earnings and capital gains in custodial accounts are subject to state and federal taxes, and you must file a tax return for the beneficiary every year.

Alternative Savings Options

It is important to consider the advantages and disadvantages before establishing a custodial account. Other options are available that might be better suited to your financial goals, including the following:

- **Trusts**

  Trusts are similar to custodial accounts except that the grantor who funds the account has more control over the money. Trust documents must be drafted by an attorney, so trusts can be complicated and expensive to set up. In addition, a trustee must be designated to administer the trust. Distributions of money to the beneficiary are made according to the terms of the trust documents beginning at whatever age the grantor chooses. There are no contribution limits or tax benefits, and the investment options are very flexible.

- **Coverdell Education Savings Accounts (ESAs)**

  ESAs, formerly known as Education IRAs, are intended to help parents to save money for their child's education. Contribution limits are relatively low, at $2,000 per year for individuals earning less than $95,000 or couples earning less than $190,000, but investment options are virtually unlimited. Although contributions to an ESA are not deductible, withdrawals that are used to pay qualified education expenses are tax free. Unlike other college savings accounts, ESAs can be used to pay for private school expenses while the child is in elementary school or high school.

- **529 Plans**

These plans are intended to provide parents and grandparents with a tax-advantaged college savings account. Contributions to 529 plans are tax deductible in many states, and the investments grow tax-deferred. As long as withdrawals are used to pay qualified education expenses, they are tax free. The main disadvantage is that the funds can only be used for approved educational purposes. If your child decides not to go to college or wants to use the money for something else, you will pay taxes on the gains plus a 10 percent penalty. Funds from custodial accounts can be transferred to a 529 plan, but you must liquidate all investments first and pay applicable taxes on any gains.

References

1. "Advantages And Disadvantages Of Custodial Accounts For College Savings," 360 Degrees of Financial Literacy, 2017.

2. "Coverdells And Custodial Accounts," FINRA, 2017.

3. "Custodial Account," Investopedia, 2017.

4. "Trust? UTMA? 529 Plan? Which Type Of Account Is Best For Your Young Child?" Laird Norton Wealth Management, May 23, 2013.

Chapter 20
Working During College

More than 70 percent of college students work while they are enrolled in school. Although most colleges recommend that full-time students limit part-time jobs to between 10 and 15 hours per week, 40 percent of undergraduates work more than 30 hours per week, and 25 percent are employed full-time. Some students have on-campus, work-study jobs that are part of a financial aid package. Others work at part-time, off-campus jobs to earn extra spending money. About one-third of students continue working at the same job they held before enrolling in college. Many companies offer tuition assistance to help cover the cost of higher education for employees who want to increase their skills.

The biggest drawback to working during college is that jobs take time that you might otherwise spend studying, participating in extracurricular or social activities, or even sleeping. After all, working at a job for 10 to 20 hours per week is the equivalent of taking one to two additional classes. If the time commitment prevents you from taking a full load of classes, staying healthy, enjoying your college experience, or graduating on time, then working during college may not be worth it.

Did You Know...

"Almost every college student works, but you can't work your way through college anymore," said Anthony P. Carnevale, lead author of *Learning While Earning: The New Normal*. The 2015 report points out that a student who works full-time for the federal minimum wage earns about $15,000 per year, which is not enough to cover tuition and room and board at most colleges.

(Source: Georgetown University Center on Education and the Workforce, Learning While Earning: The New Normal.)

However, employment during college also offers benefits that may outweigh the costs. Some of the advantages you may gain by working include the following:

- **Better academic performance**

  Studies have shown that college students who work between 1 and 12 hours per week have higher graduation rates than students who do not work. The working students tend to perform as well or even better academically than their non-working peers. Many students find that the business challenges and workplace issues they face in their jobs apply directly to their college classes and enhance the learning experience. Some students also use ideas from their college classes to solve problems in the workplace.

- **Time management skills**

  Keeping up with the demands of college and a job forces you to manage your time effectively. You learn to stay organized, stick to a schedule, prioritize tasks, and develop good work and study habits. Building these critical time-management skills in college helps prepare you for a fast-paced, demanding career after graduation.

- **Less student-loan debt**

  Most students who work during college do so in order to help pay for their education. Although many still need student loans to cover the costs of tuition and room and board, employment income can reduce the amount they need to borrow. By paying for books and basic living expenses out of their earnings, working students may be able to graduate with less student-loan debt than non-working students.

- **More independence**

  Some students must work to help cover education-related expenses. Others choose to work because they want to have cash available to spend on clothes, travel, eating out, entertainment, and other treats. If your parents are already paying for your education, you may feel guilty asking them for more funds. Earning your own spending money can give you greater independence. In addition, you can avoid the financial trap of applying for student credit cards to cover your extra expenses.

- **Money management skills**

  Students who work during college gain valuable knowledge of personal finance. Earning an income allows you to take responsibility for establishing a budget, keeping track of expenses, paying bills, and managing your money. These skills will prove valuable once you graduate from college and launch your career.

- **Career experience**

  Part-time jobs—even ones that may seem menial or meaningless—offer valuable work experience that can help you gain skills, build self-confidence, and meet potential references or networking contacts. Students who find part-time jobs or internships within their field of study also have an opportunity to clarify their career goals and add to the list of qualifications on their résumés. During job interviews, you can provide real-world examples of your ability to solve problems, work independently, and take responsibility. For many employers, work experience during college sets you apart from other recent graduates and improves your chances of landing a full-time job after graduation.

References

1. Dumbauld, Beth. "Six Things You Should Know About Working While Going To College," Straighter Line, October 20, 2016.

2. Higuera, Valencia. "Five Benefits Of Working A Job While In College," Money Crashers, 2017.

3. Levy, David. "The Benefits Of Working While In College," Edvisors, 2017.

4. "Pros And Cons Of Work-Study In College," The Prospect, 2014.

Part Four
Financial Aid And The Federal Government

Chapter 21

An Overview Of Federal Aid For Students

Federal Student Aid (FSA) is the office of the U.S. Department of Education (ED) that administers the federal government's financial aid programs for students. These programs provide around $150 billion each year in the form of grants, scholarships, work-study funds, and loans to help more than 13 million students afford to go to college. Students can use federal aid money to pay for education-related expenses, such as tuition and fees, room and board, transportation, and books and supplies. The funds are disbursed to students through more than 6,200 institutions of higher education nationwide.

Applying For Federal Student Aid

The first step in applying for federal aid is to complete the *Free Application for Federal Student Aid* (FAFSA®). The U.S. government, state governments, and colleges and universities all use information from your FAFSA® to determine your eligibility to receive need-based financial aid. The amount of need-based aid you get depends on your family's income and financial resources. The majority of applicants qualify for at least some need-based aid.

You can fill out and submit your FAFSA® online, by mail, or over the phone. The application asks for personal and financial information about you and your parents, if you are a dependent under the age of 24. You may want to gather some key documents ahead of time, such as Social Security numbers, income records, federal tax returns, bank statements, and information about assets and investments. FAFSA® applications are due several months before the start of the term or academic year when you plan to enroll, so be sure to submit it early enough to meet the deadline for your state or school.

"An Overview Of Federal Aid For Students," © 2017 Omnigraphics.

A few weeks after you submit your FAFSA®, you will receive your Student Aid Report (SAR) by email or postal mail. This report provides your Expected Family Contribution (EFC), which is a measure of your family's ability to pay your college expenses. College financial aid offices subtract your EFC from the total cost of attendance (COA) to determine how much financial aid you are eligible to receive. The COA varies depending on the college, and it includes such expenses as tuition and fees, room and board, transportation, and books and supplies.

Did You Know...

During the 2014–2015 academic year, around two-thirds of all full-time college students received federal aid. About 57 percent of this funding took the form of grants and scholarships, while 34 percent took the form of loans.

Types Of Federal Student Aid

If your EFC is less than the COA for the college you wish to attend, then you are considered to have financial need. You may qualify for federal student aid to help make up the difference. There are four types of federal need-based financial aid: grants, scholarships, work-study funds, and student loans.

Grants are considered a form of gift aid, because the funds do not need to be repaid. They are awarded to students with the greatest financial need. Other than the basic eligibility requirements for federal aid, students who receive federal grants only need to attend an accredited institution of higher education and maintain passing grades. The main federal educational grant programs include the following:

- Pell Grant—provides federal grants up to $5,730 per academic year for up to six years of study for undergraduate students with significant financial need;

- Federal Supplemental Educational Opportunity Grant (FSEOG)—provides federal grants of $100 to $4,000 for undergraduate students with exceptional financial need;

- Teacher Education Access for College and Higher Education (TEACH) Grant—provides up to $4,000 per academic year to students who agree to work as full-time teachers for at least four years after graduation in schools that serve disadvantaged children;

- Military Service Grants—provides federal grants to students with a parent who was killed while serving military duty in Iraq or Afghanistan.

Scholarships, like grants, are a form of gift aid that does not have to be repaid. Scholarships are available from a wide variety of sources, including government agencies, schools, companies, communities, individuals, and religious or social organizations. Most scholarships are merit-based, meaning that funds are awarded based on students' academic record or other achievements.

Work Study is a form of need-based federal aid that provides students with part-time jobs on or near campus to help subsidize the cost of their education. The aid is offered in exchange for work and paid directly to students. They can use the funds for education-related expenses and do not have to pay back the money they earn.

Student Loans are the most common type of financial aid provided by the federal government. Around two-thirds of students use federal loans to help pay for college. Unlike other types of federal aid, student loans must be repaid, usually with interest. Although education loans are also available from banks and other private sources, federal loans offer a number of advantages for borrowers, including: low interest rates that are fixed for the life of the loan; repayment plans that do not begin until the student completes school; maximum monthly payments based on the graduate's income; deferment options that allow students to suspend payments if they decide to return to school; and loan forgiveness under certain circumstances.

Federal student loans fall into two categories: subsidized loans, which are need-based; and unsubsidized loans, which do not require students or their families to demonstrate financial need. The main federal loan programs include the following:

- Federal Perkins Loan—a need-based, subsidized loan program that provides up to $5,500 per year for undergraduate students or $8,000 per year for graduate students at a low, fixed interest rate. Since the loan is subsidized, the federal government pays the interest while you are enrolled in college and during a six-month grace period following graduation.

- Direct Subsidized Federal Loan (also known as a Stafford Loan)—a need-based, subsidized loan program in which the amount you are eligible to borrow is determined by the school, but cannot exceed the cost of attendance. The federal government pays the interest while you remain in school, but interest accrues during the six-month grace period following graduation.

- Direct Unsubsidized Federal Loan—a non-need-based, unsubsidized loan program in which the amount you are eligible to borrow is determined by the school. Interest accrues while you are in school and during the six-month grace period before you must begin making payments. You can pay the interest as you go or have it added to the balance of your loan until after you graduate.

- Direct PLUS Loan (also known as a Parent PLUS Loan)—a non-need-based loan funded by the federal government that is available to independent graduate and professional students or the parents of dependent undergraduate students. The amount you are allowed to borrow is determined by the school and cannot exceed the cost of attendance. The interest rate and fees are higher than other federal student loans, but lower than most private loans.

Because loans must be repaid with interest over time, they are an expensive option that can affect your financial future. As a result, experts recommend using student loans as part of your college-funding plan only after you have exhausted all other financial aid options.

References

1. "Federal Student Aid At A Glance," Federal Student Aid, U.S. Department of Education, May 2016.

2. "An Overview Of Financial Aid," Best Colleges, 2017.

3. "What Is Federal Student Aid?" University of Hawaii, 2012.

Chapter 22
Applying For Federal Student Aid

Applying For Aid

To apply for federal student aid, you need to complete the FAFSA® (the *Free Application for Federal Student Aid*).

Completing and submitting the FAFSA® is free and quick, and it gives you access to the largest source of financial aid to pay for college or career school.

In addition, many states and colleges use your FAFSA® data to determine your eligibility for state and school aid, and some private financial aid providers may use your FAFSA® information to determine whether you qualify for their aid.

Why Should I Fill Out The FAFSA®?

If you don't fill out the FAFSA®, you could be missing out on a lot of financial aid! There are a number of reasons students think they shouldn't complete the FAFSA®. Here are a few:

- "I (or my parents) make too much money, so I won't qualify for aid."

- "Only students with good grades get financial aid."

- "The FAFSA® is too hard to fill out."

- "I'm too old to qualify for financial aid."

About This Chapter: Text under the heading "Applying For Aid" is excerpted from "FAFSA: Applying For Aid," Federal Student Aid, U.S. Department of Education (ED), January 5, 2017; Text beginning with the heading "The Big Changes For 2017–18" is excerpted from "FAFSA Changes For 2017–18," Federal Student Aid, U.S. Department of Education (ED), November 13, 2016.

The reality is, EVERYONE who's getting ready to go to college or career school should fill out the FAFSA®!

When Do I Fill Out The FAFSA®?

The 2016–17 FAFSA® has been available since January 1, 2016, and the 2017–18 FAFSA® launched on October 1, 2016.

There are different FAFSA® deadlines for different programs:

Table 22.1. FAFSA® Deadlines

Aid Program	Deadline Information
Federal student aid	• For the 2017–18 year, you can apply between Oct. 1, 2016, and June 30, 2018. • For the 2016–17 year, you can apply between Jan. 1, 2016, and June 30, 2017. However, there are a few federal student aid programs that have limited funds, so be sure to apply as soon as you can once the FAFSA® is available for the year you'll be attending school.
State student aid	You can find state deadlines at www.fafsa.gov or on the paper or PDF FAFSA®. Note that several states have financial aid programs with limited funds and therefore have a deadline of "as soon as possible (after the FAFSA® becomes available)."
College or career school aid	Check the school's website or contact its financial aid office. School deadlines are usually early in the year (often in February or March, although some may be even earlier now that the FAFSA® is available in October).
Other financial aid	Some programs other than government or school aid require that you file the FAFSA®. For instance, you can't get certain private scholarships unless you're eligible for a Federal Pell Grant—and you can't find out whether you're eligible for a Pell Grant unless you file a FAFSA®. If the private scholarship's application deadline is in early to mid-January, you'll need to submit your FAFSA® before that deadline.

As you can see, it's a good idea to file the FAFSA® as soon as it's available so you don't miss out on anything.

You have to fill out the FAFSA® every year you're in school in order to stay eligible for federal student aid.

Can I Get An Early Estimate Of My Aid?

You sure can! If you're not ready to file a FAFSA®, you can use *FAFSA4caster* to estimate your federal student aid.

How Do I Fill Out The FAFSA®?

There are several ways to file:

- Online at fafsa.gov is faster and easier than using paper.
- If you need a paper FAFSA®, you can
- download a PDF FAFSA® or
- order a print-out of the PDF FAFSA® by calling 877-4-ED-PUBS (877-433-7827).
- Ask the financial aid office at your college or career school if you can file it there. Some schools will use special software to submit your FAFSA® for you.

What Happens After I Fill Out The FAFSA®?

Applying isn't the last step; your FAFSA® has to be processed, and then you get an Expected Family Contribution (EFC), which your college or career school uses to figure out how much aid you can get.

The Big Changes For 2017–18

Starting with the 2017–18 *Free Application for Federal Student Aid* (FAFSA®), the following changes have been put in place:

- **Students are now able to submit a FAFSA® earlier.** Students have been able to file a 2017–18 FAFSA® since October 1, 2016, rather than beginning on January 1, 2017. The earlier submission date is a permanent change, enabling students to complete and submit a FAFSA® as early as October 1 every year. (There is NO CHANGE to the 2016–17 schedule. The FAFSA® became available January 1 as in previous years.)

- **Students now report earlier income information.** Beginning with the 2017–18 FAFSA®, students are required to report income information from an earlier tax year. For example, on the 2017–18 FAFSA®, students (and parents, as appropriate) must report their 2015 income information, rather than their 2016 income information.

Frequently Asked Questions About The 2017–18 FAFSA®

Are Deadlines Now Earlier?

The federal deadline isn't earlier, but some state and school deadlines are. Most state and school deadlines haven't changed, but be aware of this: Several states' deadlines have changed from "as soon as possible after January 1" to "as soon as possible after October 1." Find state deadlines on the FAFSA® and school deadlines on schools' websites.

Do I Have To Apply For Admission To A School Before I List It On My FAFSA®?

No. On your FAFSA®, list all the schools to which you have applied or might apply.

Will My 2016–17 FAFSA® Information Be Carried Over Onto The 2017–18 FAFSA®?

If you choose the Renewal FAFSA® option when you start your application at fafsa.gov, some basic information from your 2016–17 FAFSA® will be prepopulated in your 2017–18 FAFSA®. However, your tax and income information will not. (Too much could have changed in your life since you filled out the 2016–17 FAFSA®.)

Can I Choose To Report 2016 Information If My Family's Income Has Dropped Significantly Since We Filed 2015 Taxes?

No. You must report 2015 tax and income information, as the FAFSA® requires. If your family's financial situation has changed dramatically since then, you should complete the FAFSA® questions as required, submit the FAFSA®, then contact the school you plan to attend and discuss your situation with the financial aid office.

Do I Report My 2015 Tax And Income Information On The 2017–18 FAFSA® Now, And Then Update It Once I've Filed My 2016 Taxes?

No. Do not update after filing your taxes. The 2017–18 FAFSA® asks for 2015 tax information.

What If My Parents' (Or My) Marital Status Has Changed Since We Filed 2015 Taxes? How Do We Supply Tax And Income Information On The FAFSA®?

Here are some tips for this type of situation:

- The FAFSA® asks for marital status "as of today" (the day it's filled out). So if the student or parent is married now but wasn't in 2015 (and therefore didn't file taxes as married), the spouse's income will need to be added to the FAFSA®.

- Similarly, if the student or parent filed 2015 taxes as married but is no longer married when filling out the FAFSA®, the spouse's income will need to be subtracted.

- And if the student or parent was married when filing 2015 taxes, then got divorced and is now married to someone else, there's a bit more math to do: Subtract the ex's income, then add the new spouse's income.

- The help text in fafsa.gov will discuss all these situations.

Will I Receive Aid Offers From Schools Earlier If I Apply Earlier?

Not necessarily; some schools will make offers earlier, and others won't. And keep in mind that an early offer might be an estimated offer, so read communications from schools carefully.

Chapter 23
Estimating And Calculating Aid

The cost of a college education has increased significantly over the years. For many teens, the expense may seem to put a four-year degree out of reach. But financial aid is available from the U.S. government to help you afford college.

Did You Know...

Of the nearly $184 billion in financial aid provided to undergraduates at U.S. institutions of higher learning during the 2014–2015 academic year, 67 percent came from the federal government, 22 percent from college and universities, 6 percent from private organizations, and 5 percent from state governments.

Estimating the amount of financial aid you will be eligible to receive is an important part of planning for college. Understanding how financial aid is calculated can help you figure out the best strategies for funding your higher education.

Eligibility Criteria For Financial Aid

To qualify for financial aid, you must complete the *Free Application for Federal Student Aid* (FAFSA®) after October 1 of the year before you intend to enroll in college. FAFSA® determines your eligibility for both federal and state financial aid. To be eligible for most types of federal aid, you must demonstrate financial need. You should submit the application even if

"Estimation And Calculation Of Aid," © 2017 Omnigraphics.

you think your family income is too high for you to qualify, however, because other factors may impact your eligibility as well, such as the size of your family and the number of family members who will be enrolled in college at the same time. The basic qualification requirements for student aid include the following:

- You must be a U.S. citizen or an eligible noncitizen;

- You must have a valid Social Security number (SSN);

- If you are a male between the ages of 18 and 25, you must register with the U.S. Military Selective Service (MSS);

- You must prove you are qualified to attend college by earning a high-school diploma, getting a high-school equivalency or General Educational Development (GED) certificate, or completing a state-approved homeschool program;

- You must be accepted or enrolled at least half-time in a degree or certificate program;

- You must maintain satisfactory grades and show academic progress toward earning a degree or certificate;

- You must agree to use your federal student aid funds only for educational expenses; and

- You must not owe money on a federal student grant or be in default on a federal student loan.

Estimating Your Financial Aid

Even before you are ready to submit the FAFSA® and apply to colleges, you can estimate the amount of financial aid you will be eligible to receive by using a free, online tool called *FAFSA4caster*. This student-aid calculator provides valuable information to help you plan ahead to meet college expenses. You and your family can use it during your high-school years, or even as early as middle school, to get estimates of financial aid and create strategies for funding your education.

The *FAFSA4caster* tool works a bit like the FAFSA® itself. You answer questions about your own income and savings, along with that of your parents if you are considered a dependent. Some of the questions may require figures from your bank statements or federal tax returns. After you enter your financial information, the *FAFSA4caster* provides estimates of the amount of college funding you are likely to receive from the federal government. The sources of funding are broken down into separate amounts for Federal Pell Grants, Federal Work-Study income, Direct Subsidized Loans, and Direct Unsubsidized Loans. The financial aid amounts are displayed in a worksheet that allows you to enter more information in order to estimate the cost of attending a specific college.

Calculating Your Financial Aid

If you meet the basic eligibility criteria for federal student aid and file a FAFSA®, the information you provide is put into a complex formula to calculate your Expected Family Contribution (EFC). The EFC is an index number that each college can use to determine how much financial aid you would be eligible to receive if you attended that school.

When you apply for admission to a college, the financial aid office begins by calculating your cost of attendance (COA), which is an estimate of the total cost of attending that institution for a year. The COA typically includes:

- tuition and fees;

- room and board;

- books, supplies, transportation, and other expenses;

- costs related to a study-abroad program, if applicable.

To determine your financial need, or the amount of need-based financial aid you are eligible to receive, the school will subtract your EFC from your COA. For example, if your COA is $20,000 and your EFC is $15,000, then you would be eligible for a maximum of $5,000 in need-based federal aid. The need-based student aid programs include the Federal Pell Grant, Federal Supplemental Educational Opportunity Grant (FSEOG), Federal Perkins Loan, Direct Subsidized Loan, and Federal Work-Study.

You may also be eligible to receive non-need-based financial aid. Your EFC is not used in determining this amount. To calculate non-need-based aid, the college financial aid office takes your COA and subtracts the total amount of financial assistance you have been awarded from all sources, including federal need-based aid, private scholarships, and awards and grants offered by the college. If your COA is $20,000 and you have already received $8,000 in federal aid and scholarships, then you are eligible for a maximum of $12,000 in non-need-based aid. The federal programs for non-need-based aid include the Direct Unsubsidized Loan, Federal PLUS Loan, and Teacher Education Access for College and Higher Education (TEACH) Grant.

References

1. "Basic Eligibility Criteria," Federal Student Aid, U.S. Department of Education, 2017.

2. "Estimate Your Aid," Federal Student Aid, U.S. Department of Education, 2017.

3. "Financial Aid: FAQs," Big Future, The College Board, 2017.

4. "How Aid Is Calculated," Federal Student Aid, U.S. Department of Education, 2017.

Chapter 24

Understanding The Expected Family Contribution (EFC)

What Is The Expected Family Contribution (EFC)?

The Expected Family Contribution (EFC) is a number that determines students' eligibility for federal student aid. The EFC formulas use the financial information students provide on their *Free Application for Federal Student Aid* (FAFSA®) to calculate the EFC. Financial aid administrators (FAAs) subtract the EFC from students' cost of attendance (COA) to determine their need for the following federal student financial assistance offered by the U.S. Department of Education (the Department):

- Federal Pell Grants,

- Subsidized Stafford Loans through the William D. Ford Federal Direct Loan Program,

- Federal Supplemental Educational Opportunity Grants (FSEOG),

- Federal Perkins Loans, and

- Federal Work-Study (FWS).

The Teacher Education Assistance for College and Higher Education Grant (TEACH Grant) is a non-need-based federal program, for which a student must also use the FAFSA® to apply.

The methodology for determining the EFC is found in Part F of Title IV of the Higher Education Act of 1965, as amended (HEA). Tables used in the computation of the EFC for the 2017–2018 Award Year were published in the May 24, 2016 Federal Register (ifap.ed.gov/fregisters/FR052416.html) (81 FR 32737).

About This Chapter: This chapter includes text excerpted from "The EFC Formula, 2017–2018," Federal Student Aid, U.S. Department of Education (ED), December 20, 2016.

In Fall 2015, the President announced two major changes to the *Free Application for Federal Student Aid* (FAFSA®) process. Beginning in 2017–2018, the first change is to begin application processing on October 1, earlier than in prior cycles, and the second change is to collect and use financial information from the tax/calendar year one year earlier than in the past. This means we are collecting the 2015 tax information (again) for 2017–2018; however, it is important to note that the needs analysis calculations have been revised.

To provide the financial aid community with easy-to-access, updated information and resources relating to the 2017–2018 Early FAFSA®, Federal Student Aid created an Early FAFSA® Information page on Information for Financial Aid Professionals (IFAP).

What Is The Source Of Data Used In EFC Calculations?

All data used to calculate a student's EFC comes from the information the student provides on the FAFSA®. A student may submit a FAFSA®:

- by using FAFSA® on the Web,

- by filing an application electronically through a school, or

- by mailing a FAFSA® to the Central Processing System (CPS).

Students who applied for federal student aid in the previous award year may be eligible to reapply using a renewal FAFSA® online. Applying for federal aid is free, but to be considered for non-federal aid (such as institutional aid), students may have to fill out additional forms, which might require fees.

Applicants are encouraged to complete the FAFSA® electronically, because there are edits that reduce applicant errors and customize the questions presented based on answers to prior questions. The electronic version also contains additional instructions and help features and allows the Department to send results to the students and schools more quickly.

Who Processes The Application, And How Is A Student Notified Of His Or Her EFC?

The CPS receives the student's application data, either electronically or on the paper application, The CPS receives the student's application data, either electronically or on the paper application, and uses it to calculate an EFC. After the FAFSA® has been processed, the CPS sends the student an output document containing information about his or her application results. This document, which can be paper or electronic, is called a Student Aid Report (SAR). The SAR lists all the information from the application and indicates whether the application was complete and signed. If the application is complete and signed and there are no data conflicts, the SAR also includes the student's EFC. Students are instructed to carefully check the accuracy of the information on the SAR. All schools listed on the student's FAFSA® receive application information and processing results in an electronic file called an Institutional Student Information Record (ISIR).

Which EFC Formula Worksheet Should Be Used?

There are three regular formulas and a simplified version of each:

- Formula A for dependent students,

- Formula B for independent students **without** dependents other than a spouse, and

- Formula C for independent students **with** dependents other than a spouse.

What Is the Definition Of An Independent Student?

Because the EFC formula for a dependent student uses parental data and the two formulas for independent students do not, the first step in calculating a student's EFC is to determine his or her dependency status. For the 2017–2018 Award Year, a student is automatically determined to be independent for federal student aid if he or she meets one or more of the following criteria:

- The student was born before January 1, 1994.

- The student is married or separated (but not divorced) as of the date of the application.

- At the beginning of the 2017–2018 school year, the student will be enrolled in a master's or doctoral degree program (such as MA, MBA, MD, JD, PhD, EdD, or graduate certificate, etc.).

- The student is currently serving on active duty in the U.S. Armed Forces or is a National Guard or Reserves enlistee called into federal active duty for purposes other than training.

- The student is a veteran of the U.S. Armed Forces

- The student has or will have one or more children who receive more than half of their support from him or her between July 1, 2017 and June 30, 2018.

- The student has dependent(s) (other than children or spouse) who live with him or her and who receive more than half of their support from the student, now and through June 30, 2018.

- At any time since the student turned age 13, both of the student's parents were deceased, or the student was in foster care or was a dependent or ward of the court.

- As determined by a court in the student's state of legal residence, the student is now, or was upon reaching the age of majority, an emancipated minor (released from control by his or her parent or guardian).

- As determined by a court in the student's state of legal residence, the student is now, or was upon reaching the age of majority, in legal guardianship.

- On or after July 1, 2016, the student was determined by a high school or school district homeless liaison to be an unaccompanied youth who was homeless or was self-supporting and at risk of being homeless.

- On or after July 1, 2016, the student was determined by the director of an emergency shelter or transitional housing program funded by the U.S. Department of Housing and Urban Development (HUD) to be an unaccompanied youth who was homeless or was self-supporting and at risk of being homeless.

- At any time on or after July 1, 2016, the student was determined by a director of a runaway or homeless youth basic center or transitional living program to be an unaccompanied youth who was homeless or was self-supporting and at risk of being homeless.

- The student was determined by the college financial aid administrator to be an unaccompanied youth who is homeless or is self-supporting and at risk of being homeless.

For students who do not meet any of the above criteria but who have documented unusual circumstances, an FAA can override their dependency status from dependent to independent. For information about dependency overrides, see the Application and Verification Guide, which is part of the Federal Student Aid Handbook and can be found on the IFAP Website.

Terms Used In The Definition Of An Independent Student

Legal Dependent. Any children of the student who receive more than half of their support from the student (children do not have to live with the student), including a biological or adopted child. Also, any persons, other than a spouse, who live with the student and receive more than half of their support from the student now and will continue to receive more than half of their support from the student through June 30, 2018.

Veteran. A student who: (1) has engaged in active service in the U.S. Armed Forces (Army, Navy, Air Force, Marines, or Coast Guard), or has been a member of the National Guard or Reserves who was called to active duty for purposes other than training, or was a cadet or midshipman at one of the service academies, or attended a U.S. military academy preparatory school, and (2) was released under a condition other than dishonorable. A veteran is also a student who does not meet this definition now but will by June 30, 2018.

Which Students Qualify For The Simplified EFC Formulas?

The following criteria determine which students have their EFCs calculated by a simplified formula. Assets are not considered in the simplified EFC formulas.

For the 2017–2018 Award Year, a **dependent** student qualifies for the simplified EFC formula if both (1) and (2) are true:

(1) Anyone included in the **parents'** household size (as defined on the FAFSA®) received benefits during 2015 or 2016 from any of the designated means-tested federal benefit programs: the Medicaid Program, the Supplemental Security Income (SSI) Program, the

Supplemental Nutrition Assistance Program (SNAP), the Free and Reduced Price School Lunch Program, the Temporary Assistance for Needy Families (TANF) Program1, and the Special Supplemental Nutrition Program for Women, Infants, and Children (WIC);

OR

the student's **parents**:

- filed or were eligible to file a 2015 IRS Form 1040A or 1040EZ2,

- filed a 2015 IRS Form 1040 but were not required to do so3, or

- were not required to file any income tax return;

[1] *The TANF Program may have a different name in the student's or student's parents' state.*

[2] *For qualifying for the simplified or automatic zero EFC calculations, the following 2015 income tax forms are considered equivalent to an IRS Form 1040A or 1040EZ: the income tax return required by the tax code of the Commonwealth of Puerto Rico, Guam, American Samoa, the U.S. Virgin Islands, the Republic of the Marshall Islands, the Federated States of Micronesia, or Palau.*

[3] *Applicants who are not required to complete an IRS Form 1040, but do so solely to claim an educational tax credit are considered eligible if they meet all the other requirements for the simplified EFC formulas.*

OR

> the student's **parent** is a dislocated worker.

AND

(2) The combined 2015 income of the student's **parents** is $49,999 or less.

- For tax filers, use the parents' adjusted gross income from the tax return to determine if income is $49,999 or less.

- For non-tax filers, use the income shown on the 2015 W-2 forms of both parents (plus any other earnings from work not included on the W-2s) to determine if income is $49,999 or less.

For the 2017–2018 Award Year, an **independent** student qualifies for the simplified EFC formula if both (1) and (2) are true:

(1) Anyone included in the **student's** household size (as defined on the FAFSA®) received benefits during 2015 or 2016 from any of the designated means-tested federal benefit programs: the Medicaid Program, the SSI Program, SNAP, the Free and Reduced Price School Lunch Program, the TANF Program1, and WIC;

OR

> the student and student's spouse (if the student is married) *both*

- filed or were eligible to file a 2015 IRS Form 1040A or 1040EZ2,

- filed a 2015 IRS Form 1040 but were not required to do so3, or

- were not required to file any income tax return;

OR

> the student (or the student's spouse, if any) is a dislocated worker.

AND

(2) The student's (and spouse's) combined 2015 income is $49,999 or less.

- For tax filers, use the student's (and spouse's) adjusted gross income from the tax return to determine if income is $49,999 or less.

- For non-tax filers, use the income shown on the student's (and spouse's) 2015 W-2 forms (plus any other earnings from work not included on the W-2s) to determine if income is $49,999 or less.

Which Students Qualify For An Automatic Zero EFC Calculation?

Certain students are automatically eligible for a zero EFC. The requirements for receiving an automatic zero EFC are the same as those for the simplified EFC calculation except for these differences:

- The income threshold for the parents of dependent students and for independent students and their spouses is $25,000 or less (for an automatic zero EFC) instead of $49,999 or less (for the simplified EFC calculation), and

- For independent students, those without dependents other than a spouse cannot receive an automatic zero EFC.

Note: The income threshold for an automatic zero EFC remains at $25,000 for the 2017–2018 Award Year.

For the 2017–2018 Award Year, a **dependent student** automatically qualifies for a zero EFC if both (1) and (2) are true.

(1) Anyone included in the **parents'** household size (as defined on the FAFSA®) received benefits during 2015 or 2016 from any of the designated means-tested federal benefit programs: the Medicaid Program, the SSI Program, SNAP, the Free and Reduced Price School Lunch Program, the TANF Program1, and WIC;

OR

the student's **parents**:

- filed or were eligible to file a 2015 IRS Form 1040A or 1040EZ2,

- filed a 2015 IRS Form 1040 but were not required to do so3, or

- were not required to file any income tax return;

OR

the student's **parent** is a dislocated worker.

AND

(2) The combined 2015 income of the student's **parents** is $25,000 or less.

- For tax filers, use the parents' adjusted gross income from the tax return to determine if income is $25,000 or less.

- For non-tax filers, use the income shown on the 2015 W-2 forms of both parents (plus any other earnings from work not included on the W-2s) to determine if income is $25,000 or less.

An **independent student with dependents other than a spouse** automatically qualifies for a zero EFC if both (1) and (2) are true:

(1) Anyone included in the **student's** household size (as defined on the FAFSA®) received benefits during 2015 or 2016 from any of the designated means-tested federal benefit programs: the Medicaid Program, the SSI Program, SNAP, the Free and Reduced Price School Lunch Program, the TANF Program1, and WIC;

OR

the student and student's spouse (if the student is married) both

- filed or were eligible to file a 2015 IRS Form 1040A or 1040EZ2,

- filed a 2015 IRS Form 1040 but were not required to do so3, or

- were not required to file any income tax return;

OR

the student (or the student's spouse, if any) is a dislocated worker.

AND

(2) The student's (and spouse's) combined 2015 income is $25,000 or less.

- For tax filers, use the student's (and spouse's) adjusted gross income from the tax return to determine if income is $25,000 or less.

- For non-tax filers, use the income shown on the student's (and spouse's) 2015 W-2 forms (plus any other earnings from work not included on the W-2s) to determine if income is $25,000 or less.

Note: An **independent student without dependents other than a spouse** is not eligible for an automatic zero EFC.

Why Might A Calculation Of An EFC Using These Worksheets Differ From The EFC Reported On A Student's SAR?

When it appears that an applicant has reported inconsistent data, the CPS may make certain assumptions to resolve the inconsistency. These assumed values, which are reported on the student's SAR, are used to calculate the student's EFC. Therefore, in some cases, the EFC

produced by these worksheets may differ from the EFC produced by the CPS if the assumed values are not used.

In addition, to help reconcile EFC Formula Worksheet calculations with those of the CPS, all calculations should be carried to three decimal places and then rounded to the nearest whole numbers. Round upward for results of .500 to .999, round downward for results of .001 to .499. Rounding should be performed so that the intermediate value that is the result of each step does not have any decimal digits.

Chapter 25
Accepting And Receiving Aid

Accepting Aid

When your school financial aid office sends you an award letter, they'll ask you to indicate which financial aid you want. Look carefully at your options and make an informed decision.

I've Got An Award Letter From My School. Which Financial Aid Is The Best To Accept?

The rule is: free money first (scholarships and grants), then earned money (work-study), then borrowed money (federal student loans). Start from the top of this table and work your way down:

Table 25.1. Order Of Best Financial Aid

Order In Which To Accept Aid	Type Of Aid	What To Keep In Mind
1	Scholarships and grants	Make sure you understand the conditions you must meet (for instance, you might have to maintain a certain grade-point average in order to continue receiving a scholarship, or your TEACH Grant might turn into a loan if you don't teach for a certain number of years under specific circumstances).

About This Chapter: Text under the heading "Accepting Aid" is excerpted from "Accepting Aid," Federal Student Aid, U.S. Department of Education (ED), January 20, 2017; Text under the heading "Receiving Aid" is excerpted from "Receiving Aid," Federal Student Aid, U.S. Department of Education (ED), January 20, 2017.

Table 25.1. Continued

Order In Which To Accept Aid	Type Of Aid	What To Keep In Mind
2	Work-study	You don't have to pay the money back, but you do have to work for it, so take into account that that'll mean less time for studying. However, research has shown that students who work part-time jobs manage their time better than those who don't!
3	Federal student loans	You'll have to repay the money with interest. Subsidized loans don't start accruing (accumulating) interest until you leave school, so accept a subsidized loan before an unsubsidized loan.
4	Loans from your state government or your college	You'll have to repay the money with interest, and the terms of the loan might not be as good as those of a federal student loan. Be sure to read all the fine print before you borrow.
5	Private loans	You'll have to repay the money with interest, and the terms and conditions of the loan almost certainly will not be as good as those of a federal student loan.

I Will Need To Borrow Some Money. How Do I Decide Which Student Loans To Accept?

Accept the loans with the most favorable terms and conditions; usually, that means federal student loans and state aid offered to you.

If you have any questions or don't understand what types of loans are in your award letter, contact the school. Always ask questions and be an informed borrower. Make sure you understand what you're receiving and the repayment terms.

Is It Okay To Accept Less Loan Money Than The School Offered?

Sure! You should borrow only what you need. If your living expenses are not going to be as high as the amount estimated by your school, you have the right to turn down the loan or to request a lower loan amount. In the award letter, the school will tell you how to do this.

How Do I Tell The School What Aid I'm Accepting?

Read and follow the directions in the award letter. You might have to enter the amounts you're accepting in an online form and then submit the form. If you receive a paper award letter, you might have to sign it and mail it back to the school.

Accepting a loan listed in the award letter involves some additional steps, which vary depending on the type of loan you're receiving. Saying yes may be as simple as signing a promissory note—a contract between you and the lender that specifies terms and conditions of the loan. (If you take out a loan from the Direct Loan Program, the U.S. Department of Education (ED) will be your lender.) By signing the promissory note, you are promising to repay your student loan.

How And When Will I Get My Financial Aid?

Every school is a little different, so ask your school's financial aid staff what to expect.

Receiving Aid

You've filled out your *Free Application for Federal Student Aid* (FAFSA®), received an award letter from your school, and told the school which financial aid you want to accept. Now what?

When Will I Receive My Financial Aid?

Generally, your grant or loan will cover a full academic year and your school will disburse (pay out) your money in at least two payments called disbursements. In most cases, your school must pay you at least once per term (semester, trimester, or quarter). Schools that don't use traditional terms such as semesters or quarters usually must pay you at least twice per academic year—for instance, at the beginning and midpoint of your academic year.

- If you're a first-year undergraduate student and a first-time borrower, you may have to wait 30 days after the first day of your enrollment period (semester, trimester, etc.) for your first disbursement. Check with your school to see whether this rule applies there.

- If you're a first-time borrower of a Direct Subsidized Loan or a Direct Unsubsidized Loan, you must complete entrance counseling before you receive your first loan disbursement. Similarly, if you are a graduate or professional student taking out a Direct PLUS Loan for the first time, you must complete entrance counseling before receiving your first disbursement. If you are a parent taking out a Direct PLUS Loan to help pay for your child's education, you will not be required to participate in entrance counseling.

If you're going to have a work-study job, you'll be paid at least once a month.

How Will I Receive My Financial Aid?

It depends on what type of aid you'll be receiving—grants, student loans, work-study, or parent loans.

Grants And Student Loans

Typically, the college first applies your grant or loan money toward your tuition, fees, and (if you live on campus) room and board. Any money left over is paid to you for other expenses. You might be able to choose whether the leftover money comes to you by check, cash, a credit to your bank account, or another method.

If your loan is disbursed but then you realize that you don't need the money after all, you may cancel your loan within 120 days of the disbursement, and no interest or fees will be charged.

Work-Study

Your school must pay you directly (for instance, by cash or check) unless you request that the school

- send your payments directly to your bank account or
- use the money to pay for education-related charges (such as tuition, fees, and room and board) on your student account.

Parent (PLUS) Loans

In most cases, your child's school will disburse your loan money by crediting it to your child's school account to pay tuition, fees, room, board, and other authorized charges. If there is money left over, the school will pay it to you, usually by check. In some cases, with your permission, the school may disburse the leftover money to your child.

Chapter 26
Federal Education Grants

Grants And Scholarships

Grants and scholarships are often called "gift aid" because they are free money—financial aid that doesn't have to be repaid. Grants are often need-based, while scholarships are usually merit-based.

Grants and scholarships can come from the federal government, your state government, your college or career school, or a private or nonprofit organization. Do your research, apply for any grants or scholarships you might be eligible for, and be sure to meet application deadlines!

Certain scenarios may require that a portion or all of the grant funds be repaid, for example, if you withdraw from school before finishing an enrollment period such as a semester.

What Kinds Of Federal Grants Are Available?

The U.S. Department of Education (ED) offers a variety of federal grants to students attending four-year colleges or universities, community colleges, and career schools.

- Federal Pell Grants
- Federal Supplemental Educational Opportunity Grants (FSEOG)
- Teacher Education Assistance for College and Higher Education (TEACH) Grants
- Iraq and Afghanistan Service Grants (IASG)

About This Chapter: Text under the heading "Grants And Scholarships" is excerpted from "Grants And Scholarships," Federal Student Aid, U.S. Department of Education (ED), December 22, 2016; Text beginning with the heading "What Is A Grant?" is excerpted from "Grants 101," Grants.gov, Office of Management and Budget (OMB), April 18, 2015.

How Do I Get A Federal Grant?

Almost all of the grants (listed above) are awarded to students with financial need. If you are interested in the above stated grants, or in any federal student aid, you have to start by submitting a *Free Application for Federal Student Aid* (FAFSA®). Once you've done that, you'll work with your college or career school to find out how much you can get and when you'll get it.

What Kinds Of Scholarships Are Available, And How Do I Get One?

There are thousands of scholarships, from all kinds of organizations, and they're not hard to find. You might be able to get a scholarship for being a good student, a great basketball player, or a member of a certain church, or because your parent works for a particular company, or for some other reason.

Why Would I Have To Repay All Or Part Of A Federal Grant?

Here are some examples of why you might have to repay all or part of a federal grant:

- You withdrew early from the program for which the grant was given to you.

- Your enrollment status changed in a way that reduced your eligibility for your grant (for instance, if you switch from full-time enrollment to part-time, your grant amount will be reduced).

- You received outside scholarships or grants that reduced your need for federal student aid.

How Do I Repay A Grant Overpayment?

Your school will notify you if you must repay part of the grant. From that point, you will have 45 days to either pay that portion of the grant back in full or enter into a satisfactory repayment arrangement. If you enter into a satisfactory repayment arrangement, the school may assign the debt to ED for collection or may keep the debt and allow you to make payments directly to them.

If you do not carry out one of these options, you will lose your eligibility for further federal student aid.

What Is A Grant?

A grant is a way the government funds your ideas and projects to provide public services and stimulate the economy. Grants support critical recovery initiatives, innovative research, and many other programs listed in the Catalog of Federal Domestic Assistance (CFDA).

A grant is one of many different forms of federal financial assistance. Federal financial assistance is a broad term to refer to the various ways the U.S. government redistributes resources to eligible recipients. On Grants.gov you will find grant and cooperative agreement opportunities from federal agencies that award grants.

The Grant Lifecycle

The grant process follows a linear lifecycle that includes creating the funding opportunity, applying, making award decisions, and successfully implementing the award.

The specific actions along the lifecycle are grouped into three main phases.

1. Pre-Award Phase—Funding Opportunities and Application Review

2. Award Phase—Award Decisions and Notifications

3. Post Award—Implementation, Reporting, and Closeout

Pre-Award Phase

The pre-award phase represents the beginning of the grant lifecycle, which includes announcing opportunities, submitting applications, and reviewing applications. Below are explanations of what generally occurs during the pre-award phase.

- Funding Opportunity Announcement

- Application Review Process

Funding Opportunity Announcement

Both the grant-making agencies and prospective applicants conduct their planning processes. The awarding agencies prepare and publish Funding Opportunity Announcements (FOA) based on the related legislation and their budget.

An FOA includes all the pertinent information and requirements for an applicant to assess their eligibility, competency, and interest in the funding opportunity. How do you find these opportunities? That's where Grants.gov comes in.

You, a prospective applicant, can use the Search Grants function (www.grants.gov/web/grants/search-grants.html) to navigate through opportunities and settle on the right FOA for you. Once you select on a funding opportunity to apply for, there are two high-level steps, in addition to your own application development processes, to work on before submitting your application in Grants.gov:

1. Register to apply for grants

2. Complete your application

Register To Apply For Grants

Registering to apply for grants on Grants.gov includes several steps and types of registration, including Data Universal Number System (DUNS), SAM.gov, and Grants.gov accounts. It's not a highly complex process, but it can take 1 to 3 weeks to complete, so please register as early as you can.

Completing Your Application

Before jumping into the process of filling out the application, you (i.e., an organization or individual) should spend time analyzing your own capabilities as compared to the specific eligibility and technical requirements detailed in the application instructions. The application planning process is lengthy, but it is critical when considering the importance of carrying out government-related work and the competition you may face for funding. While the specific steps vary widely depending on the type of grant you are applying for, major components of the planning process includes developing your ideas, conducting research, writing your proposal, and completing the application in Grants.gov.

If you are interested in more specific information or training on the development of an effective proposal, there are a number of options out there. First, it is recommend perusing the awarding agencies website. Often, the awarding agency provides specific information on pre-award processes pertaining to their types of funding opportunities. It is also recommend looking at the Grant Community page (www.grants.gov/web/grants/learn-grants/grant-community.html) for additional information and upcoming grant events from across the grants sector.

Application Review Process

Once the application submission deadline passes, the awarding agencies get to work reviewing the applications. The specific process for reviewing an application varies based on the type of grant you applied for. The generally applicable steps are as follows:

- Initial screening to ensure application is complete

- Programmatic review and assessment of the substance of the applications

- Financial review of proposed budgets

- Award decision and announcement

Initial Screening Of Application

In the initial screening, sometimes called a basic minimum requirements review, the agencies will check each proposal to ensure it includes all the required elements to qualify for the grant. What the specific requirements are will vary for each grant, but common elements are eligibility, program narrative, and budget attachment. The key for the initial screening is that the agencies are looking for the presence of the required element, not the quality of the element. If your application does not meet all of these basic requirements, then your application is likely to be rejected.

Programmatic Review And Assessment Of Applications

The remaining applications undergo a thorough review and assessment for their technical and programmatic quality and competency. Again, this varies depending on the type of grant you applied for. For discretionary grants, the review is conducted by independent experts who assess the applications using the uniform rating or scoring system established by each awarding agency.

A common format is a peer review panel of at least three people, who assess and score each application independently. Then, the peer review panel will convene to discuss the merits of the applications. A series of policies and assurances are in place to maintain a fair, objective process based on material facts in the applications and without conflicts of interest (COI) for the peer reviewers. The federal agency staff monitor and participate in this review process.

Financial Review

While an application may have technical and programmatic quality, your budget also needs to be well-documented and reflect the requirements of the grant program. The federal agencies conduct a cost analysis, reviewing each line item and the overall proposed budget to ensure compliance with statutory and financial regulations. Additionally, the financial review also factors in the total budget for the grant program in relation to how much money each application requests.

Award Phase

Once the Federal agency completes the application review process, the Award Phase begins. The final award decisions rest solely in the hands of the federal agency staff with fiduciary responsibility and legal authority to enter binding agreements. Federal staff review and make award recommendations based on the programmatic and financial reviews of the applications. These recommendations are reviewed by a series of levels in the agencies to ensure high-quality, fair, and unbiased decisions.

Notice Of Award

Once the final award decisions are made, the awarding agency sends a Notice of Award (NOA) to the entities selected for funding. The NOA is the official, legally binding issuance of the award. When you or your organization accepts the grant (i.e., by signing the grant agreement or by drawing down funds) you become legally obligated to carry out the full terms and conditions of the grant.

As an award recipient, you are also subject to federal statutory and regulatory requirements and policies.

Post Award Phase

The post award phase comprises a significant amount of work over the duration of the award dates, which includes implementing the grant, reporting progress, and completing the closeout requirements. The federal agency that makes the award to you is also there to assist and ensure you or your organization complies with the grant terms and conditions. Your job is to faithfully and diligently carry out the grant program.

Reporting

The agency monitors your progress and expenditures through various programmatic and financial reporting procedures, as well as using performance metrics per the grant agreement. While the majority of award recipients carry out the grants ethically and efficiently, these monitoring procedures are necessary to maintain transparency and to prevent fraud and abuse.

The awarding agency typically has a grants management officer and program officer designated to each grant, both of which you will work with throughout the life of the grant. They are the ones who will review reports and conduct site visits, so it is recommend you build an effective line of communication with these staff members. It is better to prevent issues by talking to your grant and program officers to clarify grant terms or expectations than it is to submit a report and wait for problems to be identified and recourse initiated.

The specific reporting requirements, schedules, and systems can vary for each grant, so please review the grant terms and conditions carefully for this information.

Auditing

Federal grant-making agencies and grant recipients are audited. The Government Accountability Office (GAO), Office of Inspector General (OIG), and various departments within each Federal agency monitor and analyze policies, expenditures, and more activities within each grant-making agency. These same entities, as well as others, also monitor and analyze the performance of grant recipients.

Single Audits

The Federal awarding agency ensures non-Federal entities have a single audit conducted and submit a single audit reporting package to the Federal Audit Clearinghouse (FAC) in a timely manner. The Federal awarding agency also performs follow-up on audit findings to ensure the non-Federal entity takes appropriate and timely corrective action. As part of this process, the Federal awarding agency issues a management decision, within six months of FAC acceptance of the audit report, for audit findings that relate to Federal awards it makes to non-Federal entities.

A non-Federal entity that expends $750,000 or more in Federal awards during its fiscal year may be required to have a single audit conducted for that year. This audit is in lieu of any financial audit of Federal awards, which a non-Federal entity is required to undergo under any other Federal statute or regulation. After completion of the audit, the non-Federal entity submits the audit reporting package to the FAC within nine months after the end of the audit period. The non-Federal entity also performs follow-up and corrective action on all audit findings.

Closeout

The closeout step is where the grant process ends. In order to complete a closeout, you, the award recipient, must submit the final financial and programmatic reports. According to the OMB Uniform Grants Guidance §200.343, the receipt must submit all financial, performance, and other reports required under the grant within 90 days after the grant award expires or is terminated. The awarding agency will review these reports to ensure compliance will all the grant terms and conditions as well as to make sure you spent all the funds appropriately.

How Do I Know When A Grant Is Officially Over?

The Federal awarding agency has to confirm that the recipient has completed all of the required grant work and all the applicable administrative tasks. Until the awarding agency confirms this, you are still responsible for fulfilling all the terms of the grant. The closeout process can take several months if there are financial concerns or questions to reconcile. Also, if you or your organization acquired any property using grant funding, the closeout step is when you must make sure to handle this property exactly as the grant stipulates, which includes completing the appropriate reports on this property. Lastly, you are typically required to retain your grant records for at least three years from the date of the final expenditure report.

Chapter 27

Federal Pell Grants And Federal Supplemental Educational Opportunity Grant (FSEOG)

Federal Pell Grants

Federal Pell Grants are usually awarded only to undergraduate students. The amount of aid you can receive depends on your financial need, the cost of attendance at your school, and more.

Federal Pell Grants usually are awarded only to undergraduate students who have not earned a bachelor's or a professional degree. (In some cases, however, a student enrolled in a postbaccalaureate teacher certification program might receive a Federal Pell Grant.) You are not eligible to receive a Federal Pell Grant if you are incarcerated in a federal or state penal institution or are subject to an involuntary civil commitment upon completion of a period of incarceration for a forcible or nonforcible sexual offense. A Federal Pell Grant, unlike a loan, does not have to be repaid, except under certain circumstances.

How Much Money Can I Get?

Amounts can change yearly. For the 2016–17 award year (July 1, 2016, to June 30, 2017), the maximum award is $5,815. The amount you get, though, will depend on

- your financial need,
- your cost of attendance,

About This Chapter: Text beginning with the heading "Federal Pell Grants" is excerpted from "Federal Pell Grants," Federal Student Aid, U.S. Department of Education (ED), January 30, 2017; Text beginning with the heading "Federal Supplemental Educational Opportunity Grant (FSEOG)" is excerpted from "FSEOG (Grants)," Federal Student Aid, U.S. Department of Education (ED), January 30, 2017.

- your status as a full-time or part-time student, and

- your plans to attend school for a full academic year or less.

You may not receive Federal Pell Grant funds from more than one school at a time.

> You can receive the Federal Pell Grant for no more than 12 semesters or the equivalent (roughly six years). You'll receive a notice if you're getting close to your limit.

If you're eligible for a Federal Pell Grant, you'll receive the full amount you qualify for—each school participating in the program receives enough funds each year from the U.S. Department of Education (ED) to pay the Federal Pell Grant amounts for all its eligible students. The amount of any other student aid for which you might qualify does not affect the amount of your Federal Pell Grant.

I Heard I Might Get A Larger Federal Pell Grant If My Parent Died In Iraq Or Afghanistan. Is That Right?

It depends. If your parent or guardian was a member of the U.S. armed forces and died as a result of military service performed in Iraq or Afghanistan after the events of 9/11, you may be eligible for additional Federal Pell Grant funds if, at the time of your parent's or guardian's death, you were

- less than 24 years of age or

- enrolled in college or career school at least part-time.

If you meet these requirements and are eligible to receive a Federal Pell Grant, your eligibility will be calculated as if your Expected Family Contribution (EFC) were zero. Payments are adjusted if you are enrolled less than full time. If you meet those requirements but aren't eligible to receive a Federal Pell Grant due to your EFC being too high, you might be able to get an Iraq and Afghanistan Service Grant.

How Will I Get Paid?

Your school can apply Federal Pell Grant funds to your school costs, pay you directly, or combine these methods.

Federal Supplemental Educational Opportunity Grant (FSEOG)

A Federal Supplemental Educational Opportunity Grant (FSEOG) is a grant for undergraduate students with exceptional financial need.

To get an FSEOG, you must fill out the *Free Application for Federal Student Aid* (FAFSA®) so your college can determine how much financial need you have. Students who will receive Federal Pell Grants and have the most financial need will receive FSEOGs first. The FSEOG does not need to be repaid, except under certain circumstances. Find out why you might have to repay all or part of a federal grant.

The FSEOG program is administered directly by the financial aid office at each participating school and is therefore called "campus-based" aid. Not all schools participate. Check with your school's financial aid office to find out if the school offers the FSEOG.

How Much Money Can I Get?

You can receive between $100 and $4,000 a year, depending on your financial need, when you apply, the amount of other aid you get, and the availability of funds at your school.

Each participating school receives a certain amount of FSEOG funds each year from the U.S. Department of Education's (ED) office of Federal Student Aid. Once the full amount of the school's FSEOG funds has been awarded to students, no more FSEOG awards can be made for that year. This system works differently from the Federal Pell Grant Program, which provides funds to every eligible student.

So, make sure you apply for federal student aid as early as you can. Each school sets its own deadlines for campus-based funds. You can find a school's deadline on its website or by asking someone in its financial aid office.

How Will I Be Paid?

If you're eligible, your school will credit your student account, pay you directly, or combine these methods. Your school must disburse (pay out) funds at least once per term (semester, trimester, or quarter). Schools that do not use semesters, trimesters, or quarters must disburse funds at least twice per academic year.

Chapter 28
TEACH Grant

What Is The TEACH Grant Program?

The Teacher Education Assistance for College and Higher Education (TEACH) Grant Program provides grants of up to $4,000 per year to students who agree to teach for four years at an elementary school, secondary school, or educational service agency that serves students from low-income families and to meet other requirements. The terms and conditions of this teaching service obligation are explained in the TEACH Grant Agreement to Serve that you must sign before you receive a TEACH Grant.

> ## It's A Fact
> If you do not complete your service obligation, all TEACH Grant funds you received will be converted to a Direct Unsubsidized Loan. You must then repay this loan to the U.S. Department of Education (ED), with interest charged from the date the TEACH Grant was disbursed (paid out).

What Are The Eligibility Requirements?

To receive a TEACH Grant, you must:

- Meet the general eligibility requirements for the federal student aid programs as described at StudentAid.gov/eligibility/basic-criteria.

- Complete the *Free Application for Federal Student Aid* (FAFSA®).

About This Chapter: This chapter includes text excerpted from "Federal Student Aid TEACH Grant Program," Federal Student Aid, U.S. Department of Education (ED), October 2016.

- Be enrolled as an undergraduate, postbaccalaureate, or graduate student at a school that participates in the TEACH Grant Program.

- Be enrolled in a TEACH-Grant-eligible program.

- Meet certain academic achievement requirements (generally, scoring above the 75th percentile on one or more portions of a college admissions test or maintaining at least a 3.25 cumulative grade point average).

- Receive counseling (on ED's TEACH Grant page at https://studentloans.gov/myDirectLoan/launchTeach.action) that explains the terms and conditions of the TEACH Grant service obligation.

- Sign a TEACH Grant Agreement to Serve.

What Is A TEACH-Grant-Eligible Program?

A TEACH-Grant-eligible program is a program of study that is designed to prepare you to teach as a highly qualified teacher in a high-need field and that leads to a bachelor's or master's degree, or is a postbaccalaureate program. A two-year program that is acceptable for full credit toward a bachelor's degree is considered a program that leads to a bachelor's degree. A postbaccalaureate program is a program for students who have already earned a bachelor's degree that

1. does not lead to a graduate degree,

2. is treated as an undergraduate program, and

3. consists of courses required by a state in order for you to receive a certification or license to teach in an elementary or secondary school in that state. A postbaccalaureate program is **not** TEACH-Grant-eligible if it is offered by a school that also offers a bachelor's degree in education.

Schools that participate in the TEACH Grant Program determine which of the programs they offer are TEACH-Grant-eligible. A program that is TEACH-Grant-eligible at one school might not be TEACH-Grant-eligible at another school. Contact the financial aid office at the school you are attending (or that you plan to attend) to find out which programs at that school are eligible.

What Is The TEACH Grant Agreement To Serve?

Each year that you receive a TEACH Grant, you must sign an Agreement to Serve on ED's TEACH Grant page at https://studentloans.gov/myDirectLoan/launch Teach.action.

The TEACH Grant Agreement to Serve explains the terms and conditions of the service obligation you must agree to fulfill as a condition for receiving a TEACH Grant. By signing the Agreement to Serve, you agree to these terms and conditions and acknowledge your understanding that if you do not fulfill the service obligation, the TEACH Grant funds you received will be converted to a loan that you must repay.

What Are The Terms And Conditions Of The TEACH Grant Service Obligation?

In exchange for receiving a TEACH Grant, you must agree to the following:

- For each TEACH-Grant-eligible program for which you receive TEACH Grant funds, you must serve as a full-time teacher for a total of at least four academic years within eight years after you complete or otherwise cease to be enrolled in the program for which you received the TEACH Grant.

- You must perform the teaching service as a highly qualified teacher at a low-income school or educational service agency. The term "highly qualified teacher" is defined in Section 9101(23) of the Elementary and Secondary Education Act of 1965 and in Section 602(10) of the *Individuals with Disabilities Education Act*.

- Your teaching service must be in a high-need field.

- You must provide ED with documentation of your progress toward completing your service obligation.

- If you do not meet the requirements of your service obligation, all TEACH Grant funds you received will be converted to a Direct Unsubsidized Loan. You must repay this loan in full, with interest charged from the date of each TEACH Grant disbursement.

What Are High-Need-Fields?

High-need fields are bilingual education and English language acquisition, foreign language, mathematics, reading specialist, science, and special education, as well as any other field that has been identified as high-need by the federal government, a state government, or a local education agency, and that is included in ED's annual *Teacher Shortage Area Nationwide Listing (Nationwide List* [www.ed.gov/about/offices/list/ope/pol/tsa.doc]*)*. If you are planning to teach in a high-need field that is included in the *Nationwide List*, that field must be listed for the state where you teach either at the time you begin your qualifying teaching service or at the time you received a TEACH Grant.

How Can I Identify Schools Or Educational Service Agencies That Serve Low-Income Students?

Elementary and secondary schools (public and private) and educational service agencies serving low-income students are listed in ED's annual "Teacher Cancellation Low-Income Directory." To access the directory, visit https://tcli.ed.gov and click on the "Search" button. In addition, elementary or secondary schools operated by the Department of the Interior's Bureau of Indian Education (BIE) or operated on Indian reservations by Indian tribal groups under contract or grant with the BIE qualify as low-income schools.

Can A TEACH Grant Service Obligation Ever Be Suspended Or Canceled?

You may request a temporary suspension of the eight-year period for completing your TEACH Grant service obligation based on:

- Your enrollment in a TEACH-Grant-eligible program or your enrollment in a program that a state requires you to complete in order to receive a certification or license to teach in that state's elementary or secondary schools. For example, if you received a TEACH Grant for an undergraduate program and you later enroll in a graduate program for which you would be eligible to receive a TEACH Grant, you could receive a suspension of the eight-year period for completing your service obligation for the undergraduate program while you are enrolled in the graduate program.

- A condition that is a qualifying reason for leave under the *Family and Medical Leave Act (FMLA)*.

- A call or order to active duty status for more than 30 days as a member of the armed forces reserves, or service as a member of the National Guard on full-time National Guard duty under a call to active service in connection with a war, military operation, or national emergency.

Suspensions are granted in one-year increments, not to exceed a combined total of three years for the first two conditions listed above, or a total of three years for the third condition. If you receive a suspension, the eight-year period for completing your service obligation is put "on hold" during the suspension period. For example, if you receive a one-year suspension after two years of the eight-year period for completing your service obligation have elapsed, you would have six years left to complete your service obligation when the one-year suspension period ends.

Your TEACH Grant service obligation may be canceled (discharged) if you die or if you become totally and permanently disabled. You may also receive a discharge of some or all of your four-year teaching requirement if you are called or ordered to qualifying military active duty for a period that exceeds three years.

If I'm Interested In Receiving A TEACH Grant, Where Can I Get More Information?

Contact the financial aid office at the school where you will be enrolled to find out whether the school participates in the TEACH Grant Program and to learn about the programs of study at the school that are TEACH-Grant-eligible.

Chapter 29
Federal Versus Private Loans

If you apply for financial aid, your school will likely include student loans as part of your financial aid package. It's important to understand what types of loans you are offered. Generally, there are two types of student loans:

- Federal student loans: These loans are funded by the federal government.

- Private student loans: These loans are nonfederal loans, made by a lender such as a bank, credit union, state agency, or a school.

If you need to borrow money to pay for college or career school, start with federal student loans.

Federal student loans are:

- Direct Subsidized Loans and Direct Unsubsidized Loans;

- Direct PLUS Loans (for graduate and professional students or parents); and

- Federal Perkins Loans.

What Are The Differences Between Federal And Private Student Loans?

Federal student loans include many benefits (such as fixed interest rates and income-driven repayment plans) not typically offered with private loans. In contrast, private loans are generally more expensive than federal student loans.

The table below provides a summary of the differences.

About This Chapter: This chapter includes text excerpted from "Federal Versus Private Loans," Federal Student Aid, U.S. Department of Education (ED), January 26, 2017.

Table 29.1. Differences Between Federal And Private Student Loans

Federal Student Loans	Private Student Loans
You will not have to start repaying your federal student loans until you graduate, leave school, or change your enrollment status to less than half-time.	Many private student loans require payments while you are still in school.
The interest rate is fixed and is often lower than private loans—and much lower than some credit card interest rates.	Private student loans can have variable interest rates, some greater than 18 percent. A variable rate may substantially increase the total amount you repay.
Undergraduate students with financial need will likely qualify for a subsidized loan where the government pays the interest while you are in school on at least a half-time basis.	Private student loans are not subsidized. No one pays the interest on your loan but you.
You don't need to get a credit check for most federal student loans (except for PLUS loans). Federal student loans can help you establish a good credit record.	Private student loans may require an established credit record. The cost of a private student loan will depend on your credit score and other factors.
You won't need a cosigner to get a federal student loan in most cases.	You may need a cosigner.
Interest may be tax deductible.	Interest may not be tax deductible.
Loans can be consolidated into a Direct Consolidation Loan.	Private student loans cannot be consolidated into a Direct Consolidation Loan.
If you are having trouble repaying your loan, you may be able to temporarily postpone or lower your payments.	Private student loans may not offer forbearance or deferment options.
There are several repayment plans, including an option to tie your monthly payment to your income.	You should check with your lender to find out about your repayment options.
There is no prepayment penalty fee.	You need to make sure there are no prepayment penalty fees.
You may be eligible to have some portion of your loans forgiven if you work in public service.	It is unlikely that your lender will offer a loan forgiveness program.

Table 29.1. Continued

Federal Student Loans	Private Student Loans
Free help is available at 800-4-FED-AID (800-433-3143) and on our websites.	The Consumer Financial Protection Bureau's (CFPB) private student loan ombudsman may be able to assist you if you have concerns about your private student loan.

How Do I Get A Federal Student Loan?

To get a federal student loan, you must first complete the *Free Application for Federal Student Aid* (FAFSA®).

Chapter 30
Federal Student Loans

If you apply for financial aid, you may be offered student loans as part of your financial aid package. Federal student loans are available to help you cover your education expenses at a college or university, community college, or trade, career, or technical school. Student loans originate from the federal government or from private sources, such as a bank or financial institution. Loans made by the federal government are called "federal student loans."

What Kinds Of Federal Student Loans Are Available?

The U.S. Department of Education (ED) offers loans through the William D. Ford Federal Direct Loan (Direct Loan) Program. It is the largest federal student loan program, ED is your lender, and there are four types of Direct Loans:

1. **Direct Subsidized Loans**—For eligible undergraduate students. Generally, no interest is charged on subsidized loans while you are in school at least half-time, during the grace period, and during deferment periods. **Note:** If you are a first-time borrower on or after July 1, 2013, there is a limit on the maximum period of time (measured in academic years) that you can receive this loan type.

2. **Direct Unsubsidized Loans**—For eligible undergraduate, graduate, and professional degree students. Interest is charged on unsubsidized loans during all periods.

About This Chapter: Text in this chapter begins with excerpts from "Federal Student Loans," Federal Student Aid, U.S. Department of Education (ED), September 2015; Text under the heading "Benefits Of Federal Student Loans" is excerpted from "Why Get A Federal Student Loan?" Federal Student Aid, U.S. Department of Education (ED), November 2014.

3. **Direct PLUS Loans**—For eligible graduate or professional degree students, and for parents of dependent undergraduate students. Interest is charged on PLUS loans during all periods.

4. **Direct Consolidation Loans**—For eligible student and parent borrowers. A consolidation loan combines the borrower's eligible loans into a single loan.

Table 30.1. Types Of Federal Student Loans

Federal Loan Program	Program Details (Subject To Change)	Maximum Annual Award (Subject To Change)
Direct Subsidized Loan	• For undergraduate students who have financial need • For loans first disbursed on or after July 1, 2016, and before July 1, 2017, interest rate is 3.76 percent • You're not usually charged interest on the loan during certain periods • The U.S. Department of Education (ED) is the lender; payment is owed to ED	$5,500 depending on grade level and dependency status
Direct Unsubsidized Loan	• For undergraduate, graduate, and professional degree students; financial need is not required • For loans first disbursed on or after July 1, 2016, and before July 1, 2017: • 3.76 percent interest rate for loans made to undergraduate students, and • 5.31 percent interest rate for loans made to graduate and professional degree students • You're responsible for interest during all periods • ED is the lender; payment is owed to ED	$20,500 (less any subsidized amounts received for same period) depending on grade level and dependency status

Table 30.1. Continued

Federal Loan Program	Program Details (Subject To Change)	Maximum Annual Award (Subject To Change)
Direct PLUS Loan	• For parents of dependent undergraduate students who are borrowing money to pay for their child's education, and for graduate or professional degree students; financial need is not required • For loans first disbursed on or after July 1, 2016, and before July 1, 2017, interest rate is 6.31 percent • Borrower must not have negative credit history • ED is the lender; payment is owed to ED	Maximum amount is cost of attendance minus any other financial aid student receives
Federal Perkins Loan	• For undergraduate, graduate, and professional degree students • Eligibility depends on your financial need and availability of funds at your school; contact your school's financial aid office about eligibility • Interest rate is 5 percent • Your school is the lender; payment is owed to the school that made the loan	Undergraduate students: $5,500; graduate and professional degree students: $8,000 Total lifetime limit may not exceed $27,500 for undergraduates and $60,000 for graduate students (including amounts borrowed as an undergraduate)

(Source: "Federal Student Loan Programs," Federal Student Aid, U.S. Department of Education (ED).)

What Are The Eligibility Requirements To Receive A Direct Loan?

You must be enrolled at least half-time at a school that participates in the Direct Loan Program, and you also must meet general eligibility requirements for the federal student aid programs.

How Do I Apply For Federal Student Loans?

1. Complete **the Free Application for Federal Student Aid (FAFSA®).** The fastest and easiest way to complete the FAFSA® is online at fafsa.gov. The schools that you have identified on your FAFSA® will receive your information. Some schools have additional application procedures—check with your school's financial aid office to be sure.

2. **Receive and read your aid offer.** The schools you identified on your FAFSA® (and that have offered you admission) will send you financial aid offers that include the types and amounts of financial aid you may receive. Review your aid offers and identify any Direct Loans listed. If the schools did not include Direct Loans in their aid offers, ask their financial aid offices if you have the option to apply for them. Not all schools participate in the Direct Loan Program.

3. **Complete a Master Promissory Note (MPN).** You must complete an MPN to receive a Direct Loan. The MPN is a legal document by which you promise to repay your loans and any accrued interest and fees to ED. In most cases, a single MPN can be used for loans that you receive over several years of study.

4. **Complete entrance counseling.** Before you receive your first loan disbursement, you must complete entrance counseling. This is a mandatory information session that explains your rights and responsibilities as a borrower. It also provides great information that you'll want and need to know for the future.

How Much Can I Borrow?

The maximum amount you can borrow each school year depends on your grade level and other factors. For Direct Subsidized and Direct Unsubsidized Loans, the amount ranges from a maximum of $5,500 per year for a dependent freshman to a maximum of $20,500 per year for a graduate or professional degree student. The actual amount you are eligible to borrow each year is determined by your school and may be less than the maximum amount. There are also limits on the total amount of your loan debt.

Did You Know?

You can borrow less money than your school includes in your financial aid offer. If you need help determining how much you need to borrow, see Federal Student Loans: Be a Responsible Borrower at www.studentaid.gov/resources#responsible-borrower.

Benefits Of Federal Student Loans

Federal student loans offer you many benefits that don't typically accompany private loans. These include low fixed interest rates, income-based repayment plans, cancellation for certain types of employment, and deferment (postponement) options, including deferment of loan payments when a student returns to school. Also, private loans usually require a credit check, which most federal loans do not. For these reasons, students and parents should always exhaust federal student loan options before considering a private loan.

(Source: "Federal Student Loan Programs," Federal Student Aid, U.S. Department of Education (ED).)

Delayed repayment. Repayment doesn't start immediately. For some federal student loans you have several months after you leave school or change your enrollment status to less than half-time before your first payment is due. If you were to get a private loan or use a credit card, it's likely that you would have to begin making payments immediately.

Low interest rates. The interest rate on a federal student loan is fixed and is often lower than the interest rate on a private loan—and usually much lower than rates for most credit cards.

No interest charges. The federal government does not charge interest on some federal student loans while you are still in school and enrolled at least half-time and during certain other periods.

No credit check. You don't need a credit check (except for a PLUS loan), but one is usually required for private loans and credit cards. Private student loans may require an established credit record. The cost of a private student loan may depend on your credit score and other factors.

No cosigner is needed. You won't need a cosigner to get a federal student loan, but you may need one for most private loans.

Multiple repayment plans. Federal student loans offer a variety of repayment plans, including income-driven plans that allow your payment amount to be based on your income.

You can consolidate your federal student loans into a Direct Consolidation Loan. Loan consolidation can greatly simplify loan repayment by centralizing your loans to one bill and can lower monthly payments by giving you up to 30 years to repay your loans. And, while private student loans cannot be consolidated into a Direct Consolidation Loan, the extended period of time you to have to repay your Direct Consolidation Loan is based on the amount of your total student loan debt, including how much you owe in private student loans.

Forgiveness programs. Certain circumstances might lead to your loan being forgiven. There are forgiveness programs for teachers, government employees, and employees of many not-for-profit organizations.

Chapter 31
Subsidized And Unsubsidized Loans And Entrance Counseling

Since college is so expensive, most students can only afford it by borrowing money in the form of loans. Low-interest student loans are available from the U.S. government to help eligible students cover the costs associated with higher education. As of 2016, more than 44 million Americans had student loan debt totaling nearly $1.3 trillion. About 40 percent of these loans were used to pay for graduate or professional degrees.

Did You Know...

The average 2016 college graduate had $37,172 in student loan debt, an increase of 6 percent from the previous year, and faced at least a decade of loan payments averaging $350 per month.

The U.S. Department of Education (ED) offers two main types of loans through its Federal Student Aid program: subsidized loans and unsubsidized loans. A subsidy is a form of monetary or financial support. In a subsidized loan, the U.S. government contributes money to reduce the interest cost for student borrowers who demonstrate financial need. Although unsubsidized loans are available regardless of students' financial circumstances, borrowers are responsible for paying back the full amount of the loan, plus interest, without financial support from the federal government.

All first-time borrowers in the federal government's student loan program are required to undergo entrance counseling before they can receive their money. Since taking out a loan is a serious, long-term financial commitment, entrance counseling provides borrowers with important information about their legal rights and responsibilities, repayment options, and the consequences of failing to repay their loans.

Comparing Subsidized And Unsubsidized Loans

Federal Direct Subsidized Loans, sometimes called Stafford Loans, are intended for low-income undergraduate students. They are not available to graduate students. Since subsidized loans are a form of need-based aid, you must qualify by submitting the *Free Application for Federal Student Aid* (FAFSA®) and demonstrating financial need. Your school's financial aid office determines the amount you are eligible to receive based on your FAFSA®, but the total cannot exceed your calculated financial need.

Subsidized loans have lower annual limits than unsubsidized loans. As of 2016, the limits were $3,500 for first-year college students, $4,500 for second-year students, and $5,500 for third-year students and beyond, with a cumulative limit per student of $23,000. In addition, subsidized loans issued after July 1, 2013, have a time limit—known as the maximum eligibility period—of 150 percent of the published length of your academic program. The time limit is 3 years for a 2-year associate's degree program, for instance, and 6 years for a 4-year bachelor's degree program. You are no longer eligible to receive federally subsidized loans once the maximum eligibility period expires, although the time limit may be extended if you change to a longer academic program.

The main benefit of federally subsidized loans is that the government pays the interest on the loan under the following circumstances:

- while you are enrolled at least half-time at a four-year college or university, community college, or trade, career, or technical school;

- during periods of deferment or forbearance, when you are eligible to pause or postpone making loan payments because you go back to school, serve in the military or Peace Corps, or suffer a serious illness or financial hardship; and

- during a six-month grace period following your graduation.

Federal Direct Unsubsidized Loans do not offer any government subsidies to help cover interest costs. Instead, borrowers are responsible for paying the interest, which begins to accrue as soon as you receive your loan funds. Interest accumulates while you are in school, during the six-month grace period after graduation, and even if you receive a deferment.

Unsubsidized loans are not based on financial need, however, so it is easier to qualify. They are available to graduate as well as undergraduate students, and the annual loan limits are higher than subsidized loans. As of 2016, the limits were $5,500 for first-year undergraduate students and $9,500 for first-year graduate students. The limits increase for each additional year of schooling, with a cap of $31,000 per student. There is no maximum eligibility period for unsubsidized loans.

Subsidized and unsubsidized loans carry the same interest rates and similar fees. For the 2016–2017 academic year, the interest rate for both subsidized and unsubsidized undergraduate student loans was 3.76 percent, while the interest rate for unsubsidized graduate student loans was 5.31 percent. Both types of loans charged fees of slightly more than 1 percent of the loan amount. However, the fact that the government pays the interest on subsidized loans during your college years, the six-month grace period, and any deferments means that you should always repay unsubsidized loans first.

Entrance Counseling

All first-time recipients of federal student loans, whether subsidized or unsubsidized, are required to complete entrance counseling. This process must be completed before your school can disburse any of your loan funds. Depending on the school, you may attend an entrance counseling meeting in person at the financial aid office, pick up a packet of written materials to review at home, or get the information through an interactive, online program.

Taking out a loan is a significant, long-term financial obligation. Entrance counseling is intended to help you understand how the loan process works, the terms and conditions of your loan, and your legal rights and responsibilities as a borrower. The program also provides information about other financial resources that may be available to help pay for your education, as well as tips on budgeting and managing your college costs.

One of the most important topics discussed in entrance counseling is your obligation to repay your loans. Federal student loans must be repaid even if you do not finish your degree, are unhappy with the education you received, or cannot find a job in your field after graduation. Although your loan payments may be reduced or temporarily deferred if you encounter financial hardship or meet other requirements, federal student loan debts are not erased if you file for bankruptcy. There are only a few circumstances in which your student loan debts may be discharged or canceled, such as if you die or become permanently disabled.

In most cases, you are required to begin repaying your student loan six months after you graduate, leave school, or drop below half-time enrollment. Your loan servicer will contact you during this period to provide repayment instructions. Payments are usually due monthly for a period of 10 to 25 years, although there is no penalty for paying off the loan in advance.

Failure to repay a federal loan can have serious consequences, including collection charges, litigation, or seizure of a portion of your wages, Social Security payments, or income tax refunds. The negative credit reports associated with defaulting on a student loan can affect your ability to qualify for credit cards, car loans, or a mortgage. Therefore, it is important to understand the types of loans available and the terms and conditions associated with them in order to make smart choices about taking on debt to pay for college.

References

1. "Entrance Counseling," Federal Student Aid, U.S. Department of Education, 2017.

2. "Entrance Counseling For Federal Student Loans," Edvisor, 2017.

3. Sisolak, Paul. "What's The Difference Between Subsidized And Unsubsidized Student Loans?" Student Loan Hero, March 3, 2016.

4. "Subsidized And Unsubsidized Loans," Federal Student Aid, U.S. Department of Education, 2017.

Chapter 32
Repaying Federal Student Loans

Understanding how to repay your federal student loans can save you a lot of time and money. This chapter ways to manage repayment and answer any questions you have along the way.

Finding The Right Repayment Plan For You

There are several repayment plans available, providing the flexibility you need. Here are some things you should know:

- You'll be asked to choose a plan. If you don't choose one, you will be placed on the Standard Repayment Plan, which will have your loans paid off in 10 years.

- You can switch to a different plan at any time to suit your needs and goals.

- Your monthly payment can be based on how much you make.

How To Make A Payment

Your loan servicer handles all billing regarding your student loan, so you'll need to make payments directly to your servicer. Each servicer has its own payment process and can work with you if you need help making payments.

About This Chapter: This chapter includes text excerpted from "How To Repay Your Loans," Federal Student Aid, U.S. Department of Education (ED), January 8, 2017.

Table 32.1. Loan Servicers

Not Sure Who Your Loan Servicer Is?	Know Who Your Loan Servicer Is?	
If you don't know who your servicer is…	Visit their site to make a payment.	
	CornerStone	MOHELA
	FedLoan Servicing (PHEAA)	Navient
	Granite State–GSMR	Nelnet
	Great Lakes Educational Loan Services, Inc.	OSLA Servicing
	HESC/Edfinancial	

Never miss a payment. Got a Direct Loan? Sign up for automatic debit through your loan servicer, and your payments will be automatically taken from your bank account each month. As an added bonus, you get a 0.25 percent interest rate deduction when you enroll!

What To Do If You Can't Afford Your Payments

If you're having trouble making payments, don't ignore your loans. There are several options that can help keep your loans in good standing, even if your finances are tight.

Three Ways You Can Keep On Track With Loan Payments

1. **Change your payment due date.** Do you get paid after your student loan payment is due each month? If so, contact your loan servicer and ask whether you'd be able to switch the date your student loan payment is due.

2. **Change your repayment plan.** What you ultimately pay depends on the plan you choose and when you borrowed. If you need lower monthly payments, consider an income-driven repayment plan that'll base your monthly payment amount on how much you make.

3. **Consolidate your loans.** If you have multiple student loans, simplify the repayment process with a Direct Consolidation Loan—allowing you to combine all your federal student loans into one loan for one monthly payment.

If the options above don't work for you and you simply can't make any payments right now, you might be eligible to postpone your payments through a deferment or forbearance. However, depending on the type of loan you have, interest may still accrue (accumulate) on your loan during the time you're not making payments.

Private companies may contact you with offers to help you with your student loans for a fee. Remember, you never have to pay for help with your student loans.

Student Loan Forgiveness, Cancellation, And Discharge

There are some circumstances that may result in your no longer having to repay your federal student loan. For instance, some or all of your loan could be forgiven in exchange for your performing certain types of service such as teaching or public service. Or the obligation to make further payments on your loan might be discharged based on specific factors such as your school closing or your becoming totally and permanently disabled. Take a look at all the possibilities: Find out what circumstances qualify your loans for forgiveness, cancellation, or discharge.

Two types of forgiveness that a lot of borrowers ask about:

- Public Service Loan Forgiveness
- Teacher Loan Forgiveness

Chapter 33

Deferring (Postponing) Repayment Of Federal Student Loans

Under certain circumstances, you can receive a deferment or forbearance that allows you to temporarily postpone or reduce your federal student loan payments. Postponing or reducing your payments may help you avoid default.

You'll need to work with your loan servicer to apply for deferment or forbearance; and be sure to keep making payments on your loan until the deferment or forbearance is in place.

Deferment

What Is Deferment?

A deferment is a period during which repayment of the principal and interest of your loan is temporarily delayed.

What Happens To My Loan During Deferment?

During a deferment, you do not need to make payments. What's more, depending on the type of loan you have, the federal government may pay the interest on your loan during a period of deferment.

The government may pay the interest on your

- Federal Perkins Loan,

- Direct Subsidized Loan, and/or

About This Chapter: This chapter includes text excerpted from "Deferment And Forbearance," Federal Student Aid, U.S. Department of Education (ED), January 26, 2017.

- Subsidized Federal Stafford Loan.

The government does not pay the interest on your unsubsidized loans (or on any Parent Loan for Undergraduate Students (PLUS) loans). You are responsible for paying the interest that accrues (accumulates) during the deferment period, but your payment is not due during the deferment period. If you don't pay the interest on your loan during deferment, it may be capitalized (added to your principal balance), and the amount you pay in the future will be higher.

Am I Eligible For A Loan Deferment?

The following table provides situations that may make you eligible for a deferment of your federal student loan.

Table 33.1. Loan Deferment

Situations When You May Apply For Deferment	Deferment Available? (And For How Long, If Applicable)		
	Direct Loans	**FFEL loans**	**Perkins Loans**
During a period of at least half-time enrollment in college or career school	Yes	Yes	Yes
During a period of study in an approved graduate fellowship program or in an approved rehabilitation training program for the disabled	Yes	Yes	Yes
During a period of unemployment or inability to find full-time employment	Yes (for up to 3 years)	Yes (for up to 3 years)	Yes (for up to 3 years)
During a period of economic hardship (includes Peace Corps service)	Yes (for up to 3 years)	Yes (for up to 3 years)	Yes (for up to 3 years)
During a period of service qualifying for Perkins Loan discharge/cancellation	No	No	Yes
During a period of active duty military service during a war, military operation, or national emergency	Yes	Yes	Yes

Table 33.1. Cotinued

Situations When You May Apply For Deferment	Deferment Available? (And For How Long, If Applicable)		
	Direct Loans	FFEL loans	Perkins Loans
During the 13 months following the conclusion of qualifying active duty military service, or until you return to enrollment on at least a half-time basis, whichever is earlier, if you are a member of the National Guard or other reserve component of the U.S. armed forces and you were called or ordered to active duty while enrolled at least half-time at an eligible school or within six months of having been enrolled at least half-time	Yes	Yes	Yes

If you are a Direct Loan or Federal Family Education Loan (FFEL) Program borrower who has a loan that was first disbursed (paid to you or on your behalf) before July 1, 1993, you may be eligible for additional deferments for such situations as teaching in a teacher shortage area, public service, being a working mother, parental leave, or temporary disability.

How Do I Request A Deferment?

Most deferments are not automatic, and you will likely need to submit a request to your loan servicer, the organization that handles your loan account. If you are enrolled in school at least half-time and you would like to request an in-school deferment, you'll need to contact your school's financial aid office as well as your loan servicer.

Your deferment request should be submitted to the organization to which you make your loan payments.

- Direct Loans and FFEL Program loans: contact your loan servicer

- Perkins Loans: contact the school you were attending when you received the loan

Forbearance

What Is Forbearance?

If you can't make your scheduled loan payments, but don't qualify for a deferment, your loan servicer may be able to grant you a forbearance. With forbearance, you may be able to stop making payments or reduce your monthly payment for up to 12 months. Interest will continue to accrue on your subsidized and unsubsidized loans (including all PLUS loans).

There are two types of forbearances:

1. Discretionary

2. Mandatory

Discretionary Forbearance

For discretionary forbearances, your lender decides whether to grant forbearance or not.

You can request a discretionary forbearance for the following reasons:

- Financial hardship

- Illness

Mandatory Forbearance

For mandatory forbearances, if you meet the eligibility criteria for the forbearance, your lender is required to grant the forbearance.

You can request a mandatory forbearance for the following reasons:

- You are serving in a medical or dental internship or residency program, and you meet specific requirements.

- The total amount you owe each month for all the student loans you received is 20 percent or more of your total monthly gross income (additional conditions apply).

- You are serving in a national service position for which you received a national service award.

- You are performing teaching service that would qualify for teacher loan forgiveness.

- You qualify for partial repayment of your loans under the U.S. Department of Defense (DoD) Student Loan Repayment Program (SLRP).

- You are a member of the National Guard and have been activated by a governor, but you are not eligible for a military deferment.

How Do I Request A Forbearance?

Receiving loan forbearance is not automatic. You must apply by making a request to your loan servicer. In some cases, you must provide documentation to support your request.

What Happens To The Interest On My Loan During Forbearance?

Interest will continue to be charged on all loan types, including subsidized loans.

You can pay the interest during forbearance or allow the interest to accrue (accumulate). If you don't pay the interest on your loan during forbearance, it may be capitalized (added to your principal balance), and the amount you pay in the future will be higher.

> You MUST continue making payments on your student loan until you have been notified that your request for deferment or forbearance has been granted. If you stop paying and your deferment or forbearance is not approved, you will become delinquent and you may default on your loan.

Do I Have Options Besides Deferment Or Forbearance?

Always contact your loan servicer immediately if you are having trouble making your student loan payment. If you don't qualify for deferment or forbearance, you may be able to change your repayment plan. There may be a repayment plan that offers lower payments than you're currently making.

Chapter 34
Loan Cancellation (Forgiveness) Of Federal Student Loans

The Public Service Loan Forgiveness (PSLF) Program forgives the remaining balance on your Direct Loans after you have made 120 qualifying monthly payments under a qualifying repayment plan while working full-time for a qualifying employer.

> If you are employed by a government or not-for-profit organization, you may be able to receive loan forgiveness under the Public Service Loan Forgiveness Program.

What Is Qualifying Employment?

Qualifying employment for the PSLF Program is not about the specific job that you do for your employer. Rather, it is about who your employer is. Employment with the following types of organizations qualifies for PSLF:

- Government organizations at any level (federal, state, local, or tribal)

- Not-for-profit organizations that are tax-exempt under Section 501(c)(3) of the Internal Revenue Code (IRC)

- Other types of not-for-profit organizations that provide certain types of qualifying public services

Serving in a full-time AmeriCorps or Peace Corps position also counts as qualifying employment for the PSLF Program.

About This Chapter: This chapter includes text excerpted from "Forgiveness, Cancellation, And Discharge," Federal Student Aid, U.S. Department of Education (ED), January 8, 2017.

The following types of employers do not qualify for PSLF:

- Labor unions

- Partisan political organizations

- For-profit organizations

- Non-profit organizations that are not tax-exempt under Section 501(c)(3) of the Internal Revenue Code and that do not provide a qualifying service

What Is Considered Full-Time Employment?

For PSLF, you are generally considered to work full-time if you meet your employer's definition of full-time or work at least 30 hours per week, whichever is greater.

If you are employed in more than one qualifying part-time job at the same time, you may meet the full-time employment requirement if you work a combined average of at least 30 hours per week with your employers.

For borrowers who are employed by not-for-profit organizations, time spent on religious instruction, worship services, or any form of proselytizing may not be counted toward meeting the full-time employment requirement.

Which Types Of Federal Student Loans Qualify For PSLF?

A qualifying loan for PSLF is any loan you received under the William D. Ford Federal Direct Loan (Direct Loan) Program.

You may have received loans under other federal student loan programs, such as the Federal Family Education Loan (FFEL) Program or the Federal Perkins Loan (Perkins Loan) Program. Loans from these programs do not qualify for PSLF, but they may become eligible if you consolidate them into a Direct Consolidation Loan. However, only qualifying payments that you make on the new Direct Consolidation Loan can be counted toward the 120 payments required for PSLF. Any payments you made on the FFEL Program loans or Perkins Loans before you consolidated them don't count.

If you have both Direct Loans and other types of federal student loans that you want to consolidate to take advantage of PSLF, it's important to understand that if you consolidate your existing Direct Loans with the other loans, you will lose credit for any qualifying PSLF payments you made on your Direct Loans before they were consolidated. In this situation, you may want to leave your existing Direct Loans out of the consolidation and consolidate only your other federal student loans.

If you don't know which types of federal student loans you have, log in to My Federal Student Aid (www.studentaid.ed.gov/sa/?login=true) to get that information. Generally, if you see a loan type with "Direct" in the name on My Federal Student Aid, then it is a Direct Loan; otherwise, it is a loan made under another federal student loan program.

What Is A Qualifying Monthly Payment?

A qualifying monthly payment is a payment that you make

- after October 1, 2007;

- under a qualifying repayment plan;

- for the full amount due as shown on your bill;

- no later than 15 days after your due date; and

- while you are employed full-time by a qualifying employer.

You can make qualifying monthly payments only during periods when you are required to make a payment. Therefore, you cannot make a qualifying monthly payment while your loans are in

- an in-school status,

- the grace period,

- a deferment,

- a forbearance, or

- default.

Your 120 qualifying monthly payments do not need to be consecutive.

If you make a monthly payment for more than the amount you are required to pay, you should keep in mind that you can receive credit for only one payment per month, no matter how much you pay. You can't qualify for PSLF faster by making larger payments. However, if you do want to pay more than your required monthly payment amount, you should contact your servicer and ask that the extra amount not be applied to cover future payments. Otherwise, you may end up being paid ahead, and you can't receive credit for a qualifying PSLF payment during a month when no payment is due.

There are special rules that allow borrowers who are AmeriCorps or Peace Corps volunteers to use their Segal Education Award or Peace Corps transition payment to make a single "lump sum" payment that may count for up to 12 qualifying PSLF payments.

The best way to ensure that you are making qualifying payments is to sign up for automatic debit with your loan servicer.

What Is A Qualifying Repayment Plan?

Qualifying repayment plans include all of the income-driven repayment plans (plans that base your monthly payment on your income) and the 10-year Standard Repayment Plan.

Even though the 10-year Standard Repayment Plan is a qualifying repayment plan for PSLF, you will not receive PSLF unless you make the majority of your 120 qualifying monthly payments under an income-driven repayment plan. If you are in repayment on the 10-year Standard Repayment Plan during the entire time you are working toward PSLF, you will have no remaining balance left to forgive after you have made 120 qualifying PSLF payments. Therefore, if you are seeking PSLF and are not already repaying under an income-driven repayment plan, you should change to an income-driven repayment plan as soon as possible.

How Do I Know I'm On The Right Track To Receive PSLF?

Because you have to make 120 qualifying monthly payments, it will take at least 10 years for you to become eligible for PSLF. To help you determine if you are on the right track as early as possible, we (FSA) have created an Employment Certification for Public Service Loan Forgiveness form (Employment Certification form) that you can submit periodically while you are working toward meeting the PSLF eligibility requirements. We will use the information you provide on the form to let you know if you are making qualifying PSLF payments.

Although you are not required to do so, we encourage you to submit the Employment Certification form annually or whenever you change jobs, so that we can help you track your progress toward meeting the PSLF eligibility requirements. If you do not periodically submit the form, then at the time you apply for forgiveness you will be required to submit an Employment Certification form for each employer where you worked while making the required 120 qualifying monthly payments.

If you would like us to track your progress as you work toward making the 120 qualifying monthly payments for PSLF, send the completed form, with your employer's certification, to

FedLoan Servicing (PHEAA), the U.S. Department of Education's (ED's) federal loan servicer for the PSLF Program.

We will take the following actions after we receive your Employment Certification form:

- We will review your Employment Certification form to ensure that it is complete, and to determine whether your employment is qualifying employment for the PSLF Program.

- We will notify you if the form you submitted is incomplete or if we cannot determine, based on the information provided on the form, whether your employment qualifies. We may ask you to provide additional information or documentation to help us determine whether you were employed by a qualifying public service organization.

- If we determine that your employer is not an eligible public service organization, we will notify you that your employment does not qualify. If you believe there is additional information that would establish the eligibility of your employer, you will have the opportunity to provide that information.

- If we determine that your employment qualifies, and if some or all of your federal student loans that are owned by the U.S. Department of Education are not already serviced by FedLoan Servicing (PHEAA), those loans will be transferred to FedLoan Servicing (PHEAA). You will then have a single federal loan servicer for all of your federally held loans. You will receive a notice if your loans are transferred.

- If we determine that your employment qualifies, we will then review your payment history (including any payments you made to another federal loan servicer before your loans were transferred) to determine how many payments made during the period of employment certified on the Employment Certification form are qualifying monthly payments for PSLF. We will then inform you that your employment qualifies and notify you of the total number of qualifying payments you have made, and how many payments you must still make before you can qualify for PSLF.

Will I Automatically Receive PSLF After I've Made 120 Qualifying Monthly Payments?

No. After you make your 120th qualifying monthly payment, you will need to submit the PSLF application to receive loan forgiveness. The application is under development and will be available prior to October 2017, the date when the first borrowers will become eligible for PSLF. You must be working for a qualified public service organization at the time you submit the application for forgiveness and at the time the remaining balance on your loan is forgiven.

Note that loan amounts forgiven under the PSLF Program are not considered income by the Internal Revenue Service. Therefore, you will not have to pay federal income tax on the amount of your Direct Loans that is forgiven after you have made the 120 qualifying payments.

Chapter 35
Loan Servicers

A loan servicer is a company that handles the billing and other services on your federal student loan. The loan servicer will work with you on repayment plans and loan consolidation and will assist you with other tasks related to your federal student loan. It is important to maintain contact with your loan servicer. If your circumstances change at any time during your repayment period, your loan servicer will be able to help.

Do I Select My Loan Servicer?

No. Your loan is assigned to a loan servicer by the U.S. Department of Education (ED) after your loan amount is first disbursed (paid out). The loan has been disbursed when your school transfers your loan money to your school account, gives money to you directly, or a combination of both. Your loan is usually disbursed in at least two payments, and your loan servicer will contact you after the first payment is made to you.

Whom Do I Contact To Get Information About My Loan?

If your loan is for the current or upcoming school year, contact your school's financial aid office directly for information about

- loan status,
- loan cancellation within 120 days of disbursement, and

About This Chapter: This chapter includes text excerpted from "Loan Servicers," Federal Student Aid, U.S. Department of Education (ED), August 9, 2016.

- loan disbursement amounts and timing.

Only your school's financial aid office can provide this information.

If your loan was disbursed in a past school year and you're still in school, contact your loan servicer when you

- change your name, address, or phone number;

- graduate;

- drop below half-time enrollment;

- stop going to school; or

- transfer to another school.

If you're no longer in school, contact your loan servicer when you

- change your name, address, or phone number;

- need help making your loan payment;

- have a question about your bill; or

- have other questions about your student loan.

Who Is My Loan Servicer?

Visit My Federal Student Aid (studentaid.ed.gov/sa/?login=true) to view information about all of the federal student loans you have received and to find contact information for the loan servicer or lender for your loans.

The following are loan servicers for federally held loans made through the William D. Ford Federal Direct Loan (Direct Loan) Program and the Federal Family Education Loan (FFEL) Program.

Table 35.1. Loan Servicers

Loan Servicer	Contact
CornerStone	800-663-1662
FedLoan Servicing (PHEAA)	800-699-2908
Granite State – GSMR	888-556-0022
Great Lakes Educational Loan Services, Inc.	800-236-4300
HESC/Edfinancial	855-337-6884

Table 35.1. Continued

Loan Servicer	Contact
MOHELA	888-866-4352
Navient	800-722-1300
Nelnet	888-486-4722
OSLA Servicing	866-264-9762

Will ED Ever Transfer My Federally Held Loans To A Different Servicer?

Possibly. In some cases, ED needs to transfer loans from one servicer to another servicer on the federal loan servicer team. ED transfers loans as part of its efforts to ensure that all borrowers are provided with customer service and repayment support. If ED needs to transfer your federal student loans from your assigned servicer to another servicer, your loans will still be owned by ED. The "transfer" to another servicer on ED's federal loan servicer team simply means that a new servicer will provide the support you need to fully repay your loans.

Here's what you should expect if your loan is transferred to a new servicer:

- You may receive an email or a letter from your assigned servicer when your loans are transferred to the new servicer.

- You will receive a welcome letter from the new servicer after your loans are added to the new servicer's system. This notice will provide you with the contact information for the new servicer and inform you of actions that you may need to take.

- All of your loan information will be transferred from your assigned servicer to your new servicer.

- There will be no change in the terms of your loans.

- Your previous loan servicer and new loan servicer will work together to make sure that all payments you make during the transfer process are credited to your loan account with the new servicer.

After you receive the welcome letter from your new servicer, you should do the following:

- Begin sending your loan payments to your new servicer. If you use a bank or bill paying service to make your loan payments, update the new servicer's contact information with the bank or bill paying service.

- Follow the new servicer's instructions for creating an online account so that you can more easily communicate with the new servicer and keep track of your loan account.

Whom Do I Contact For Information About My Federal Perkins Loan?

If you have Federal Perkins Loans, here's whom to contact for repayment information:

- Contact the school where you received your Federal Perkins Loan for details about repaying your loan. Your school may be the servicer for your loan.

- Contact the Educational Computer Systems, Inc. (ECSI) Federal Perkins Loan Servicer at 866-313-3797 if you know that your Federal Perkins Loan has been assigned to ED.

Whom Do I Contact For Information About My FFEL Program Loan That Isn't Owned By ED?

If you have privately-owned FFEL Program loans, contact your lender for details about repayment options and tools for your FFEL Program loans that are not owned by ED.

Whom Do I Contact for Information About My Health Education Assistance Loan (HEAL) Program Loan?

If you're not in default on your Health Education Assistance Loan (HEAL) Program loan, contact your loan servicer for help with account-related questions. Use the contact information your loan servicer provided to you.

If you're in default on your HEAL Program loan, contact the Debt Collection Center for help with account-related questions.

> It is no longer possible to obtain a new HEAL Program loan. The making of new HEAL Program loans was discontinued on September 30, 1998.

What Should I Do If I Am Contacted By Someone Who Wants To Charge Me Fees To Consolidate My Federal Student Loans Or To Apply For An Income-Based Repayment Plan?

Contact your federal loan servicer; these services and more can be completed by your servicer for free! If you are contacted by a company asking you to pay "enrollment," "subscription," or "maintenance" fees to enroll you in a federal repayment plan or forgiveness program, you should walk away.

Chapter 36
Federal Work-Study And Education For Unemployed Workers Programs

Federal Work-Study (FWS) provides part-time jobs for undergraduate and graduate students with financial need, allowing them to earn money to help pay education expenses. The program encourages community service work and work related to the student's course of study.

Here's a quick overview of Federal Work-Study:

- It provides part-time employment while you are enrolled in school.

- It's available to undergraduate, graduate, and professional students with financial need.

- It's available to full-time or part-time students.

- It's administered by schools participating in the Federal Work-Study Program. Check with your school's financial aid office to find out if your school participates.

What Kinds Of Jobs Are There?

The Federal Work-Study Program emphasizes employment in civic education and work related to your course of study, whenever possible.

Are Jobs On Campus Or Off Campus?

Both. If you work on campus, you'll usually work for your school. If you work off campus, your employer will usually be a private nonprofit organization or a public agency, and the work performed must be in the public interest.

About this chapter: Text in this chapter begins with the excerpts from "Work-Study Jobs," Federal Student Aid, U.S. Department of Education (ED), November 30, 2016; Text under the heading "Federal Work-Study (FWS) Program" is excerpted from "Federal Work-Study (FWS) Program," U.S. Department of Education (ED), April 17, 2014.

Some schools might have agreements with private for-profit employers for work-study jobs. These jobs must be relevant to your course of study (to the maximum extent possible). If you attend a proprietary school (i.e., a for-profit institution), there may be further restrictions on the types of jobs you can be assigned.

If you're interested in getting a Federal Work-Study job while you're enrolled in college or career school, make sure you apply for aid early. Schools that participate in the Federal Work-Study Program award funds on a first come, first served basis.

How Much Can I Earn?

You'll earn at least the current federal minimum wage. However, you may earn more depending on the type of work you do and the skills required for the position.

Your total work-study award depends on:

- when you apply,
- your level of financial need, and
- your school's funding level.

How Will I Be Paid?

How you're paid depends partly on whether you're an undergraduate or graduate student.

- If you are an undergraduate student, you're paid by the hour.
- If you are a graduate or professional student, you're paid by the hour or by salary, depending on the work you do.
- Your school must pay you at least once a month.
- Your school must pay you directly unless you request that the school
- send your payments directly to your bank account or
- use the money to pay for your education-related institutional charges such as tuition, fees, and room and board.

Can I Work As Many Hours As I Want?

No. The amount you earn can't exceed your total Federal Work-Study award. When assigning work hours, your employer or your school's financial aid office will consider your class schedule and your academic progress.

Federal Work-Study (FWS) Program

Purpose

The FWS Program provides funds for part-time employment to help needy students to finance the costs of postsecondary education. Students can receive FWS funds at approximately 3,400 participating postsecondary institutions.

A participating institution applies each year for FWS funding by submitting a Fiscal Operations Report and Application to Participate (FISAP) to the U.S. Department of Education (ED). Using a statutory formula, the Department allocates funds based on the institution's previous funding level and the aggregate need of eligible students in attendance in the prior year. In most cases, the school or the employer must pay up to a 50 percent share of a student's wages under FWS. (In some cases, such as FWS jobs as reading or mathematics tutors, the federal share of the wages can be as high as 100 percent.)

Students may be employed by: the institution itself; a federal, state, or local public agency; a private nonprofit organization; or a private for-profit organization. Institutions must use at least 7 percent of their Work-Study allocation to support students working in community service jobs, including: reading tutors for preschool age or elementary school children; mathematics tutors for students enrolled in elementary school through ninth grade; literacy tutors in a family literacy project performing family literacy activities; or emergency preparedness and response.

Students must file a *Free Application for Federal Student Aid* (FAFSA®) as part of the application process for FWS assistance. The FAFSA® can be completed on the Web at www.fafsa. ed.gov.

Eligibility

Who May Apply: (by category) Individuals, Institutions of Higher Education (IHEs)

Who May Apply: (specifically) IHEs may apply for an allocation of funds to be awarded to undergraduate, vocational, and graduate students enrolled or accepted for enrollment at participating schools.

Chapter 37
Education Tax Credits

Education tax credits can help offset the costs of education. The American Opportunity (Hope Credit extended) and the Lifetime Learning Credit are education credits you can subtract in full from the federal income tax, not just deduct from taxable income.

American Opportunity Tax Credit

Under the American Recovery and Reinvestment Act (ARRA), more parents and students will qualify for the American Opportunity Tax Credit to help pay for college expenses.

The American Opportunity Tax Credit (AOTC) modifies the existing Hope Credit. The AOTC makes the Hope Credit available to a broader range of taxpayers, including many with higher incomes and those who owe no tax. It also adds required course materials to the list of qualifying expenses and allows the credit to be claimed for four postsecondary education years instead of two. Many of those eligible will qualify for the maximum annual credit of $2,500 per student.

The full credit is available to individuals whose modified adjusted gross income is $80,000 or less, or $160,000 or less for married couples filing a joint return. The credit is phased out for taxpayers with incomes above these levels. These income limits are higher than under the existing Hope and Lifetime Learning Credits.

The AOTC applied to tax years 2009 and 2010 under ARRA. The credit was extended to apply for tax years 2011 and 2012 by the Tax Relief and Job Creation Act of 2010. The American Taxpayer Relief Act of 2012 extended the AOTC for five years through December 2017.

About This Chapter: This chapter includes text excerpted from "Education Credits," Internal Revenue Service (IRS), February 25, 2016.

Tax Benefits For Education: Information Center

Tax credits, deductions and savings plans can help taxpayers with their expenses for higher education.

- A tax credit reduces the amount of income tax you may have to pay.

- A deduction reduces the amount of your income that is subject to tax, thus generally reducing the amount of tax you may have to pay.

- Certain savings plans allow the accumulated earnings to grow tax-free until money is taken out (known as a distribution), or allow the distribution to be tax-free, or both.

- An exclusion from income means that you won't have to pay income tax on the benefit you're receiving, but you also won't be able to use that same tax-free benefit for a deduction or credit.

Credits

An education credit helps with the cost of higher education by reducing the amount of tax owed on your tax return. If the credit reduces your tax to less than zero, you may get a refund. There are two education credits available: the American opportunity tax credit and the lifetime learning credit.

Who Can Claim An Education Credit?

There are additional rules for each credit, but you must meet all three of the following for either credit:

1. You, your dependent or a third party pays qualified education expenses for higher education.

2. An eligible student must be enrolled at an eligible educational institution.

3. The eligible student is yourself, your spouse or a dependent you list on your tax return.

If you're eligible to claim the lifetime learning credit and are also eligible to claim the American opportunity credit for the same student in the same year, you can choose to claim either credit, but not both. You can't claim the AOTC if you were a nonresident alien for any part of the tax year unless you elect to be treated as a resident alien for federal tax purposes.

The law requires that both you and your qualifying student have a valid Social Security number (SSN) or Individual Taxpayer Identification Number (ITIN), issued before the due date for your tax return, in order to claim the AOTC.

Deductions

Tuition And Fees Deduction

You may be able to deduct qualified education expenses paid during the year for yourself, your spouse or your dependent. You cannot claim this deduction if your filing status is married filing separately or if another person can claim an exemption for you as a dependent on his or her tax return. The qualified expenses must be for higher education.

The tuition and fees deduction can reduce the amount of your income subject to tax by up to $4,000. This deduction, reported on Form 8917, Tuition and Fees Deduction, is taken as an adjustment to income. This means you can claim this deduction even if you do not itemize deductions on Schedule A (Form 1040). This deduction may be beneficial to you if, for example, you don't qualify for the American opportunity or lifetime learning credits.

You may be able to take one of the education credits for your education expenses instead of a tuition and fees deduction. You can choose the one that will give you the lower tax. You cannot claim the tuition and fees deduction as well as an education credit for the same expense.

Student Loan Interest Deduction

Generally, personal interest you pay, other than certain mortgage interest, is not deductible on your tax return. However, if your modified adjusted gross income (MAGI) is less than $80,000 ($160,000 if filing a joint return), there is a special deduction allowed for paying interest on a student loan (also known as an education loan) used for higher education. Student loan interest is interest you paid during the year on a qualified student loan. It includes both required and voluntary interest payments.

For most taxpayers, MAGI is the adjusted gross income as figured on their federal income tax return before subtracting any deduction for student loan interest. This deduction can reduce the amount of your income subject to tax by up to $2,500.

The student loan interest deduction is taken as an adjustment to income. This means you can claim this deduction even if you do not itemize deductions on Form 1040's Schedule A.

Qualified Student Loan

This is a loan you took out solely to pay qualified education expenses (defined later) that were:

- For you, your spouse, or a person who was your dependent when you took out the loan.

- Paid or incurred within a reasonable period of time before or after you took out the loan.

- For education provided during an academic period for an eligible student.

Loans from the following sources are not qualified student loans:

- A related person.

- A qualified employer plan.

Qualified Education Expenses

For purposes of the student loan interest deduction, these expenses are the total costs of attending an eligible educational institution, including graduate school. They include amounts paid for the following items:

- Tuition and fees.

- Room and board.

- Books, supplies and equipment.

- Other necessary expenses (such as transportation).

The cost of room and board qualifies only to the extent that it is not more than the greater of:

- The allowance for room and board, as determined by the eligible educational institution, that was included in the cost of attendance (for federal financial aid purposes) for a particular academic period and living arrangement of the student, or

- The actual amount charged if the student is residing in housing owned or operated by the eligible educational institution.

Business Deduction For Work-Related Education

If you are an employee and can itemize your deductions, you may be able to claim a deduction for the expenses you pay for your work-related education. Your deduction will be the amount by which your qualifying work-related education expenses plus other job and certain miscellaneous expenses is greater than 2 percent of your adjusted gross income. An itemized deduction may reduce the amount of your income subject to tax.

If you are self-employed, you deduct your expenses for qualifying work-related education directly from your self-employment income. This reduces the amount of your income subject to both income tax and self-employment tax.

Your work-related education expenses may also qualify you for other tax benefits, such as the American opportunity credit, tuition and fees deduction and the lifetime learning credit. You may qualify for these other benefits even if you do not meet the requirements listed above. You cannot claim this deduction as well as the tuition and fees deduction for the same expense, nor can you claim this deduction as well as an education credit for the same expense.

To claim a business deduction for work-related education, you must:

- Be working.

- Itemize your deductions on Schedule A (Form 1040 or 1040NR) if you are an employee.

- File Schedule C (Form 1040), Schedule C-EZ (Form 1040), or Schedule F (Form 1040) if you are self-employed.

- Have expenses for education that meet the requirements discussed under Qualifying Work-Related Education, below.

Qualifying Work-Related Education

You can deduct the costs of qualifying work-related education as business expenses. This is education that meets at least one of the following two tests:

- The education is required by your employer or the law to keep your present salary, status or job. The required education must serve a bona fide business purpose of your employer.

- The education maintains or improves skills needed in your present work.

However, even if the education meets one or both of the above tests, it is not qualifying work-related education if it:

- Is needed to meet the minimum educational requirements of your present trade or business or

- Is part of a program of study that will qualify you for a new trade or business.

You can deduct the costs of qualifying work-related education as a business expense even if the education could lead to a degree.

Education Required By Employer Or By Law

Education you need to meet the minimum educational requirements for your present trade or business is not qualifying work-related education. Once you have met the minimum educational requirements for your job, your employer or the law may require you to get more education. This additional education is qualifying work-related education if all three of the following requirements are met.

- It is required for you to keep your present salary, status or job.

- The requirement serves a business purpose of your employer.

- The education is not part of a program that will qualify you for a new trade or business.

When you get more education than your employer or the law requires, the additional education can be qualifying work-related education only if it maintains or improves skills required in your present work.

Education To Maintain Or Improve Skills

If your education is not required by your employer or the law, it can be qualifying work-related education only if it maintains or improves skills needed in your present work. This could include refresher courses, courses on current developments and academic or vocational courses.

Savings Plans

Qualified Tuition Programs (529 plans)

States may establish and maintain programs that allow you to either prepay or contribute to an account for paying a student's qualified education expenses at a postsecondary institution. Eligible educational institutions may establish and maintain programs that allow you to prepay a student's qualified education expenses. If you prepay tuition, the student (designated beneficiary) will be entitled to a waiver or a payment of qualified education expenses. You can't deduct either payments or contributions to a Qualified Tuition Programs. For information on a specific QTP, you will need to contact the state agency or eligible educational institution that established and maintains it.

No tax is due on a distribution from a QTP unless the amount distributed is greater than the beneficiary's adjusted qualified education expenses. Qualified expenses include required tuition and fees, books, supplies and equipment including computer or peripheral equipment, computer software and Internet access and related services if used primarily by the student enrolled at an eligible education institution. Someone who is at least a half-time student, room and board may also qualify.

Coverdell Education Savings Account

A Coverdell Education Savings Account (ESA) can be used to pay either qualified higher education expenses or qualified elementary and secondary education expenses. Income limits apply to contributors, and the total contributions for the beneficiary of this account cannot be more than $2,000 in any year, no matter how many accounts have been established. A beneficiary is someone who is under age 18 or is a special needs beneficiary.

Contributions to a Coverdell ESA are not deductible, but amounts deposited in the account grow tax-free until distributed. The beneficiary will not owe tax on the distributions if they are less than a beneficiary's qualified education expenses at an eligible institution. This benefit applies to qualified higher education expenses as well as to qualified elementary and secondary education expenses.

Here are some things to remember about distributions from Coverdell accounts:

- Distributions are tax-free as long as they are used for qualified education expenses, such as tuition and fees, required books, supplies and equipment and qualified expenses for room and board.

- There is no tax on distributions if they are for enrollment or attendance at an eligible educational institution. This includes any public, private or religious school that provides elementary or secondary education as determined under state law. Virtually all accredited public, nonprofit and proprietary (privately owned profit-making) postsecondary institutions are eligible.

- Education tax credits can be claimed in the same year the beneficiary takes a tax-free distribution from a Coverdell ESA, as long as the same expenses are not used for both benefits.

- If the distribution exceeds qualified education expenses, a portion will be taxable to the beneficiary and will usually be subject to an additional 10 percent tax. Exceptions to the additional 10 percent tax include the death or disability of the beneficiary or if the beneficiary receives a qualified scholarship.

Scholarships And Fellowships

A scholarship is generally an amount paid or allowed to, or for the benefit of, a student at an educational institution to aid in the pursuit of studies. The student may be either an undergraduate or a graduate. A fellowship is generally an amount paid for the benefit of an individual to aid in the pursuit of study or research. Generally, whether the amount is tax-free or taxable depends on the expense paid with the amount and whether you are a degree candidate.

A scholarship or fellowship is tax-free only if you meet the following conditions:

- You are a candidate for a degree at an eligible educational institution.

- You use the scholarship or fellowship to pay qualified education expenses.

Qualified Education Expenses

For purposes of tax-free scholarships and fellowships, these are expenses for:

- Tuition and fees required to enroll at or attend an eligible educational institution.

- Course-related expenses, such as fees, books, supplies, and equipment that are required for the courses at the eligible educational institution. These items must be required of all students in your course of instruction.

However, in order for these to be qualified education expenses, the terms of the scholarship or fellowship cannot require that it be used for other purposes, such as room and board, or specify that it cannot be used for tuition or course-related expenses.

Expenses That Don't Qualify

Qualified education expenses do not include the cost of:

- Room and board

- Travel

- Research

- Clerical help

- Equipment and other expenses that are not required for enrollment in or attendance at an eligible educational institution.

This is true even if the fee must be paid to the institution as a condition of enrollment or attendance. Scholarship or fellowship amounts used to pay these costs are taxable.

Exclusions From Income

You may exclude certain educational assistance benefits from your income. That means that you won't have to pay any tax on them. However, it also means that you can't use any of the tax-free education expenses as the basis for any other deduction or credit, including the lifetime learning credit.

Employer-Provided Educational Assistance

If you receive educational assistance benefits from your employer under an educational assistance program, you can exclude up to $5,250 of those benefits each year. This means your employer should not include the benefits with your wages, tips, and other compensation shown in box 1 of your Form W-2.

Educational Assistance Program

To qualify as an educational assistance program, the plan must be written and must meet certain other requirements. Your employer can tell you whether there is a qualified program where you work.

Educational Assistance Benefits

Tax-free educational assistance benefits include payments for tuition, fees and similar expenses, books, supplies, and equipment. The payments may be for either undergraduate- or graduate-level courses. The payments do not have to be for work-related courses. Educational assistance benefits do not include payments for the following items.

- Meals, lodging, or transportation.

- Tools or supplies (other than textbooks) that you can keep after completing the course of instruction.

- Courses involving sports, games, or hobbies unless they:

- Have a reasonable relationship to the business of your employer, or

- Are required as part of a degree program.

Benefits Over $5,250

If your employer pays more than $5,250 for educational benefits for you during the year, you must generally pay tax on the amount over $5,250. Your employer should include in your wages (Form W-2, box 1) the amount that you must include in income.

Working Condition Fringe Benefit

However, if the benefits over $5,250 also qualify as a working condition fringe benefit, your employer does not have to include them in your wages. A working condition fringe benefit is a benefit which, had you paid for it, you could deduct as an employee business expense.

Education Credits Can Help At Tax Time

Five Ways To Offset Education Costs

College can be very expensive. To help students and their parents, the Internal Revenue Service (IRS) offers the following five ways to offset education costs.

1. **The American Opportunity Credit** This credit can help parents and students pay part of the cost of the first four years of college. The American Recovery and Reinvestment Act modifies the existing Hope Credit for tax years 2009 and 2010, making it available to a broader range of taxpayers. Eligible taxpayers may qualify for the maximum annual credit of $2,500 per student. Generally, 40 percent of the credit is refundable, which means that you may be able to receive up to $1,000, even if you owe no taxes.

2. **The Hope Credit** The credit can help students and parents pay part of the cost of the first two years of college. This credit generally applies to 2008 and earlier tax years. However, for tax year 2009 a special expanded Hope Credit of up to $3,600 may be claimed for a student attending college in a Midwestern disaster area as long as you do not claim an American Opportunity Tax Credit for any other student in 2009.

3. **The Lifetime Learning Credit** This credit can help pay for undergraduate, graduate and professional degree courses—including courses to improve job skills—regardless of the number of years in the program. Eligible taxpayers may qualify for up to $2,000—$4,000 if a student in a Midwestern disaster area—per tax return.

4. **Enhanced benefits for 529 college savings plans** Certain computer technology purchases are now added to the list of college expenses that can be paid for by a qualified tuition program, commonly referred to as a 529 plan. For 2009 and 2010, the law expands the definition of qualified higher education expenses to include expenses for computer technology and equipment or Internet access and related services.

5. **Tuition and fees deduction** Students and their parents may be able to deduct qualified college tuition and related expenses of up to $4,000. This deduction is an adjustment to income, which means the deduction will reduce the amount of your income subject to tax. The Tuition and Fees Deduction may be beneficial to you if you do not qualify for the American opportunity, Hope, or lifetime learning credits.

You cannot claim the American Opportunity and the Hope and Lifetime Learning Credits for the same student in the same year. You also cannot claim any of the credits if you claim a tuition and fees deduction for the same student in the same year. To qualify for an education credit, you must pay postsecondary tuition and certain related expenses for yourself, your spouse or your dependent. The credit may be claimed by the parent or the student, but not by both. Students who are claimed as a dependent cannot claim the credit.

Part Five
Other Sources Of Financial Aid

Chapter 38
Finding And Applying For A Scholarship

Scholarships are gifts. They don't need to be repaid. There are thousands of them, offered by schools, employers, individuals, private companies, nonprofits, communities, religious groups, and professional and social organizations.

What Kinds Of Scholarships Are Available?

Some scholarships for college are merit-based. You earn them by meeting or exceeding certain standards set by the scholarship-giver. Merit scholarships might be awarded based on academic achievement or on a combination of academics and a special talent, trait, or interest. Other scholarships are based on financial need.

Many scholarships are geared toward particular groups of people; for instance, there are scholarships for women or high school seniors. And some are available because of where you or your parent work, or because you come from a certain background (for instance, there are scholarships for military families).

A scholarship might cover the entire cost of your tuition, or it might be a one-time award of a few hundred dollars. Either way, it's worth applying for, because it'll help reduce the cost of your education.

How Do I Find Scholarships?

You can learn about scholarships in several ways, including contacting the financial aid office at the school you plan to attend and checking information in a public library or online.

About This Chapter: This chapter includes text excerpted from "Finding And Applying For Scholarships," Federal Student Aid, U.S. Department of Education (ED), February 2, 2017.

But be careful. Make sure scholarship information and offers you receive are legitimate; and remember that you don't have to pay to find scholarships or other financial aid.

Try these free sources of information about scholarships:

- the financial aid office at a college or career school

- a high school or TRIO counselor

- the U.S. Department of Labor's (DOL) FREE scholarship search tool

- federal agencies

- your state grant agency

- your library's reference section

- foundations, religious or community organizations, local businesses, or civic groups

- organizations (including professional associations) related to your field of interest

- ethnicity-based organizations

- your employer or your parents' employers

When Do I Apply For Scholarships?

That depends on each scholarship's deadline. Some deadlines are as early as a year before college starts, so if you're in high school now, you should be researching and applying for scholarships during the summer between your junior and senior years. But if you've missed that window, don't give up!

How Do I Apply For Scholarships?

Each scholarship has its own requirements. The scholarship's website should give you an idea of who qualifies for the scholarship and how to apply. Make sure you read the application carefully, fill it out completely, and meet the application deadline.

How Do I Get My Scholarship Money?

That depends on the scholarship. The money might go directly to your college, where it will be applied to any tuition, fees, or other amounts you owe, and then any leftover funds given to you. Or it might be sent directly to you in a check. The scholarship provider should tell you what to expect when it informs you that you've been awarded the scholarship. If not, make sure to ask.

How Does A Scholarship Affect My Other Student Aid?

A scholarship will affect your other student aid because all your student aid added together can't be more than your cost of attendance at your college or career school. So, you'll need to let your school know if you've been awarded a scholarship so that the financial aid office can subtract that amount from your cost of attendance (and from certain other aid, such as loans, that you might have been offered). Then, any amount left can be covered by other financial aid for which you're eligible.

Chapter 39
Avoiding Scholarship Scams

Need money for college? Just about everyone does, and with the high cost of education, most students and their families need to rely on scholarships and other sources of financial aid to help pay the bills. Luckily, even a slight amount of research will show that there are many, many sources of scholarship funding available. Unfortunately, as with virtually any kind of economic transaction, students seeking scholarships need to be wary of unscrupulous individuals looking to rope them into money-losing scams.

How To Spot A Scholarship Scam

According to the Federal Trade Commission (FTC), the country's consumer protection agency, there are numerous methods that underhanded companies and individuals use to defraud students and parents. It's impossible to learn about each of them in detail, since these people are constantly testing new strategies and changing their approaches. But there are some conditions, sales pitches, and phrases that should raise a red flag indicating that something is not right. These include:

- **Guaranteed scholarships.** This is one of the come-ons that is used most often. And why not? It sounds like you already won. But bear in mind that no one representing a legitimate scholarship-funding organization will make this promise. Almost all scholarships have some requirements, like academic performance, financial need, volunteering, career goals, or club membership. And there are too many variables for them to know in advance who will end up receiving an award.

"Avoiding Scholarship Scams," © 2017 Omnigraphics.

- **Money-back guarantees.** This usually goes along with the promise of a scholarship. The scammer will require a fee in advance, guaranteeing to refund the money if he or she can't deliver the scholarship. Then, when the scholarship—if there ever was one—fails to materialize, there are so many conditions on the refund that it's impossible for the consumer ever to see that money again.

- **Up-front fees.** Legitimate scholarship-granting organization don't normally charge a fee for an application. On those rare occasions that there is one, it will be a very small amount. Be aware, however, that there are services that charge a fee to match you with a scholarship for which you qualify. If you go this route, do enough advance research to make sure you're not dealing with a scammer.

- **Unsolicited offers.** "You've been chosen!" That's great to hear if you've applied for a scholarship, but if you read those words in an unsolicited letter or email, be suspicious. The sender could be phishing for personal information or setting you up to pay an advance fee, which will turn out to be non-refundable.

- **Exclusive information.** Scholarship information is readily available online or from the granting organizations. Anyone claiming to have exclusive access to private sources or a secret database is almost certainly trying to scam you. Most scholarship money comes from the federal government and from individual colleges. Those sources, plus any private granting organizations, want their information easily accessible so they can get the largest possible number of good candidates.

- **Free scholarship seminars.** Similar to those offers of a free dinner with an informational seminar that try to hook people into investment scams or vacation condos, the intention here is to make you think you'll be learning about how get scholarship money. But in all likelihood the scammer intends to end the seminar with an offer to get you financial aid in exchange for a "guaranteed refundable" advance fee.

- **Limited-time offers.** All legitimate scholarships have deadlines, but this is different. Here, the scammer pressures you for a quick decision to pay an advance fee before the offer runs out. Be aware that these scams often come as part of an unsolicited offer. Real scholarship-granting organizations never pressure students to apply, and they generally allow plenty of time for you to complete the application.

- **Requests for sensitive personal information.** Obviously, all scholarship applications will ask for some personal details, such as name, contact information, and date of birth. But never provide your social security number, checking or savings account numbers, or other information that could help a scammer or identity thief. If you actually get a scholarship, some of this information may be requested at that time, but never on an application.

Think It's A Scam? Look And Listen For These Tell-Tale Lines

- "The scholarship is guaranteed or your money back."
- "You can't get this information anywhere else."
- "I just need your credit card or bank account number to hold this scholarship."
- "We'll do all the work. You just pay a processing fee."
- "The scholarship will cost some money."
- "You've been selected" by a "national foundation" to receive a scholarship—or "You're a finalist" in a contest you never entered.

(Source: "Scholarship And Financial Aid Scams," Federal Trade Commission (FTC).)

Tips On Avoiding A Scholarship Scam

Avoiding scholarship scams is primarily a matter of common sense ("if it sounds too good, it probably is") and arming yourself with enough knowledge about the kinds of fraudulent tactics noted above to sidestep the scammers. In addition, there are many sources of assistance that can help point students and parents in the direction of legitimate scholarships, including guidance counselors, school or community librarians, online research, and the colleges or granting organizations themselves. But here are a few general suggestions for protecting yourself from fraudulent scholarships:

- **Don't pay any fees up front.** The goal of any scam is to get your money, and to get it as quickly as possible. The scammers will try to make the charges sound perfectly reasonable, calling them "application fees" or "services charges." But legitimate granting organizations don't generally require any money to apply, especially a large amount of money.

- **Never volunteer personal information.** Providing highly personal information—especially financial information—on an application form or web page is just asking for trouble. There's no justifiable reason for any granting organization to require these details at application time.

- **Stick with reputable sources.** It's usually easy spot a reputable scholarship sources. They're generally colleges, government departments, fraternal organizations, or other groups that you've heard of. Scammers often set up websites made to look like they're run by a legitimate granting organization, but they're exposed as soon as they ask for money or personal information.

- **Don't respond to unsolicited offers.** Genuine scholarships get more applicants than they can support. There's no reason for them to use mass-mailings, email blasts, pop-up ads, or phone solicitation to find students to take their money.

- **Be wary of seminars.** If you decide to attend an informational seminar, proceed cautiously. Investigate the hosting organization ahead of time by checking it out online or speaking to a guidance counselor. Don't pay for anything at the seminar. If you're interested in their services, ask for contact information, and tell them you'll get back to them. If they respond by turning up the pressure, leave.

- **Ask a lot of questions.** Legitimate scholarship providers have brick-and-mortar addresses and published phone numbers, and they are almost always very easy to contact. They also have identifiable representatives, often with their names listed on websites or letterheads, who are happy to answer questions from potential applicants.

- **Do your homework.** A number of government and college websites can guide you in your search for a scholarship. Follow their recommendations, and carefully check out any sources you find on your won. Often a simple Google search will turn up complaints from people who've been scammed by the same granting organization you're investigating.

- **Keep accurate records.** Set up an email folder for any strings of correspondence you have about scholarships, keep notes on phone conversations, and make photocopies of hard-copy offers or letters. For one thing, this will help you keep straight where things stand with each scholarship you're investigating, and for another this information might come in handy if you do uncover a scam and want to report it to the authorities.

- **Ask, "Is this too good to be true?"** Trust your instincts. If someone appears shady, avoids answering questions, or attempts to use one of the scams mentioned above, be wary, and definitely don't give them any money.

In the final analysis, it's important to remember that billions of dollars in scholarships are granted each year to millions of students from government sources, colleges and universities, foundations, corporations, churches, professional groups, chambers of commerce, and many other organizations.

If you believe you've come across a scholarship scam or think you've been contacted by a scammer, you can file a complaint with your state attorney general's office or with the Federal Trade Commission at ftccomplaintassistant.gov.

Don't hesitate to cross a potential scholarship off your list if you suspect a scam, because there are plenty more available.

References

1. "Avoiding Scholarship Scams," The College Board, n.d.

2. "Avoiding Scholarship Scams," CollegeScholarships.org, n.d.

3. "Avoid Scholarship Scams," InternationalStudent.org, n.d

4. "How To Avoid And Protect Yourself From Scholarship Scams," Finaid.org, n.d.

5. Hoyt, Elizabeth. "Scholarship Scam Red Flags," Fastweb.com, October 8, 2016.

6. "Scholarship and Financial Aid Scams," FTC.gov, May 2012.

Chapter 40
The Nursing Scholarship Program

The NURSE Corps Scholarship Program is administered by the Bureau of Health Workforce (BHW). This program supports the mission of BHW and the Health Resources and Services Administration (HRSA), which is to improve health and achieve health equity through access to quality services, a skilled health workforce, and innovative programs.

What Is The NURSE Corps Scholarship Program?

The purpose of the NURSE Corps Scholarship Program is to provide scholarships to nursing students in exchange for a minimum 2-year full-time service commitment (or part-time equivalent), at an eligible healthcare facility with a critical shortage of nurses. Scholarships are awarded competitively and consist of payment for tuition, required school fees, Other Reasonable Costs and a monthly support stipend. Applicants are strongly encouraged to explore the types of nursing opportunities that exist in critical shortage facilities before applying to the program. All participants will be expected to fulfill their service obligation in the discipline and funding preference for which they were awarded.

Up to fifty percent of NURSE Corps Scholarship Program funds will be made available for nurse practitioners (NPs) to address key issues pertaining to the expanding need for healthcare.

About This Chapter: This chapter includes text excerpted from "NURSE Corps Scholarship Program—Fiscal Year 2016 Application and Program Guidance," Bureau Of Health Workforce (BHW), Health Resources and Services Administration (HRSA), March 2016.

What Are The Benefits Of The NURSE Corps Scholarship Program?

- Service: NURSE Corps Scholarship Program participants will have the opportunity to increase access to care by delivering nursing services in eligible healthcare facilities with a critical shortage of nurses.

- Scholarship: NURSE Corps Scholarship Program provides the following:

- Funds to support nursing school tuition and fees;

- An annual payment for Other Reasonable Costs to cover expenses for books, clinical supplies, and instruments; and

- Monthly stipends to cover living expenses.

Eligibility Requirements

Am I Eligible?

To be eligible for a scholarship, a NURSE Corps Scholarship Program applicant must:

1. Be a U.S. citizen (either U.S. born or naturalized), U.S. national, or a Lawful Permanent Resident.

> **Note:**
>
> A driver's license and social security card are NOT proof of U.S. citizenship or status as a U.S. National or Lawful Permanent Resident.

2. Be enrolled or accepted for enrollment as a full-time or part-time student in an accredited nursing degree program at one of the following:

    - **An associate degree school of nursing:** A department, division, or other administrative unit in a junior college, community college, college, or university which provides primarily or exclusively a two-year program of education in professional nursing and allied subjects leading to an associate degree in nursing or to an equivalent degree and is an accredited program.

    - **A collegiate school of nursing:** A department, division, or the administrative unit in a college or university which provides primarily or exclusively a program of education in professional nursing and related subjects leading to a degree of bachelor of arts, bachelor of science, bachelor of nursing, graduate degree in nursing, or to an equivalent degree, and including advanced training related to such program of education provided by such school and is an accredited program.

- **A diploma school of nursing:** A school affiliated with a hospital or university, or an independent school, which provides primarily or exclusively a program of education in professional nursing and allied subjects leading to a diploma or to an equivalent evidence of completion and is an accredited program.

- **Accredited Program.** The NURSE Corps Scholarship Program considers a nursing program to be accredited if it is accredited by a national or regional nurse education accrediting agency or state approval agency recognized by the Secretary of the U.S. Department of Education (ED).

3. Is enrolled in or accepted for enrollment in a school of nursing located in a state, the District of Columbia, or a U.S. Territory.

- **Located in a State, the District of Columbia, or a U.S. Territory.** The schools and educational programs for which scholarship support is requested must be in one of the 50 States, the District of Columbia, the Commonwealth of Puerto Rico, the Commonwealth of the Northern Marianas, the U.S. Virgin Islands, the Territory of Guam, the Territory of American Samoa, the Republic of Palau, the Republic of the Marshall Islands, or the Federated States of Micronesia. A student attending a school outside of these areas is not eligible for the NURSE Corps Scholarship Program, even though the student may be a citizen/national/lawful permanent resident of the United States.

4. Begin taking classes for the nursing degree program in which you are enrolled or accepted on or before September 30, 2016.

5. Submit a complete application and signed contract. An applicant will be deemed ineligible if the applicant:

- Has any judgment liens against his or her property arising from a debt owed to the United States;

- Defaulted on a prior service obligation to the Federal government, a State or local government, or other entity, even if the applicant subsequently satisfied that obligation through service, monetary payment, or other means.

- Is excluded, debarred, suspended, or disqualified by a Federal Agency; OR

- **Has an existing service obligation.** An applicant who is already obligated to a Federal, State, or other entity for professional practice or service after academic training is not eligible for a NURSE Corps Scholarship Program award. An exception may be made if the entity to which the obligation is owed provides documentation that there is no potential conflict in fulfilling the service commitment to the NURSE Corps Scholarship Program and that the NURSE Corps Scholarship Program service commitment will be served first. A NURSE Corps Scholarship Program participant who subsequently enters into another service commitment and is not immediately available after completion of the participant's degree to fulfill his/her NURSE Corps Scholarship Program service commitment will be subject to the breach-of-contract provisions. The applicant may still apply as long as all service obligations are completed by the date the applicant submits the NURSE Corps Scholarship Program application.

Understanding The Contract And Length Of The Service Commitment

How Many Years Of School Does The Contract Cover?

The NURSE Corps Scholarship Program award and contract is for the 2016–2017 academic year (July 1, 2016–June 30, 2017). Any funding provided after June 30, 2017, is considered another contract year. Any additional school years (Optional Contracts) requested by the applicant and agreed to by the Secretary or his/her designee is indicated in the executed contracts. Support will be provided during the academic years agreed to in the executed contracts (not to exceed 4 years), beginning with the 2016–2017 academic year and will be based on the cost of the initial school of record (i.e., the school attended at the time the initial contract is executed).

Application funding may not be deferred. Awards are for consecutive academic terms.

Can I Request Additional Scholarship Support After I Receive My Award?

Additional scholarship support will only be provided for the same nursing degree that the NURSE Corps Scholarship Program participant's original contract was funded. To request additional scholarship support for the 2017–2018 year or any subsequent academic years, the NURSE Corps Scholarship Program participant must submit a signed contract for that academic year and a report verifying that he/she is still in an acceptable level of academic standing.

The participant may also request optional contracts for subsequent academic years while pursuing the same nursing degree, program, and specialty on the original contract through graduation for a maximum of 4 academic years of support. The NURSE Corps Scholarship Program will notify the participant when this submission is due.

The granting of continuation awards depends upon the availability of funds for the NURSE Corps SP and is contingent upon the participant's:

1. Continued eligibility to participate in the NURSE Corps Scholarship Program (e.g., acceptable level of academic standing, not repeating coursework, etc.). Please be advised that a credit check will be conducted as part of the eligibility process;

2. Compliance with policies and procedures established by the NURSE Corps Scholarship Program for requesting continued support; AND

3. Past compliance with program policies and requirements.

Participants requesting continued support must be able to financially support themselves until the scholarship benefit payment schedule can be reinstated. If a continuation award is granted, the first payment may not be received until mid-November but will include stipends retroactive to July 1 and the annual Other Reasonable Costs (ORC) payment.

Can I Terminate My NURSE Corps Scholarship Program Contract?

The Secretary of Health and Human Services or his/her designee may terminate a NURSE Corps SP contract for an academic year if, on or before June 1 of the school year, the participant:

1. submits a written request to terminate his/her contract for that academic year; and

2. repays all amounts paid to, or on behalf of, that participant (tuition, stipends and Other Reasonable Cost) for that academic year. If a scholarship participant does not meet these requirements, he/she will incur a minimum 2-year service commitment for the full or partial year of support received.

How Long Is My Service Commitment?

All participants incur, at a minimum, a 2-year full-time service obligation (or part-time equivalent) and may have a longer service obligation, as shown in Table 41.1.

Participants who sign "Full-Time Student" contracts incur an obligation to provide one year of full-time service for each full or partial school year of support received beyond two years as set forth in the table below. For example, a student who receives a full year of support (12 months) the first school year, a partial year of support (6 months) the second school year, and a full year of support the third school year will owe the equivalent of 3 years of full-time clinical service. If a participant receives support for one year or less, there is still an obligation to serve two years

Table 41.1. Years Of Service Obligation

Years Of Scholarship Support	Years Of Service Obligation
Up to 1 Full-Time School Year (2016–2017)	2 Years Full-Time
Up to 2 Full-Time School Years (2016–2018)	2 Years Full-Time
Up to 3 Full-Time School Years (2016–2019)	3 Years Full-Time
Up to 4 Full-Time School Years (2016–2020)	4 Years Full-Time

Participants who sign "Part-Time Student" contracts will have their part-time enrollment aggregated to determine the full-time equivalent.

Program Requirements

What Are The Requirements While I Am In School?

1. **Maintain Enrollment.** The NURSE Corps Scholarship Program participant must maintain enrollment in the nursing program until the program is complete. Every NURSE Corps Scholarship Program participant must verify his/her enrollment status through the Customer Service Portal for each term (semester, quarter). In this process, an appropriate school official must certify the participant's full-time (part-time, if approved) enrollment, and submit a list of the courses and credit hours each term for which the Nurse Corps Scholarship Program will receive an invoice and describe the tuition and fees. The participant must also upload an unofficial transcript. Participants who fail to complete and submit their enrollment verification through the Customer Service Portal each academic term could jeopardize their scholarship and stipend. Participants not in compliance may be recommended for default.

2. **Maintain an Acceptable Level of Academic Standing.** A scholarship participant must be in an acceptable level of academic standing, or the level at which a student retains eligibility to continue attending school under the school's standards and practices, for the duration of the academic year. Applicants on academic probation are not considered to be in an acceptable level of academic standing by the NURSE Corps Scholarship Program.

3. **Notify NURSE Corps Scholarship Program of Any Changes in Enrollment Status.**
   A participant is required to notify the NURSE Corps Scholarship Program through the Customer Service Portal as soon as one of the following events is anticipated:

- Repeat course work for which the NURSE Corps Scholarship Program has already made payments;

- A change in the applicant's graduation date;

- A leave of absence approved by the school;

- Withdrawal or dismissal from school;

- A change from full-time student status as determined by the school's registrar, to a less than full-time student status for participants who sign "Full-Time Student" Contracts (a change from part-time student status for participants who sign "Part-Time Student" Contracts).

- Voluntary withdrawal from courses during an academic term; OR

- A transfer to another school or program.

Tuition, Required Fees, Other Reasonable Costs, And Stipend

The NURSE Corps Scholarship Program uses a Data Collection Worksheet (DCW) to collect information on tuition, fees, and student expenses for the current and upcoming school years. A school official will be asked to complete a DCW for each applicant considered for an award. This information will be used to determine award calculations including: Annual Tuition (both In-state and Out-of-state), Eligible Program Fees, Books, and Other Reasonable Costs (e.g., Clinical Supplies/Instruments, and Uniforms) for the entire academic year (including estimated summer fees). If the school official does not complete the DCW, program participants may experience delays in the process of their future tuition payments to their institutions.

Please note, once submitted, information on the DCW cannot be changed after the award is made.

Scholars are responsible for making sure their school official is aware of NURSE Corps Scholarship Program specific invoicing and payment requirements. Invoicing information will be provided to all scholars upon award. All educational institutions will be required to submit an invoice to the NURSE Corps Scholarship Program for the payment of tuition and eligible fees for each term that the student is enrolled. All funds will be disbursed electronically; therefore, each institution must make sure it is registered with the System for Award Management (SAM) at the following web address: www.sam.gov.

The first payment for new NURSE Corps Scholarship Program awardees will be made no later than November 2016 and will include stipend payments retroactive to July 1, 2016, and the annual payment for Other Reasonable Costs.

What Costs Does The NURSE Corps Scholarship Program Cover?

1. Tuition and Required Fees

   - **Tuition and eligible required fees will be paid directly to the nursing school.** The nursing school or the school's authorized financial office must submit an invoice to the NURSE Corps Scholarship Program for payment of tuition and fees for each term. Any fees on the invoice that are included in the Other Reasonable Costs (discussed below) will not be approved for payment to the nursing school.

   - **Summer sessions.** NURSE Corps Scholarship Program will only pay tuition and fees for required courses in summer school sessions when (1) summer session is an academic term normally required by the school for all students in the same program and (2) the summer session is in progress during the participant's contract period.

   - **Repeated coursework.** The NURSE Corps Scholarship Program will not pay tuition and fees for repeated coursework for which the NURSE Corps Scholarship Program has previously made a payment (e.g., cost of the repeated course, overload fees). If the repeated course work does not delay the participant's graduation date, the scholarship payments for other tuition and fees may continue. The decision to continue scholarship payments while a participant is repeating coursework will be made at the discretion of the NURSE Corps Scholarship Program. Participants who must repeat coursework should immediately contact the NURSE Corps Scholarship Program via the Customer Service Portal or risk losing their monthly stipend payments.

   - **Increases in tuition or required fees.** Payments for any increases in tuition or required fees that are reported by the school after the award has been made are not guaranteed and are subject to the availability of funds.

   - **Attending more than one school.** For participants enrolled in programs that require taking classes at more than one school/campus, please be advised that payments will only be made to other institutions which have degree program agreements with the nursing institution as indicated on the NURSE Corps Scholarship Program application and only for courses required as part of the degree program.

- **The NURSE Corps Scholarship Program will pay for ONLY the courses that are required for graduation.** The NURSE Corps Scholarship Program will not pay for additional courses beyond those required for graduation. Also, the NURSE Corps Scholarship Program will not pay for tuition costs or fees unrelated to the degree/program, such as membership dues for student societies/associations, loan processing fees, penalty or late fees, and other similar expenses.

- **Transfers to other academic institutions are strongly discouraged.** Transfers to other academic institutions are strongly discouraged once the applicant has been accepted into the NURSE Corps Scholarship Program. Transfers will be considered on a case-by-case basis and only for exceptional circumstances. Transfers must be approved by the NURSE Corps Scholarship Program in advance to ensure continued eligibility for funding. Scholarship awards are based on the cost of attendance at the initial school of record for all school year contracts executed during the FY 2016 application cycle. If a transfer is approved, the NURSE Corps Scholarship Program will not cover any increase in tuition and/or fees for the new institution; the participant will be responsible for the difference. Changes in type of nursing program will not be approved.

2. **Other Reasonable Costs (ORC)**

- The ORC is an additional, annual payment provided directly to each NURSE Corps Scholarship Program participant to assist in the payment of books, clinical supplies/instruments, and uniforms. This information is obtained directly from the institution and is determined independently for each application. ORC payments will vary from student to student depending on the student's program and graduation date.

- The ORC payment will be reduced proportionately for students who plan to attend less than a full school year (e.g., December graduates) and for part-time students.

3. **Stipend Amount**

- During the 2016–2017 academic year, the NURSE Corps Scholarship Program will pay each full-time student a monthly amount of $1,330.00 (before Federal taxes). A part-time student will receive a proportionately reduced stipend amount.

- The stipend payments may be delayed or placed on hold if requested NURSE Corps Scholarship Program documents—invoices, enrollment verification forms, transcripts, etc.—have not been received. Stipend payments may also be stopped if a student is repeating coursework that has already been paid for by the NURSE Corps Scholarship Program.

- Stipend payments will stop the month the nursing course work is completed or when the contract ends, whichever comes first.

Receipt of the stipend payment does not mean that the NURSE Corps Scholarship Program participant is employed by the Federal Government or participates in any of the benefits available to Federal employees.

Chapter 41

The National Health Service Corps Scholarship

What Is The National Health Service Corps (NHSC) Scholarship Program (SP)?

The NHSC SP is a competitive federal program that awards scholarships to students pursuing eligible primary care health professions training leading to:

- A degree in medicine (allopathic or osteopathic)

- A degree in dentistry; or

- A postgraduate degree or postgraduate certificate from a school or program in nurse-midwifery education, physician assistant (PA) education, or nurse practitioner (NP) education specializing in adult medicine, family medicine, geriatrics, pediatrics, psychiatric-mental health, or women's health.

In return, scholars commit to providing primary care health services in underserved communities. Administered by the Bureau of Health Workforce (BHW) in the Health Resources and Services Administration (HRSA) of the U.S. Department of Health and Human Services (HHS), the program provides support to students who seek financial assistance to complete primary care health professions education.

The NHSC SP pays for tuition and various other reasonable education-related expenses and also provides a monthly stipend to assist with living expenses in exchange for a minimum of two years of full-time service. The service obligation must be completed at an NHSC-approved site in a Health Professional Shortage Area (HPSA) of greatest need. The total

About This Chapter: This chapter includes text excerpted from "National Health Service Corps Scholarship Program," Health Resources and Services Administration (HRSA), March 2016.

number of years of full-time service a scholar is obligated to serve will depend on the number of school years of NHSC SP support received by the scholar, not to exceed 4 school years.

NHSC scholars are required to fulfill their NHSC service obligation at NHSC-approved sites located in HPSAs of greatest need. A HPSA is a geographic area, population group, public or nonprofit private medical facility or other public facility for the delivery of health services (including a Federal or State correctional institution), which is determined by the HHS Secretary to have a shortage of health professionals. Information considered when designating a HPSA includes health provider to population ratios, rates of poverty, and access to available healthcare services. The HPSA locations may be anywhere in the United States, the Commonwealth of Puerto Rico, the Territory of Guam, the Commonwealth of the Northern Marianas, the U.S. Virgin Islands, the Territory of American Samoa, the Republic of Palau, the Republic of the Marshall Islands, or the Federated States of Micronesia.

A commitment to participate in the NHSC SP is significant, as is the need for primary care in the underserved communities across the United States and the U.S. territories. Applicants will be evaluated with respect to their demonstrated interest in primary care, their qualifications to participate in the NHSC SP, and their commitment to serving the underserved. The NHSC SP is seeking well-prepared applicants who demonstrate geographic flexibility and a strong interest in providing primary health services to underserved populations nationally.

> Only those students who are committed to practicing primary care and are able to relocate based on the needs of the NHSC in underserved communities should consider becoming a scholar in the NHSC SP.

What Are The Benefits Of The NHSC SP?

1. **Service.** Scholars will join the thousands of current and former NHSC clinicians who provide primary healthcare services to communities in need.

2. **Payment of Educational Expenses.** The NHSC SP provides the following financial support for full-time enrollment in an eligible primary care health professions degree training program for up to 4 school years:

   • Payment of tuition and eligible fees;

   • An annual payment for other reasonable educational costs; and

   • Monthly stipends, for up to 4 school years, to assist with living expenses while pursuing the health professions degree educational training program.

Eligibility Requirements, Selection Factors, And Funding Priorities

Am I Eligible?

To be eligible for a scholarship, all applicants must:

1. **Be a U.S. Citizen (either U.S. born or naturalized) or U.S. National.** To be eligible for an NHSC scholarship, applicants must present proof of U.S. citizenship or status as a U.S. national. This may include a copy of a birth certificate issued by a city, county, or state agency in the United States, the ID page of a U.S. passport, or a certificate of citizenship or naturalization. A permanent resident card, driver's license, marriage certificate, or social security card is not acceptable proof of U.S. citizenship or status as a U.S. national.

2. **Be enrolled or accepted for enrollment as a full-time student.** To be considered for a scholarship award for the 2016–2017 school year, classes **must begin** on or before September 30, 2016. Applicants planning to be on a leave of absence from school that will preclude full-time class attendance on or before September 30, 2016 should not submit an application this year, but may apply for the 2017–2018 academic year.

    Full-time. A full-time student is defined as a student enrolled for a sufficient number of credit hours in any academic term to complete the course of study within the number of academic terms normally required at the school. Any courses that are not required to complete the qualifying degree program will not count towards the hours required for full-time status and will not be supported by the NHSC SP.

3. **Be attending or accepted to attend one of the following accredited schools or programs located in a state, the District of Columbia, or a U.S. territory:**

    - Physician

        - A school of allopathic or osteopathic medicine, pursuing an M.D. or D.O. degree; and

        - Accredited by the Liaison Committee on Medical Education (LCME) [sponsored by the American Medical Association (AMA) and the Association of American Medical Colleges (AAMC)] or the American Osteopathic Association (AOA), Commission on Osteopathic College Accreditation (COCA).

- Dentist

  - A school of dentistry, pursuing a D.D.S. or D.M.D. degree; and

  - Accredited by the American Dental Association (ADA), Commission on Dental Accreditation (CODA).

- Nurse Practitioner

  - A school or program of nurse practitioner education, pursuing a postgraduate degree or postgraduate certificate;

  - Accredited by the Accreditation Commission for Education in Nursing (ACEN) or the Commission on Collegiate Nursing Education (CCNE); and

  - Leading to national certification as a nurse practitioner specializing in adult medicine, family medicine, geriatrics, primary care pediatrics, psychiatric-mental health, or women's health by the American Nurses Credentialing Center (ANCC), the American Academy of Nurse Practitioners (AANP), or the Pediatric Nursing Certification Board (PNCB).

- Nurse-Midwife

  - A school or program of nurse-midwifery education, pursuing a postgraduate degree or postgraduate certificate;

  - Accredited by the American College of Nurse-Midwives (ACNM), Division of Accreditation; and

  - Leading to national certification by the American Midwifery Certification Board (AMCB).

- Physician Assistant

  - A school or program of primary care physician assistant education, pursuing a postgraduate degree or postgraduate certificate;

  - Accredited by the Accreditation Review Commission on Education for the Physician Assistant (ARC-PA) AND the affiliated school must be accredited by a U.S. Department of Education (ED) nationally recognized regional or state institutional accrediting agency; and

  - Leading to national certification by the National Commission on Certification of Physician Assistants (NCCPA).

Located in a state, the District of Columbia, or a U.S. territory. Eligible schools and educational programs for which scholarship support is provided must be in a state (includes the 50 states, the District of Columbia, the Commonwealth of Puerto Rico, the Commonwealth of the Northern Marianas, the U.S. Virgin Islands, the Territory of Guam, the Territory of American Samoa, the Republic of Palau, the Republic of the Marshall Islands, and the Federated States of Micronesia).

Students attending schools outside of these geographic areas are not eligible for NHSC scholarships, even though they may be citizens or nationals of the United States.

4. **Be eligible for federal employment.** Most NHSC scholars should expect to serve their obligations as a salaried, non-federal employee of public or private entities approved by the NHSC SP. However, there may be vacancies that require federal employment, including a security clearance. In light of the potential for federal employment, an applicant must be eligible to hold an appointment as a Commissioned Officer of the U.S. Public Health Service (USPHS) or be eligible for a federal civil service appointment.

5. **Not have an existing service obligation.** Applicants who are already obligated to a Federal, State, or other entity for professional practice or service after academic training are not eligible for NHSC scholarship awards unless the entity to which the obligation is owed provides a written statement satisfactory to the HHS Secretary that

    *   there is no potential conflict in fulfilling the NHSC SP obligation and the entity's obligation, and

    *   the NHSC SP obligation will be served first.

    Scholars who subsequently incur other service obligations and are not immediately available after completion of their training to fulfill their NHSC SP service obligation will be subject to the breach-of-contract provisions.

    Exception: Individuals in a Reserve component of the Armed Forces including the National Guard are **eligible** to participate in the NHSC SP. Reservists should understand the following:

    *   Military training or service performed by reservists will not satisfy the NHSC SP service obligation. If a scholar's military training and/or service, in combination with the scholar's other absences from the service site, will exceed 7 weeks per service year,

the scholar should request a suspension. The NHSC SP service obligation end date will be extended to compensate for the break in service.

- If the approved NHSC site where the reservist is serving at the time of his/her deployment is unable to reemploy that reservist, the NHSC SP will assist the reservist in finding another NHSC-approved site to complete his/her remaining service obligation.

6. **Submit a complete application.** Each applicant must complete an online application and submit a résumé, two letters of recommendation, a report verifying acceptance or enrollment in good standing in an eligible health professions school, and school transcripts. Each applicant is also required to respond to three essay questions. These documents will be used to evaluate an applicant's qualifications to participate in the NHSC SP. If selected, individuals will be required to review and submit a signed contract indicating they agree to provide primary care in a HPSA of greatest need in exchange for a scholarship.

Applicants are **ineligible** if they are:

- Pursuing a non-primary care specialty. (For example, enrolled or accepted for enrollment in a program with a surgical or emergency medicine focus.)

- In the pre-professional phase of their health professions education. (For example, taking undergraduate pre-requisites for admission to a health professions training program.)

How Does The NHSC SP Determine Who Will Receive Scholarship Support?

Among eligible applicants, the NHSC SP determines scholarship awardees using various selection factors and funding priorities.

Selection Factors

1. **History of honoring prior legal obligations.** NHSC SP applicants who have a history of not honoring prior legal obligations, as evidenced by one or more of the following factors, may not be selected:

- Default on any federal payment obligations (e.g., Health Education Assistance Loans (HEAL), Nursing Student Loans (NSL), Federal Housing Administration loans (FHA), federal income tax liabilities, federally guaranteed/insured loans (such as student or home mortgage loans, etc.) or any non-federal payment obligations (e.g., court-ordered child support payments) even if the applicant is currently considered to be in good standing by that creditor;

- Default on a prior service obligation to the Federal Government, a state or local government, or other entity, even if the applicant subsequently satisfied that obligation through service, monetary payment or other means; OR

- Charge-off/Write-off of any federal or non-federal debt as uncollectible or had any federal service or payment obligation waived.

2. **Academic performance.** Demonstrates the ability to excel and maintain good academic standing while in school.

3. **Commitment to a Career in Primary Care and Working in Underserved Communities.** Demonstrates a strong commitment to the field of primary care; interest/motivation to provide care to underserved communities; and relevant work experience and/or activities (i.e., community service, research, and internships) that have prepared the applicant to work with underserved populations. This factor is reviewed through the following:

   - **Essay Questions.** An applicant's responses to the essay questions aid in the review process and help gauge an applicant's interest in primary care and commitment to working in underserved communities.

   - **Recommendation Letters.** Provide a detailed description of the applicant's performance in school; education/work achievements; community/civic or other non-academic achievements; ability to work and communicate constructively with others from diverse backgrounds; and interest and motivation to serve underserved populations through work experience, course work, special projects, research, etc.

4. **Not have any judgment liens arising from a federal debt.**

5. **Not be currently excluded, debarred, suspended, or disqualified by a federal agency.** Before entering into a scholarship contract, an applicant must report if he or she is currently excluded, debarred, suspended or disqualified by a federal agency. The applicant should sign the Certification that is applicable to his/her situation. As a condition of participating in the NHSC SP, a scholar must agree to provide immediate written notice to the NHSC SP if the scholar learns that he/she failed to make a required disclosure or that a disclosure is now required due to changed circumstances.

Chapter 42
College-Bound Athletes

Over one thousand U.S. colleges and universities offer opportunities for talented students to play for the college team as a means of paying for their education.

The key to being successful in your search for athletic scholarships is to meticulously research your options and look for the right opportunities. Some points to consider as you begin your search:

- Start early. The application process is competitive and requires careful planning. Start your research approximately 18 to 24 months prior to the date you plan to attend a university in the United States.

- Graduate from secondary school or high school. Find your country in the National Collegiate Athletic Association (NCAA) International Standards for Student Athletes.

- Find a school. See the National Collegiate Athletic Association (NCAA) Sport Listing to find participating U.S. institutions.

Sports scholarships

- National Association of Intercollegiate Athletics (NAIA)

- National Junior College Athletic Association (NJCAA)

- beRecruited

- Athletic Scholarships

About This Chapter: Text in this chapter begins with excerpts from "Athletic Scholarships," EducationUSA, U.S. Department of State (DOS), March 25, 2015; Text under the heading "The ABC Of Sports Scholarships" is excerpted from "Quick Guide," EducationUSA, U.S. Department of State (DOS), April 2016.

You may also want to think about drafting a sports CV, bio, or résumé that includes your athletic accomplishments and recording videos of your performance in games/events. Start thinking about letters of reference from your coaches and other mentors to help them express how they view your potential to succeed and represent the institution with a sports or athletic scholarship.

The ABC Of Sports Scholarships

Over 150,000 sports scholarships are awarded to men and women in 35 sports annually. Scholarships range from US$1,000 to over US$30,000 each year, with an average amount of US$10,000. Regardless of whether or not students receive a sports scholarship, they must register with the athletic association they hope to be playing in (e.g., NCAA, NAIA).

Register With Athletic Associations

Early in Year 11, begin the registration process. The appropriate association can be found on each university's website.

- **National Collegiate Athletic Association (NCAA)** (www.ncaa.org)

    - Division I and II: register with the NCAA Eligibility Center at www.eligibilitycenter.org

    - Division III: no registration required; contact Division III universities/colleges directly regarding admission standards and financial aid.

- **National Association of Intercollegiate Athletics (NAIA)** (www.playnaia.org)

- **National Junior College Athletic Association (NJCAA)** (www.njcaa.org).

Research Universities

Research the universities and sports programs that interest you. Consider both the academics and sports aspects. The admissions process is separate from the sports recruiting process, so you will need to apply to the college/university at the end of Year 12 and be admitted on your academic credentials, regardless of your sporting ability. Generally, we recommend applying to 6–8 schools.

Contact Coaches

Send a short introductory email to as many as 50 coaches at the universities. This email should include:

- Your name, gender and date of birth

- Date of graduation and high school's name

- The month and year you are hoping to start university so the coach knows when to consider you for his/her team

- Sporting awards you have won

- Level of team you play on—state or national

- Position you play

- Name and contact details of your current coach

- SAT/ACT results if you have them

- A link to a short video of you playing your sport.

SAT/ACT Test

- Take the SAT (www.collegeboard.org) or ACT test (www.actstudent.org) and request your scores to be sent to the NCAA or NAIA.

- When you register for the SAT or ACT use NCAA Eligibility Center code 9999 to ensure they are reported directly to the Eligibility Center. For NAIA use code 9876. Test scores MUST come from the testing agencies.

National Collegiate Athletic Association (NCAA)

The National Collegiate Athletic Association (NCAA) is a non-profit organization whose members include more than 1,200 universities and colleges in the United States. It has three divisions, administers 23 sports and enforces the rules which are made by its member institutions. There are three divisions in the NCAA—Division I, II and III. Each member university/college decides which one of these divisions it belongs to. That decision is made by matching its enrolment, financial situation and fan support with the requirements for each division.

All college-bound student-athletes who wish to compete in NCAA Division I or II must have their academic and amateurism credentials certified by the NCAA Eligibility Center (www.eligibilitycenter.org). There are no sports-based scholarships available at Division III institutions, so eligibility requirements are determined by each institution.

National Association Of Intercollegiate Athletics (NAIA)

Founded in 1937, the National Association of Intercollegiate Athletics (NAIA) is a governing body of small athletics programs that are dedicated to character-driven intercollegiate athletics. The student-athlete is the centre of all NAIA experiences and each year more than 60,000 student-athletes have the opportunity to play college sports at NAIA member institutions. More than 260 colleges and universities make up the NAIA, offering 13 sports and 23 national championships. NAIA student-athletes are awarded nearly $500 million in athletic scholarships annually.

Registration with the NAIA Eligibility Center is required (www.playnaia.org). Early registration (e.g., by Year 12) is recommended as it assists student-athletes in making contact with NAIA coaches. The Guide for the College-Bound Student-Athlete, available on the NAIA website, provides answers to many frequently asked questions.

The National Junior College Athletic Association (NJCAA)

NJCAA founded in 1938, is an association of Community Colleges and Junior Colleges dedicated to promoting a national program of athletic participation in two-year institutions. There are 525 member colleges divided into 24 separate geographic regions offering 26 sports across three divisions. Member colleges are permitted to participate in any division and may choose to participate across multiple divisions in various sports (e.g., Division I for Men's Baseball and Division II for Golf).

The NJCAA does not have an "eligibility clock" nor age limit. Students are allowed two seasons of competition in any sport at an NJCAA college if they have not participated at any intercollegiate level during two seasons previously.

Due to the complexity of the NJCAA eligibility rules, it is recommended that potential student-athletes discuss their athletic eligibility with the athletic personnel at the NJCAA college they are interested in attending. Further details are available on the NJCAA website www.njcaa.org.

Chapter 43

College Funding For Disadvantaged Students And Students With Disabilities

Grants To Help Improve Outcomes Of Individuals With Disabilities

The U.S. Department of Education's (ED) Office of Special Education and Rehabilitative Services (OSERS) announced more than $121 million in grants to help improve the outcomes of individuals with disabilities—from cradle through career. The investments are aimed at promoting inclusion, equity and opportunity for all children and adults with disabilities to help ensure their economic self-sufficiency, independent living and full community participation.

U.S. Secretary of Education mentioned "These investments are significant in assisting individuals with disabilities to reach their full potential, We want all individuals with disabilities to succeed and these investments symbolize our values and commitment as a nation toward achieving excellence for all."

Among the grants is $54 million from OSERS' Office of Special Education Programs (OSEP) to support research, demonstrations, technical assistance, technology, personnel development and parent-training and information centers. The OSEP grants include $8.7 million to WestED in San Francisco to create a Center for Systemic Improvement (CSI). The $8.7 million grant becomes the largest technical assistance (TA) investment ever

---

About This Chapter: Text under the heading "Grants To Help Improve Outcomes Of Individuals With Disabilities" is excerpted from "$121 Million Awarded In Grants To Help Improve Outcomes Of Individuals With Disabilities," U.S. Department of Education (ED), October 8, 2014; Text under the heading "Federal TRIO Programs" is excerpted from "Federal TRIO Programs," U.S. Department of Education (ED), January 27, 2017.

funded by OSERS. The focus of this national center will be to provide assistance to states to help build their capacity to support local school districts and early intervention services programs in improving educational results and functional outcomes for children with disabilities. CSI will help states implement the Department's Results Driven Accountability framework by strategically delivering the assistance necessary to implement bold, innovative and systemic reforms that raise expectations for academic achievement and improve outcomes.

Besides special education, OSERS' Rehabilitation Services Administration (RSA) awarded $47 million to fund its comprehensive and coordinated programs of vocational rehabilitation, supported employment and independent living for individuals with disabilities. And, OSERS' National Institute on Disability and Rehabilitation Research (NIDRR) distributed $19 million to institutions of higher education and private and non-profit organizations for innovative, cutting-edge research projects.

Federal TRIO Programs

The Federal TRIO Programs (TRIO) are Federal outreach and student services programs designed to identify and provide services for individuals from disadvantaged backgrounds. TRIO includes eight programs targeted to serve and assist low-income individuals, first-generation college students, and individuals with disabilities to progress through the academic pipeline from middle school to postbaccalaureate programs. TRIO also includes a training program for directors and staff of TRIO projects.

The recipients of the grants, depending on the specific program, are institutions of higher education, public and private agencies and organizations including community-based organizations with experience in serving disadvantaged youth and secondary schools. Combinations of such institutions, agencies, and organizations may also apply for grants. These entities plan, develop and carry out the services for students. While individual students are served by these entities, they may not apply for grants under these programs. Additionally, in order to be served by one of these programs, a student must be eligible to receive services and be accepted into a funded project that serves the institution or school that student is attending or the area in which the student lives.

Educational Opportunity Centers

The Educational Opportunity Centers (EOC) program provides counseling and information on college admissions to qualified adults who want to enter or continue a program of postsecondary education. The program also provides services to improve the financial and economic literacy of participants. An important objective of the program is to counsel participants on financial aid options, including basic financial planning skills, and to assist in the application process. The goal of the EOC program is to increase the number of adult participants who enroll in postsecondary education institutions.

Ronald E. McNair Postbaccalaureate Achievement

Through a grant competition, funds are awarded to institutions of higher education to prepare eligible participants for doctoral studies through involvement in research and other scholarly activities. Participants are from disadvantaged backgrounds and have demonstrated strong academic potential. Institutions work closely with participants as they complete their undergraduate requirements. Institutions encourage participants to enroll in graduate programs and then track their progress through to the successful completion of advanced degrees. The goal is to increase the attainment of Ph.D. degrees by students from underrepresented segments of society.

Student Support Services

Through a grant competition, funds are awarded to institutions of higher education to provide opportunities for academic development, assist students with basic college requirements, and to motivate students toward the successful completion of their postsecondary education. Student Support Services (SSS) projects also may provide grant aid to current SSS participants who are receiving Federal Pell Grants (# 84.063). The goal of SSS is to increase the college retention and graduation rates of its participants.

Talent Search Program

The Talent Search program identifies and assists individuals from disadvantaged backgrounds who have the potential to succeed in higher education. The program provides academic, career, and financial counseling to its participants and encourages them to graduate from high school and continue on to and complete their postsecondary education. The program publicizes the availability of financial aid and assist participant with the postsecondary application process. Talent Search also encourages persons who have not completed education programs at the secondary or postsecondary level to enter or reenter and complete postsecondary education. The goal of Talent Search is to increase the number of youth from disadvantaged backgrounds who complete high school and enroll in and complete their postsecondary education.

Upward Bound Program

Upward Bound provides fundamental support to participants in their preparation for college entrance. The program provides opportunities for participants to succeed in their precollege performance and ultimately in their higher education pursuits. Upward Bound serves: high school students from low-income families; and high school students from families in which neither parent holds a bachelor's degree. The goal of Upward Bound is to increase the rate at which participants complete secondary education and enroll in and graduate from institutions of postsecondary education.

Upward Bound Math-Science

The Upward Bound Math and Science program is designed to strengthen the math and science skills of participating students. The goal of the program is to help students recognize and develop their potential to excel in math and science and to encourage them to pursue postsecondary degrees in math and science, and ultimately careers in the math and science profession.

Chapter 44

Institutional Education Grants

Institutional Aid

Many colleges and universities, both public and private, provide grant aid to undergraduates to help them pay for all or part of the tuition and fees charged by the institution. This practice, often referred to as "tuition discounting," has grown rapidly in recent years. Depending on the type and selectivity of the institution, institutional aid is awarded for different reasons. Some institutions aim to promote access to low-income and otherwise disadvantaged students, others use institutional aid to increase the enrollment of meritorious students, and still others use it to increase tuition revenues. Many institutions are trying to accomplish more than one of these goals simultaneously. Through the packaging of need-based and merit-based aid, different institutions use different strategies. For example, a need-within-merit strategy uses merit criteria, but prioritizes the recipients on the basis of need, whereas a merit-within-need strategy awards aid on the basis of need, but prioritizes the recipients on the basis of merit.

Academic Merit, Financial Need, And Institutional Grant Aid Among First-Year Students

Institutional aid can be awarded on the basis of financial need, academic merit, or both need and merit. In addition, depending on the selectivity of the institution, institutional aid packages and amounts may vary.

About This Chapter: This chapter includes text excerpted from "What Colleges Contribute," National Center For Education Statistics (NCES), U.S. Department of Education (ED), May 4, 2015.

Many of the differences observed in institutional grant aid awards are related to the selectivity of the institution. For example, in both public and private not-for-profit institutions, the likelihood of awarding institutional aid in very selective institutions do not vary significantly with students' academic merit, whereas in less selective institutions, it did. In less selective institutions, as students' high school academic merit increased, so did their likelihood of receiving institutional grant aid.

Differences by institution selectivity were also evident when examining the relationship between institutional aid awards and students' financial need, especially in the private sector. In very selective private not-for-profit institutions, as students' financial need rose, so did their likelihood of receiving institutional grant aid, from 21 percent of those with low financial need, to 59 percent with moderate need, to 66 percent with high need. In less selective institutions, on the other hand, while there was an association between institutional aid awards and financial need, fully one-half (51 percent) of students with low financial need received institutional grant aid, as did 71 percent of both those with moderate and high need.

In both less selective and very selective public institutions, students' likelihood of receiving institutional grant aid was clearly associated with their financial need. Students with no financial need were less likely to receive institutional grant aid than their counterparts with high need. However, students with no financial need were more likely to receive institutional grant aid in less selective institutions than in very selective institutions, whereas those with high need were more likely to receive aid in very selective institutions.

When looking at students' financial need in relation to their high school academic merit, positive associations between students' financial need and the likelihood of receiving institutional aid awards remained for those who had achieved no higher than moderate levels of high school academic merit. This was observed for all institution types, including less selective private not-for-profit institutions: at such institutions, among those who had achieved moderate levels of academic merit, 69 percent with high need received institutional grant aid, compared with 47 percent with low need. However, as discussed below, for students who had achieved high levels of academic merit, whether or not they received institutional grant aid in less selective institutions did not vary significantly with their financial need.

Students With High Academic Merit

Students enrolled in less selective institutions who had achieved high academic merit in high school were more likely to receive institutional grant aid than their high-merit counterparts in very selective institutions. This was observed for both public institutions (52 vs. 27

percent) and private not-for-profit institutions (87 vs. 51 percent). However, in less selective institutions, no association could be detected between the likelihood of high-merit students receiving institutional grant aid and their financial need.6 In private not-for profit less selective institutions, for example, roughly 9-in-10 high-merit students received institutional grant aid regardless of their financial need. In very selective institutions, on the other hand, high-merit students with high financial need were more likely to receive institutional aid than their counterparts with low (or no) need.

For high-merit students who received institutional grant aid, the average amount received as a percentage of tuition varied by institution selectivity in private not-for-profit institutions: those in very selective institutions received about 58 percent of their tuition amounts, compared with 46 percent in less selective institutions. However, in the same sector, only in very selective institutions did the amount of institutional aid received vary by aid recipients' financial need. Specifically, in very selective institutions, high-merit recipients with high financial need received enough institutional grant aid to pay for about two-thirds of their tuition, compared with about one-half of tuition for high-merit recipients with moderate or low need. In less selective private not-for-profit institutions, on the other hand, no difference in the average amounts received by high-merit recipients could be detected among students in terms of their financial need.

Tuition in public institutions is typically much lower than it is in comparable private not-for-profit institutions. Due to large variations in the amounts received, in particular for students with no financial need, statistical differences in aid amounts could be detected only for high-merit aid recipients in less selective public institutions. Among such students, those with high need received enough aid to pay 96 percent of their tuition, compared with recipients with moderate need who received only enough aid to pay 64 percent of their tuition.

Chapter 45
Private Education Loans

More than two-thirds of college students must borrow money to help cover the costs of their education. The vast majority of student loans (91% as of 2014) come from lending programs funded by the U.S. government. Federal education loans are a good option for students and their families because they offer low, fixed interest rates and generous borrower protections. You are allowed to defer or postpone repaying your loan under certain circumstances, for instance, and you can apply to adjust the amount of your payments based on your income. But federal loan programs place annual and cumulative limits on how much you can borrow, so some students must seek additional financing in the form of private education loans.

Private or alternative education loans are funded by private, commercial lenders, such as banks, credit unions, credit card companies, and online lenders. Some of the most prominent companies that offer private student loans include Citizens Bank, College Ave, Common Bond, Discover, Navient, PNC Bank, Sallie Mae, SoFi, and Wells Fargo. Private student loan programs vary widely in terms of the interest rates, fees, loan limits, loan terms, and repayment options they offer. Since commercial lenders are in business to make a profit, however, private student loans are usually more expensive for borrowers than federal student loans.

Apply For Federal Student Loans First

College financial aid officers recommend considering private student loans only after you have exhausted all other options for covering the costs of your education, including savings, scholarships, grants, work-study income, and federal student loans. Before applying for private loans, you should fill out and submit the *Free Application for Federal Student Aid* (FAFSA®).

"Private Education Loans," © 2017 Omnigraphics.

Both the federal and state governments use FAFSA® information to determine whether you qualify for government assistance based on financial need. Even if you are not eligible for need-based financial aid, you can still qualify for unsubsidized federal student loans, which are not based on financial need.

The amount you can borrow in federal student loans depends on your cost to attend college, how much other financial aid you receive, your year in school, and whether you are considered a dependent of your parents. If you borrow the maximum amount and still cannot meet your college expenses, then you may have to take out private student loans. Private loans are also the only option available to graduates of medical school or law school who need funds to cover the cost of obtaining professional qualifications, such as taking the bar exam or finding a medical residency. Federal student loans are not available for these purposes.

Factors To Consider With Private Loans

If you decide that you need to take out a private education loan, it is important to compare the interest rates, fees, borrower protections, repayment plans, and customer service offered by various lenders. Here are some important factors to consider:

- **Your credit history and co-signers**

  Keep in mind that the final cost of the loan and the amount you are able to borrow will be based on your credit history. Private lenders prefer borrowers who have good credit, a solid employment history, and enough cash or assets on hand to make loan payments in an emergency. As a result, many college students can only obtain private loans if a parent or guardian co-signs the loan agreement.

- **Interest rates**

  The interest rates on private student loans may be fixed or variable. Fixed interest rates remain the same for the entire life of the loan. Variable rates, on the other hand, carry some risk because they can increase or decrease depending on general economic conditions. Some lenders offer low, introductory interest rates while you are in school that increase once you graduate. Others offer discounted interest rates following a certain number of on-time payments.

- **Fees**

  The fees charged by lenders can add to the cost of the loan. Experts point out that every 3 percent to 4 percent increase in loan fees is roughly equivalent to paying a 1 percent higher interest rate. Most lenders reserve the most favorable interest rates and lowest fees for customers with excellent credit histories, and only about 20 percent of borrowers qualify. If you have poor credit, you should expect to pay up to 6 percent higher interest rates and 9 percent higher fees than lenders advertise for their best customers.

- **Borrower protections**

  Private education loan packages can include various options for borrowers. Some lenders offer options for you to defer payments while you are enrolled in school, during a six-month grace period after you graduate, or later if you experience financial hardship. Other lenders offer flexible repayment plans that are based on your income. In most cases, however, adding these sorts of options will increase the cost of the loan.

Did You Know...

According to the Institute for College Access and Success, 47 percent of private student loan borrowers failed to maximize their use of safer, more affordable federal student loans before applying for private loans during the 2011–2012 academic year.

Many colleges will provide students with a list of preferred lenders for private education loans. Although schools are not allowed to recommend a specific lender, these lists usually only include lenders that offer fair loan terms and good customer service. Research each lender option, compare the features of various loans carefully, and only borrow what you need and can manage to repay.

References

1. "Nine Best Private Student Loan Options In 2017," NerdWallet, 2017.

2. "Private Education Loan Checklist," Office of Financial Aid, Brown University, November 2015.

3. "Private Education Loans," FinAid, 2017.

Chapter 46

AmeriCorps Education Awards

The Segal AmeriCorps Education Award is a postservice benefit received by individuals who complete terms of national service in approved AmeriCorps programs, such as AmeriCorps VISTA, AmeriCorps NCCC, or AmeriCorps State and National. The award is named after Eli Segal, one of the pioneers of the national service movement and the first CEO of the federal Corporation for National and Community Service (CNCS).

A person who serves in an AmeriCorps program is known as an AmeriCorps member. AmeriCorps members serving in full-time terms of national service are required to complete the service within 12 months. Upon successful completion of the service, members are eligible to receive a Segal AmeriCorps Education Award.

The education award may be used to pay educational costs at eligible postsecondary educational institutions (including many technical schools and GI-Bill approved educational programs), as well as to repay qualified student loans. The dollar amount of a full-time education award is tied to the maximum amount of the U.S. Department of Education's (ED) Pell Grant. Since the amount of a Pell Grant can change from year to year, the amount of an education award can vary from year to year. Currently, AmeriCorps members may earn up to the value of two full-time education awards and have seven years from the date they earned each award to use it.

Members can divide up an award and use portions of it at different times before it expires, as long as it is for authorized expenditures. A person could, for example, apply a portion of it to existing qualified student loans and save the remainder to pay for authorized college costs a few years down the road.

About This Chapter: This chapter includes text excerpted from "Segal AmeriCorps Education Award," Corporation for National and Community Service (CNCS), May 25, 2016.

Since the program's founding in 1994, almost 1 million AmeriCorps members have earned more than $2.4 billion in education awards.

AmeriCorps VISTA members are uniquely eligible to earn an end-of-year cash stipend in lieu of an education award.

Legislation was passed in 2009 to allow certain senior AmeriCorps members to transfer their education awards to their children or grandchildren under specific conditions.

The Internal Revenue Service (IRS) has determined that payments made from an education award are considered to be included in a member's taxable income in the tax year the payment was made to the school or loan holder. Interest payments are also considered taxable income.

The award, which was designed to encourage AmeriCorps alumni to seek postsecondary education opportunities, serves as a powerful recruitment tool for individuals to join AmeriCorps. Studies show that AmeriCorps alumni, with their commitment to service, also make excellent students. A growing number of higher education institutions are "matching" the education award with scholarships and/or academic credits in order to encourage AmeriCorps alumni to enroll in their institutions.

Amount, Eligibility, And Limitations Of Education Awards

Award Amount

The amount of a full-time education award is equivalent to the maximum value of the Pell Grant for the award year in which the term of national service is approved. Prior to fiscal year 2010, the amount of an education award had remained the same since the AmeriCorps program began.

The amount of the Pell Grant can change every year. Therefore, the amount of a full-time award can change in the future. However, once a member earns an award, the dollar value of that particular award will not increase. For all programs, award amounts for part-time terms of service vary based upon the length of the required term of service.

As a reference, here is a chart that shows the amounts of education awards for various types of national service positions that are approved (effective) in fiscal year 2017, which begins October 1, 2016.

Table 46.1. Segal Education Award Amounts Effective October 1, 2016

Participation Type	Minimum # Of Hours	Amount
Full-Time	1,700	$5,815.00
Half-Time	900	$2,907.50
Reduced Half-Time	675	$2,215.24
Quarter-Time	450	$1,538.36
Minimal-Time and Summer Associate	300	$1,230.69

Members should check with their programs or project sponsors to confirm the amount of the awards for which they are eligible.

Eligibility To Receive An Award

You are eligible for a Segal AmeriCorps Education Award if you successfully complete a term of service with one of the following approved AmeriCorps programs in accordance with your member contract:

- AmeriCorps State and National Program
- AmeriCorps VISTA Program
- AmeriCorps NCCC Program

There are limitations on both the number of terms an individual can serve in each of the three programs and limits on the value of education awards a person can receive. A member serving in a full-time term of service is required to complete the service within 12 months.

Special Option For VISTA Members

As an alternative to the Segal AmeriCorps Education Award, AmeriCorps VISTA members may choose to receive a postservice cash stipend at the end of their service. VISTA alumni who chose the stipend may also be eligible for up to 15 percent cancelation on certain types of loans for their service. AmeriCorps VISTA members who choose to receive an education award for their service are not eligible to receive this cancelation; only those members who elect the cash stipend.

You can contact the U.S. Department of Education's (ED's) Federal Student Aid Information Center to determine what student loans may be eligible for this type of cancelation and to receive forms. Their toll-free number is 800-433-3243.

Limits On The Number Of Terms You Can Serve

Currently, the maximum numbers of terms that an individual can serve in each AmeriCorps program are:

- four terms for AmeriCorps State and National programs

- five one-year terms for VISTA programs

- two terms for NCCC programs

For AmeriCorps State and National programs, each term of service for which an individual earned any education award counts as one term of service in computing the limits on the term limitations. This includes terms for which a member earned a full-time, half-time, and any other type of part-time or prorated education award. A pro-rated education award is an award that may be earned when an individual, for reasons beyond his or her control, cannot complete the entire service period.

Generally, if you are released for cause before completing your term of service and do not receive an education award, that term counts as one of your terms served.

Limit On The Value Of Education Awards You Can Receive

There is a limit on the value of education awards that an individual is allowed to receive. The "value" of an education award is distinct from the dollar "amount" of an award. By law, an individual may not receive more than the aggregate (or total) value of two full-time education awards.

The value of an education award refers to the service opportunity offered by a particular term of service, such as full-time, half-time, and summer terms of service. As examples, the value of a full-time award is always "1.0"; the value of a half-time award is always "0.5." While the dollar amount of an award for a particular term of service may change over time, the value of that award remains constant.

The value of every education award received is calculated by taking the actual amount of the education award received for the service and dividing it by the amount of a full-time award in the fiscal year in which the national service position was approved.

Current and former AmeriCorps members can keep track of the value of education awards they have received through their accounts in the online system, *My AmeriCorps*. In their accounts, each award they have earned shows both the award amount and the award value.

Education Award Payments

You have seven years to use the education award from the date of your completion of AmeriCorps service. You can divide up your award and use portions of it at different times, as long as it is for authorized expenditures within the specified time period. You could, for example, apply a portion of it to existing qualified student loans, and save the remainder to pay for authorized college costs a few years down the road.

The Trust cannot make payments to anyone other than eligible schools and qualified loan holders. See your financial aid counselor for information on how they handle disbursements and reimbursements.

If you withdraw from the school where you have used the education award, the school may be required to refund the Trust. If any refund is owed, it is credited to your education award account, and is subject to the award's original expiration date (seven years from the date the award was earned).

> Under certain circumstances, you can use the education award to study outside the United States.

Award Transfers

The Serve America Act allows for the transfer of AmeriCorps State and National and Silver Service education awards under specific conditions which are stated in the Act. The individuals who have earned the awards have to have been at least 55 years old when they began their terms of service and each person to whom an award is transferred has to be the transferring individual's child (including step-child), grandchild (including step-grandchild), or foster child.

Each award can be transferred only once. The entire unspent balance can be transferred or a portion of the balance can be transferred.

To transfer an award, an individual must:

- have earned an education award in an AmeriCorps State and National or a Silver Scholar term of service;

- have been at least 55 years of age before beginning the term of service for the subject award;

- have begun this term of service on or after October 1, 2009;

- transfer the award before the original expiration date;

- designate all or a portion of the unused award for the transfer; and

- complete the forms authorizing the transfer, which includes providing information and certifying eligibility to make the transfer.

Taxes

The IRS has determined that payments made from an education award are considered to be included in a member's taxable income in the year the payment is made to the school or loan holder. Interest payments are also considered taxable income. This increase in your income could affect your tax liability for that year.

Chapter 47

The Peace Corps And Leadership Experience

Changing Lives The World Over

The Peace Corps is a service opportunity for motivated changemakers to immerse themselves in a community abroad, working side by side with local leaders to tackle the most pressing challenges of our generation.

The Peace Corps Mission

To promote world peace and friendship by fulfilling three goals:

1. To help the people of interested countries in meeting their need for trained men and women.

2. To help promote a better understanding of Americans on the part of the peoples served.

3. To help promote a better understanding of other peoples on the part of Americans.

History

For more than five decades, Peace Corps Volunteers in 140 countries have demonstrated ingenuity, creativity, and grit to solve critical challenges alongside community leaders.

Through the years, Peace Corps Volunteers have been connected by their passion for service and love for their host countries.

About This Chapter: Text beginning with the heading "Changing Lives The World Over" is excerpted from "Changing Lives The World Over," Peace Corps, January 27, 2017; Text under the heading "Frequently Asked Questions" is excerpted from "Peace Corps And Repayment Of Your Federal Student Loans," Federal Student Aid, U.S. Department of Education (ED), December 22, 2016.

The transformative impact of the Peace Corps on the communities they serve and the Volunteers themselves can be measured in many ways. A shared cup of tea with a host mother that leads to a greater understanding of Americans. A new school library built, or a safe latrine where there wasn't one before. A young boy prepared to serve his own community, a young girl who sees herself as equal to her male classmates. A Volunteer with a clear career path and a lifelong passion. Here are just some of the ways the Peace Corps measures impact.

In the field

- Fighting HIV/AIDS
- Fighting Hunger
- Protecting the Environment
- Improving Access to Technology

In the community

Peace Corps Volunteers leave a legacy in the lives of the community members they reach, educate, and inspire. Some of those young people grow up to be extraordinary leaders, including engineers, doctors, and government officials.

In career success

Returned Peace Corps Volunteers have gone on to achieve extraordinary success in all kinds of fields.

Some, inspired by their service, stay in education or health-related professions, or choose to join the Foreign Service. Others pursue careers in business, from entrepreneurial startups to management at major companies.

Returned Peace Corps Volunteers are working as journalists, writers, members of Congress, and even astronauts.

Leadership

The Peace Corps is an independent agency within the executive branch of the United States government.

The President of the United States appoints the Peace Corps Director and deputy director, and the appointments must be confirmed by the U.S. Senate.

Initially established by President John F. Kennedy by Executive Order on March 1, 1961, the Peace Corps was formally authorized by the Congress on September 22, 1961, with passage of the Peace Corps Act.

The Peace Corps enjoys bipartisan support in Congress. Senators and representatives from both parties have served as Volunteers.

The Senate Committee on Foreign Relations and House Committee on Foreign Affairs are charged with general oversight of the activities and programs of the Peace Corps. The Peace Corps' annual budget is determined each year by the congressional budget and appropriations process. Funding for the Peace Corps is included in the State, Foreign Operations, and Related Programs Appropriations bill. Generally, the Peace Corps budget is about 1 percent of the foreign operations budget. The Peace Corps is continuously working to provide the highest quality support to Volunteers, particularly in the areas of health, safety, and security.

Strategic Partners Of The Peace Corps

The Peace Corps is passionate about working with strategic partners to strengthen the impact of their mission, both at home and abroad.

Through their collaborations, they have provided new opportunities for Volunteers and their communities, exchanged knowledge and best practices in development, and funded projects that make a difference in the countries where they work.

Peace Corps are committed to working with organizations across the public and private sectors to create high-impact strategic partnerships. Here are some of their current collaborators:

- Nonprofits

- Corporations and local businesses

- National and local governments

- Philanthropic institutions

- Academic institutions

They are always interested in developing new relationships that optimize their mutual strengths. Here are some of their successful partnership areas:

- Programming or field-based collaboration

- Support for projects developed and implemented by Volunteers and their communities

- Recruitment of Volunteers
- Career development opportunities for returned Volunteers

Global Initiatives

Their work at the forefront of change is turning the world's challenges into shared triumphs.

U.S. Government Let Girls Learn Initiative

Educating girls is essential to healthy and thriving communities but, globally, 62 million girls are not in school, and barriers to adolescent girls completing school are particularly significant. In some countries, fewer than 10 percent of teenage girls complete secondary school. Since the launch of Let Girls Learn, Peace Corps Volunteers around the world have responded to the call to make a difference in their communities of service.

President's Malaria Initiative

Peace Corps Volunteers are advancing President's Malaria Initiative through the agency's Stomping Out Malaria in Africa initiative. Volunteers in 22 Peace Corps programs across Africa are collaborating to eradicate malaria by carrying out malaria prevention, diagnosis, and treatment education campaigns at the community level.

Global Food Security And Feed The Future

In partnership with the U.S. Agency for International Development (USAID), Peace Corps Volunteers are supporting the President's Feed the Future initiative by promoting sustainable methods for local people to assure their own food security through increased agricultural productivity, improved economic opportunity, and improved health and nutrition.

President's Emergency Plan For AIDS Relief

Through the President's Emergency Plan for AIDS Relief (PEPFAR), Peace Corps Volunteers continue to implement PEPFAR's Blueprint to an AIDS-free generation through the targeted goals of scaling up prevention and treatment; implementing evidence-based interventions for populations at greatest risk; promoting sustainability, efficiency, and effectiveness; strengthening local healthcare and support systems; and driving results with science.

Benefits

Peace Corps service asks a lot of you. But it also has a lot to give. While you serve others, you will be gaining benefits that last through your Volunteer service and well beyond.

Financial Benefits

The Peace Corps provides each Volunteer with housing and a living stipend that enables them to live in a manner similar to people in their community of service. Unlike other international volunteer programs, there is no charge to participate in the Peace Corps. There is no application fee, although costs may only be partially covered for required medical examinations during the application process.

Upon completion of two years of service, the Peace Corps provides each Volunteer with more than $8,000 (pre-tax) to help with the transition to life back home. This money is yours to use as you wish.

Student Loan Benefits

Student loans are your responsibility while you are in service, but certain public student loans may be eligible for deferment or for Public Service Loan Forgiveness by your lender.

Perkins loans may be eligible for partial cancellation by your lender.

While serving, Volunteers are still responsible for any student loans they have. But, there may be benefits available to you, including deferment, partial cancellation, income-driven repayment, or forgiveness. Potential benefits depend on the type of loan you have (federal or private), the specific loan you have (Perkins, Stafford, Federal Direct, Federal Direct Consolidated, etc.), and what you intend to do after service. Research your options carefully, as you may not be eligible for all benefits and your individual circumstances will determine the best option for you.

(Source: "Student Loan Information," Peace Corps.)

Travel Benefits

The Peace Corps covers the cost of transportation to and from the country of service. Each Volunteer receives two paid vacation days per month of service, and many use this time to travel to nearby countries. Some invite family or friends to visit so they can share their experience of the host country. And, of course, Volunteers can use this time for a visit home (at their own expense). Paid leave is available in the event of family emergencies.

Medical And Dental Benefits

The Peace Corps provides medical and dental care that covers all related expenses during service, including preventative care, and issues incurred during your training period, service, or on vacation. In the case of a health problem that cannot be treated in your host country, you will be sent to a nearby country or the United States at no cost to you.

Returned Volunteers may be eligible for workers' compensation for injuries incurred during their service, although this program is managed by the U.S. Department of Labor (DOL) and not by the Peace Corps.

Career Benefits

The Peace Corps provides rigorous technical training at the start of service, which includes in-depth intercultural and language instruction, usually from a native speaker.

Throughout service, Volunteers have regular opportunities to gain new skills related to work, language, culture, and safety. This training makes returned Peace Corps Volunteers highly in demand by corporate, nonprofit, and government employers seeking candidates with the skills required in today's global economy.

Public Loan Service Forgiveness

Peace Corps Volunteer service is considered qualifying employment for the Department of Education's Public Service Loan Forgiveness (PSLF) Program. If you are working full-time for a qualifying employer, PSLF forgives the remainder of certain federal loans after 120 monthly payments are made under a qualifying repayment plan. Under a qualifying repayment plan, your payments could be $0 per month while volunteering. Signing up at the beginning of your service allows you to make the greatest number of qualifying payments.

(Source: "Student Loan Information," Peace Corps.)

The Peace Corps offers career support specifically tailored to Volunteers when they return home to help them prepare for their next step:

- Help translating their field experience to prospective employers

- Advantages in federal employment and hiring benefits related to noncompetitive eligibility and possible credit toward retirement should they meet qualifications

- Access to job announcements, résumé services, and career fairs

- Other special eligibility for hiring preferences by organizations designated as Employers of National Service

Returned Peace Corps Volunteers have gone on to successful careers in all kinds of fields, from international development to business to the arts.

Graduate School Benefits

Graduate schools recognize the valuable service experience returned Peace Corps Volunteers bring to underserved communities at home. The Paul D. Coverdell Fellows program partners offer returned Peace Corps Volunteers reduced tuition, assistantships, and stipends at more than 90 participating universities and colleges.

Federal Loans

If you have federal student loans, such as Stafford, Perkins, direct, and consolidated loans, you may be eligible for deferment, partial cancellation, income-driven repayment, or eligibility for the Public Loan Service Forgiveness Program during Peace Corps service. Volunteers with Perkins loans may be eligible for a 15–70 percent cancellation benefit.

Private Loans

If you have a private loan, you will need to contact your loan servicer to see if they provide any student loan relief for Peace Corps Volunteer service.

(Source: "Student Loan Information," Peace Corps.)

Become Part Of A Vibrant Network

More than 220,000 Americans have served as Peace Corps Volunteers, making for a highly active and diverse alumni network.

Frequently Asked Questions

I Want To Serve In The Peace Corps, But I'm Concerned About How I Will Repay My Federal Student Loans. Can I Still Join?

If you are serving in the Peace Corps, you have a number of options to help manage the repayment of your federal student loans. You may be eligible to defer repaying them for the duration of your service or enter an income-driven repayment plan, described under question 3 below. Also, your service in the Peace Corps may count toward your eligibility for Public

Service Loan Forgiveness (PSLF), but you must plan ahead. Only loans received under the William D. Ford Federal Direct Loan (Direct Loan) Program are eligible for PSLF. Other federal student loans may become eligible for PSLF if you consolidate them into a Direct Consolidation Loan.

Note: These options do not apply to private education loans. Separate arrangements must be made regarding repayment of those loans

What Is Public Service Loan Forgiveness (PSLF)?

PSLF is intended to encourage individuals to enter and to continue to work full-time in public service employment. Under the PSLF program, you may qualify for forgiveness of the remaining balance of your Direct Loans after you've made 120 qualifying payments (i.e., 10 years' worth of payments) on those loans while employed full-time by certain types of public service employers. Serving in the Peace Corps is considered qualifying employment for the PSLF Program. You do not need to make consecutive payments on your loans to qualify for PSLF, so if you leave your PSLF-qualifying employment but eventually return to public service, your prior qualifying payments continue to count toward the 120 monthly payment total.

How Can I Use My Peace Corps Service To Qualify For Loan Forgiveness?

If you serve full-time in the Peace Corps, you can qualify for PSLF in two ways:

First, you can make qualifying payments under a qualifying repayment plan just like any other Direct Loan borrower seeking PSLF. You would make payments on your Direct Loan for the full duration of your service. Also, to increase the likelihood that you will qualify for loan forgiveness, you should repay your loan under the Pay As You Earn (PAYE), Income-Based Repayment (IBR), or Income-Contingent Repayment (ICR) plans (the "income-driven repayment plans") because these plans are most likely to result in an outstanding balance after you make 120 qualifying payments.

Payments under income-driven repayment plans are based on your annual income, family size, and the amount of your eligible loans. You must submit annual verification of your income and family size to remain eligible under these plans. Note that as those who serve in the Peace Corps do not make significant income, payments under the income-driven plans can be as low as zero dollars per month. Any month your scheduled payment is zero dollars under an income-driven repayment plan, it still counts as a qualifying payment for PSLF. If your scheduled payment is greater than zero dollars per month under the same type of plan, you must make that full payment, and it must be made on time for it to qualify for PSLF.

Second, you can apply for an economic hardship deferment for the period of your Peace Corps service and then use the transition payment you receive after completing your service to make a lump sum payment on your Direct Loan. The lump sum payment, if made within six months of receiving your transition payment, will result in up to 12 qualifying payments for PSLF. The number of qualifying payments you make is determined by dividing the amount of your lump sum payment by the amount of your scheduled monthly payment at the time you entered Peace Corps service, but you may not make more than 12 monthly payments toward the PSLF payment requirement. For example, if, when you entered the Peace Corps, you were required to make a monthly payment of $400 and you requested the economic hardship deferment, you could make a lump sum payment of $4,800 from your transition payment and thus be credited for the maximum of 12 qualifying monthly payments toward PSLF forgiveness. If you serve in the Peace Corps for less than 12 months, you can make only the number of payments equal to the number of months you served. For example, a borrower who serves for six months can use the lump sum to make a maximum of six qualifying payments regardless of the amount of the lump sum payment.

For most borrowers serving in the Peace Corps, declining the deferment and continuing to make monthly payments under an income-driven repayment plan will result in more PSLF-qualifying payments at a significantly lower cost to the borrower than using the transition payment.

I Am Interested In An Income-Driven Repayment Plan To Make Qualifying PSLF Payments During My Peace Corps Service. Are There Other Considerations When Repaying Under These Plans?

Yes. Repaying under an income-driven repayment plan will extend your overall repayment period if you decide later not to pursue or are not eligible for PSLF and will result in increased interest charges. In addition, although any outstanding balance left after 20 or 25 years of repayment under an income-driven repayment plan is forgiven, this amount is considered taxable income for the borrower by the Internal Revenue Service, whereas amounts forgiven under PSLF are not considered taxable income.

What Loans Are Eligible For PSLF? Is There Any Way To Qualify For PSLF If I Have Loans Through The Federal Family Education Loan (FFEL) Program Or Federal Perkins Loan Program?

Only loans you have received under the Direct Loan Program are eligible for PSLF. Loans you received under the FFEL Program, the Perkins Loan Program, or any other federal student loan program are not directly eligible for PSLF. If you have FFEL loans, you may consolidate them into a Direct Consolidation Loan to take advantage of PSLF. You'll want to keep in mind that only the qualifying payments you make on the new Direct Consolidation Loan while working in qualifying public service will count toward the required 120 qualifying payments for PSLF. Payments made on your FFEL loans before you consolidated them, even if they were made during qualifying service, do not count as qualifying PSLF payments.

In addition, any payments that you made on a Direct Loan that qualified towards PSLF will no longer count if you consolidate that loan into a Direct Consolidation Loan. In other words, consolidating a loan means you reset the number of qualifying payments you have made to zero, and you will need to make 120 new payments to qualify for PSLF. It is also important to note that to qualify to repay under the IBR or PAYE plans, you must not include any PLUS loans made to parents in your Direct Consolidation Loan. If you are not sure what kinds of loans you have, contact your loan servicer or check NSLDS.

As with FFEL loans, you may consolidate a Perkins Loan into a Direct Consolidation Loan. Before doing so, you should check with the school where you received your Perkins Loan or with your loan servicer to determine whether or not you qualify for loan cancellation under the Perkins Loan Program. Perkins loan borrowers may receive loan cancellation for eligible service in a variety of public service positions, including service in the Peace Corps. A Perkins borrower may receive partial cancellation of interest and principal for each 12-month period of Peace Corps service for up to four years.

What Should I Do If I've Consolidated A PLUS Loan (Made To Parents) With Other Federal Student Loans In A Direct Consolidation Loan?

The IBR and PAYE plans are not available to borrowers of PLUS Loans made to parents or Direct Consolidation Loans that repaid a PLUS Loan made to parents. However, a Direct Consolidation Loan that repaid PLUS Loans made to parents may be repaid under the ICR Plan, which is also a PSLF-eligible repayment plan.

I Think I Will Qualify For Loan Forgiveness Under PSLF. How Can I Keep Track Of My Eligibility?

It will take at least 10 years for you to make the 120 payments necessary to qualify for PSLF. To assist you in tracking your periods of qualifying employment and payments, the Department of Education has created the Employment Certification for Public Service Loan Forgiveness form (Employment Certification form) for you to complete and submit.

I Think I Will Qualify For Loan Forgiveness Under PSLF. What Steps Should I Follow?

First, check NSLDS to verify that your loans are Direct Loans. Any Direct Loan will have "Direct" in the loan type name. If after checking NSLDS, you are still not sure your federal student loans are Direct Loans, contact the loan servicer (also listed in NSLDS). If you have FFEL Program loans or Perkins Loans, consider consolidating them. Apply for a Direct Consolidation Loan at StudentLoans.gov.

Next, decide which method you will use to make your qualifying payments. If you are going to enter an income-driven repayment plan, first check that you will be able to afford any payment you must make under those plans. Use the Repayment Estimator at StudentAid.gov/repayment-estimator to determine which of these plans may be right for you. If you decide to use an income-driven repayment plan, apply online for that plan at StudentLoans.gov. If you decide to request a deferment of your federal student loans, contact your loan servicer or visit its website to download and complete the Economic Hardship Deferment form.

After you've served in the Peace Corps for a year or when you have finished your service, complete the Employment Certification form for PSLF at StudentAid.gov/publicservice. This will allow you to confirm that your employment and payments qualify for PSLF.

If you use your Peace Corps transition payment to make PSLF-qualifying payments, tell your loan servicer that your payment is not intended to cover future installments, or it may affect your ability to make qualifying payments in the future. Continue making monthly payments on your loan. You may submit the Employment Certification form either before or after making the lump sum payment. When you submit the form, it may help to include a record of the date and amount of your transition payment, the date and amount of your PSLF-qualifying lump sum payment, and a statement that you served in the Peace Corps and intend for your lump sum payment to count toward PSLF. After you complete this process, FedLoan Servicing at www.myfedloan.org will send you notification that provides the number of qualifying payments you've made.

What If I Do Not Plan To Pursue Public Service Or PSLF? How Should I Handle My Federal Student Loans While Serving In Peace Corps?

How you handle your federal student loan payments during your Peace Corps service depends on your personal circumstances and the amount of your loan. For example, if you have significant personal savings and a small loan balance, it may make financial sense for you to make larger payments under a plan, such as the 10-year Standard Repayment Plan, during your Peace Corps service. Making smaller, income-driven payments during your Peace Corps service may result in a larger loan balance that will either need to be repaid or forgiven. If you have a higher loan balance and you are concerned about affording repayment during your service, an income-driven repayment plan or a deferment may be advisable even if you do not plan to pursue PSLF.

In all cases, stay current on your student loan payments during your service. If you do not enroll in an income-driven repayment plan or request an economic hardship deferment and fail to make payments, you may default on your student loans. A default on your loan would have significant consequences, including fees and penalties that will increase your student loan balance and result in negative reports on your credit history. If you do not believe you can afford your regular monthly payments during Peace Corps service, entering an income-driven repayment plan may result in a monthly payment of zero dollars that would avoid a default. The examples at the end of this document show different borrower repayment scenarios that may inform your decision-making.

Chapter 48
Military Service And Education Benefits

Many benefits are available to advance the education and skills of Veterans and Service-members. Spouses and family members may also be eligible for education and training assistance in fact, 25 percent of those benefitting from U.S. Department of Veterans Affairs's (VA) education programs are non-Veterans. Some might find they're eligible for more than one benefit or that one program is more suited to certain education and training goals than another.

Learn about these and other education and training programs administered by VA or start your application now:

- The Post-9/11 GI Bill offers higher education and training benefits to Veterans, Servicemembers, and their families who served after September 10, 2001.

- The Montgomery GI Bill assists active duty and Reservists with the pursuit of higher education degrees, certificates, and other education and training.

- These other VA education and training programs offer various education and training benefits or increased benefits to certain Reservists and Veterans and their survivors and dependents:

- Reserve Educational Assistance Program (REAP)

- Veterans Educational Assistance Program (VEAP)

- Survivors and Dependents Educational Assistance Program (DEA)

- National Testing Program

- National Call to Service Program

About This Chapter: Text in this chapter begins with the excerpts from "Education Programs," U.S. Department of Veterans Affairs (VA), February 27, 2015; Text under the heading "Aid For Military Families" is excerpted from "Aid For Military Families," Federal Student Aid, U.S. Department of Education (ED), November 13, 2016.

Aid For Military Families

Both the federal government and nonprofit organizations offer money for college to veterans, future military personnel, active duty personnel, or those related to veterans or active duty personnel.

What Financial Aid Does The Government Offer For Military Service Or For Family Members Of Military Personnel?

Below are a few sources of financial aid that you might want to consider. You also should explore todaysmilitary.com's list of educational benefits for service members.

Reserve Officers' Training Corps (ROTC) Scholarships

These scholarships are awarded on the basis of merit rather than financial need:

- Army ROTC scholarships are offered at hundreds of colleges. Application packets, information about eligibility, and the telephone number of an ROTC advisor in your area are available from College Army ROTC (www.goarmy.com/rotc.html) or 800-USA-ROTC (800-872-7682).

- The Air Force ROTC college scholarship program targets students pursuing certain foreign language and technical degrees, although students entering a wide variety of majors may be accepted. Information about Air Force ROTC scholarships is available from Air Force ROTC College Scholarship Section (www.afrotc.com) or 866-4-AFROTC (866-423-7682).

- Navy ROTC offers both two-year and four-year scholarships, with options to join the Navy, the Marines, or the Navy Nursing Corps (NC). For information and applications, contact Naval Reserve Officers Training Corps (www.nrotc.navy.mil) or 800-NAV-ROTC (800-628-7682).

- The Marine Officer NROTC Program pays your way through college at approved schools and offers an additional scholarship if you attend one of a list of approved Historically Black Colleges and Universities (HBCUs).

Department Of Veterans Affairs (VA) Education Benefits

The VA offers education benefits for veterans and for their widows and dependents on its GI Bill site.

Iraq And Afghanistan Service Grant Or Additional Federal Pell Grant Funds

If your parent or guardian died as a result of military service in Iraq or Afghanistan after the events of 9/11, you may be eligible for additional aid. To be eligible, at the time of your parent's or guardian's death, you must have been less than 24 years old or enrolled at least part-time at a college or career school. Payments will be adjusted if you are enrolled less than full-time.

- **Federal Pell Grants:** If you meet the requirements above and are eligible to receive a Pell Grant, you will receive an Expected Family Contribution (EFC) of zero, which maximizes your Pell Grant eligibility and can increase your eligibility for other federal student aid programs.

- **Iraq and Afghanistan Service Grants:** If you meet the requirements above but are not eligible for a Pell Grant based on your EFC, you will be eligible to receive the Iraq and Afghanistan Service Grant (IASG). The maximum amount of the Iraq and Afghanistan Service Grant is the same as the maximum Pell Grant award. Your EFC will not be affected, and therefore neither will your eligibility for any need-based federal student aid.

Limited Interest Rates, No Accrual Of Interest, And Deferment Of Student Loans

To receive the benefits below, contact your loan servicer for information about the documentation you must provide to show that you qualify.

- Under the Servicemembers Civil Relief Act (SCRA), if you took out student loans prior to entering the military or being called to active duty, the interest rate on those loans will be limited to 6 percent during your active duty military service. This applies to both federal and private student loans (and other loans as well).

- For all Direct Loans first disbursed on or after October 1, 2008, no interest will be charged for a period of no more than 60 months while you are serving on active duty or performing qualifying National Guard duty during a war, other military operation, or national emergency and are serving in an area of hostilities qualifying for special pay. For Direct Consolidation Loans, this benefit applies to the portion of the consolidation loan that repaid loans first disbursed on or after October 1, 2008.

- You will qualify for deferment of repayment on any of your federal loans while serving on active duty in the military, or performing qualifying National Guard duty, during a war, military operation, or national emergency. If your period of active duty service includes October 1, 2007, or begins on or after that date, your deferment will be extended for an additional 180 days after the demobilization date for each period of qualifying service.

- If you are a member of the National Guard or other reserve component of the U.S. armed forces (current or retired) and you are called or ordered to active duty while you are enrolled at least half-time at an eligible school or within six months of having been enrolled at least half-time, you qualify for deferment of repayment on your federal student loans during the 13 months following the end of your active duty service, or until you return to school on at least a half-time basis, whichever is earlier.

What Financial Aid Do Veterans Service Organizations Offer For Military Service Or For Family Members Of Military Personnel?

The following major national organizations offer scholarships primarily to active duty military, veterans, and/or their families:

- American Legion
- AMVETS (or American Veterans)
- Paralyzed Veterans of America (PVA)
- Veterans of Foreign Wars (VFW)

There are many smaller veterans service organizations around the country that might offer scholarships. Check with your local organization or try a scholarship search.

How Can I Submit A Complaint About How My College Or Career School Is Administering My Financial Aid?

Do you believe your school is not administering federal student aid funds properly? Here's some information that might help you determine how to solve your problem or submit a complaint.

Your college or career school—not the U.S. Department of Education (ED)—will distribute your financial aid. If you have questions about why your aid hasn't been paid out yet, or why it wasn't the amount you expected, contact your school.

IF: You believe your school violated its own policy or federal regulations in its administration of the federal student aid programs—for instance, if

- your school calculated your eligibility for federal student grants, loans, or work-study incorrectly;
- your school disbursed (paid out) your aid or your credit balance incorrectly (in the wrong amount, at the wrong time, or not at all);

- your school doesn't have a financial aid administrator (yet is participating in the federal student aid programs), doesn't have policies or procedures for administering the federal student aid programs, or has policies but isn't following them;

- your school or its representative has made false or misleading statements about the school's educational programs, financial charges, employability of graduates, etc.; and if you have tried to work things out with the school but have been unable to... THEN: You may contact the Federal Student Aid Feedback System or call 844-651-0077.

How Can I Learn More About Military Service?

Contact a recruiter to learn more about service with the following military branches' websites:

- www.marines.com

- www.navy.com

- www.goarmy.com

- www.airforce.com

- www.gocoastguard.com

Part Six
If You Need More Information

Chapter 49
Directory Of Financial Aid Resources

National Sources Of Student Aid

American Indian College Fund (AICF)
8333 Greenwood Blvd.
Denver, CO 80221
Toll-Free: 800-776-FUND (800-776-3863)
Phone: 303-426-8900
Fax: 303-426-1200
Website: www.collegefund.org
E-mail: info@collegefund.org

AmeriCorps
1201 New York Ave., N.W.
Washington, DC 20525
Phone: 202-606-5000
TTY: 800-833-3722
Website: www.nationalservice.gov/programs/americorps
E-mail: questions@americorps.gov

Horatio Alger Association of Distinguished Americans
99 Canal Center Plaza, Ste. 320
Alexandria, VA 22314
Toll-Free: 844-422-4200
Phone: 703-684-9444
Fax: 703-684-9445
Website: www.horatioalger.org

Resources in this chapter were compiled from several sources deemed reliable, February 2017.

National Association for the Advancement of Colored People (NAACP)
4805 Mt. Hope Dr.
Baltimore, MD 21215
Toll-Free: 877-NAACP-98 (877-622-2798)
Phone: 410-580-5777
Website: www.naacp.org

National Merit Scholarship (NMSC)
1560 Sherman Ave., Ste. 200
Evanston, IL 60201-4897
Phone: 847-866-5100
Website: www.nationalmerit.org

Peace Corps
1111 20th St., N.W.
Washington, DC 20526
Toll-free: 855-855-1961
Website: www.peacecorps.gov

Scholarship America
One Scholarship Way
Saint Peter, MN 56082
Toll-Free: 800-537-4180
Phone: 507-931-1682
Website: www.scholarshipamerica.org

SLM Corporation (Sallie Mae Bank)
P.O. Box 3319
Wilmington, DE 19804-4319
Toll-Free: 800-4-SALLIE (800-472-5543)
Phone: 844-827-7478
Fax: 855-756-2011
Website: www.salliemae.com
E-mail: SchoolAssist@salliemae.com

United Negro College Fund (UNCF)
1805 Seventh St., N.W.
Washington, DC 20001
Toll-Free: 800-331-2244
Website: www.action.uncf.org

Online Scholarship Search Services

Adventures In Education
Website: www.adventuresineducation.org/HighSchool/Scholarships/index.cfm

BrokeScholar
Website: www.brokescholar.com

College Board
Website: www.collegeboard.org

College Data
Website: www.collegedata.com/cs/search/scholar/scholar_search_tmpl.jhtml

CSO College Center
Website: www.csocollegecenter.org

FastAid
Website: www.fastaid.com

FastWeb
Website: www.fastweb.com/college-scholarships

GoCollege
Website: www.gocollege.com/financial-aid/scholarships

NextStudent
Website: www.nextstudent.com

Peterson's Financial Aid
Website: www.petersons.com

Sallie Mae's Scholarship Search
Website: www.salliemae.com

Scholarships.com
Website: www.scholarships.com

Additional Information About Planning For Higher Education

American Association of Community Colleges (AACC)
One Dupont Cir., N.W., Ste. 410
Washington, DC 20036
Phone: 202-728-0200
Fax: 202-833-2467
Website: www.aacc.nche.edu

American College Testing (ACT)
Phone: 319-337-1000
Website: www.act.org

American Council on Education (ACE)
One Dupont Cir., N.W.
Washington, DC 20036
Phone: 202-939-9300
Website: www.acenet.edu

College Board
250 Vesey St.
New York, NY 10281
Phone: 212-713-8000
Website: www.collegeboard.org

Council for Opportunity in Education (COE)
1025 Vermont Ave., N.W., Ste. 900
Washington, DC 20005-3516
Phone: 202-347-7430
Fax: 202-347-0786
Website: www.coenet.us

Distance Education and Training Council (DEAC)
1101 17th St., N.W., Ste. 808
Washington, DC 20036
Phone: 202-234-5100
Fax: 202-332-1386
Website: www.deac.org

Let's Get Ready!

50 Bdwy.
25th Fl.
New York, NY 10004
Phone: 646-808-2760
Fax: 646-808-2770
Website: www.letsgetready.org
E-mail: info@letsgetready.org

Mapping Your Future

Toll-Free: 800-374-4072
Website: www.mappingyourfuture.org

National Association for College Admission Counseling (NACAC)

1050 N. Highland St., Ste. 400
Arlington, VA 22201
Toll-Free: 800-822-6285
Phone: 703-836-2222
Fax: 703-243-9375
Website: www.nacacnet.org
E-mail: info@nacacnet.org

National Association for Equal Opportunity in Higher Education (NAFEO)

1800 K St., N.W., Ste. 900
Washington, DC 20006-2202
Phone: 202-552-3300
Fax: 202-552-3330
Website: www.nafeo.org

National Association of Student Financial Aid Administrators (NASFAA)

1101 Connecticut Ave. N.W., Ste. 1100
Washington, DC 20036-4303
Phone: 202-785-0453
Fax: 202-785-1487
Website: www.nasfaa.org
E-mail: info@nasfaa.org

National Center for Education Statistics (NCES)
550 12th St., S.W.
Washington, DC 20202
Phone: 202-403-5551
Website: www.nces.ed.gov

National Collegiate Athletic Association (NCAA)
700 W. Washington St.
P.O. Box 6222
Indianapolis, IN 46206-6222
Phone: 317-917-6222
Fax: 317-917-6888
Website: www.ncaa.org

Saving For College
1151 Pittsford Victor Rd., Ste. 103
Pittsford, NY 14534
Website: www.savingforcollege.com

Texas Guaranteed Student Loan Corporation (TGSLC)
301 Sundance Pkwy.
Round Rock, TX 78681
Toll-Free: 800-252-9743
Phone: 519-219-5700
Website: www.tgslc.org

U.S. Department of Education (ED)
400 Maryland Ave., S.W.
Washington, DC 20202
Toll-Free: 800-USA-LEARN (800-872-5327}
Phone: 319-337-5665
Toll-Free TTY: 800-730-8913
Website: www.ed.gov

Chapter 50
Directory Of State Higher Education Agencies

Alabama

Alabama Commission on Higher Education (ACHE)
100 N. Union St.
Montgomery, AL 36104-3758
Toll-Free: 800-960-7773
Phone: 334-242-1998
Fax: 334-242-0268
Website: www.ache.alabama.gov

Alaska

Alaska Commission on Postsecondary Education (ACPE)
P.O. Box 110505
Juneau, AK 99811-0505
Toll-Free: 800-441-2962
Phone: 907-465-2962
Fax: 907-465-5316
TTY: 907-465-3143
Website: www.acpe.alaska.gov
E-mail: ACPE@alaska.gov

Resources in this chapter were compiled from several sources deemed reliable, February 2017.

Arizona

Arizona Commission for Postsecondary Education (ACPE)

2020 N. Central Ave., Ste. 650
Phoenix, AZ 85004
Phone: 602-258-2435
Fax: 602-258-2483
Website: www.highered.az.gov

Arkansas

Arkansas Department of Higher Education (ADHE)

423 Main St., Ste. 400
Little Rock, AR 72201
Phone: 501-371-2000
Website: www.adhe.edu
E-mail: ADHE_Info@adhe.edu

California

California Student Aid Commission (CSAC)

P.O. Box 419026
Rancho Cordova, CA 95741-9026
Toll-Free: 888-224-7268
Fax: 916-464-8002
Website: www.csac.ca.gov
E-mail: studentsupport@csac.ca.gov

Colorado

Colorado Commission on Higher Education (CCHE)

1560 Bdwy., Ste. 1600
Denver, CO 80202
Phone: 303-866-2723
Fax: 303-866-4266
Website: www.highered.colorado.gov

Connecticut

Connecticut Department of Higher Education

450 Columbus Blvd., Ste. 510
Hartford, CT 06103-1841
Phone: 860-947-1800
Fax: 860-947-1310
Website: www.ctdhe.org

Delaware

Delaware Higher Education Commission (DHEC)

The Townsend Building
401 Federal St., Ste. 2
Dover, DE 19901
Toll-Free: 800-292-7935
Phone: 302-735-4120
Fax: 302-739-5894
Website: www.doe.k12.de.us/domain/226
E-mail: dheo@doe.k12.de.us

District of Columbia

Office of the State Superintendent of Education (OSSE)

810 First St., N.E.
Ninth Fl.
Washington, DC 20002
Phone: 202-727-6436
Website: www.seo.dc.gov

Florida

Office of Student Financial Assistance (OSFA)

Florida Department of Education
Local Metro Area
Tallahassee, Fl
Toll-Free: 800-366-3475
Phone: 850-410-5200
Website: www.floridastudentfinancialaid.org
E-mail: OSFAStudentLoans@fldoe.org

Georgia

Georgia Student Finance Commission (GSFC)
2082 E. Exchange Pl.
Tucker, GA 30084
Toll-Free: 800-436-7442
Phone: 770-724-9000
Fax: 770-724-9089
Website: www.gsfc.georgia.gov

Hawaii

University of Hawaii System (UH)
Office of Student Affairs
2444 Dole St.
Bachman Annex 9, Rm. 5
Honolulu, HI 96822-2399
Phone: 808-956-8753
Website: www.hawaii.edu

Idaho

Idaho State Board of Education (ISDE)
650 W. State St.
Third Fl.
Boise, ID 83702
Phone: 208-334-2270
Fax: 208-334-2632
Website: www.boardofed.idaho.gov/scholarships
E-mail: board@osbe.idaho.gov

Illinois

Illinois Student Assistance Commission (ISAC)
1755 Lake Cook Rd.
Deerfield, IL 60015-5209
Toll-Free: 800-899-4722 (800-899-ISAC)
Fax: 847-831-8549
Website: www.collegeillinois.org
E-mail: isac.studentservices@isac.illinois.gov

Indiana

Indiana Commission for Higher Education (CHE)
101 W. Ohio St.. Ste. 300
Indianapolis, IN 46204-4206
Toll-Free: 888-528-4719
Phone: 317-464-4400
Fax: 317-232-3260
Website: www.in.gov

Iowa

Iowa College Student Aid Commission
430 E. Grand Ave.
Third Fl.
Des Moines, IA 50309-1920
Toll-Free: 877-272-4456
Phone: 515-725-3400
Fax: 515-725-3401
Website: www.iowacollegeaid.gov
E-mail: info@iowacollegeaid.gov

Kansas

Kansas Board of Regents
1000 S.W. Jackson St., Ste. 520
Topeka, KS 66612-1368
Phone: 785-296-3421
Fax: 785-296-0983
Website: www.kansasregents.org

Kentucky

Kentucky Higher Education Assistance Authority (KHEAA)
Frankfort, KY 40602
Toll-Free: 800-928-8926
Phone: 502-696-7200
Website: www.kheaa.com

Louisiana

Louisiana Office of Student Financial Assistance (LOSFA)
602 N. Fifth St.
Baton Rouge, LA 70802
Toll-Free: 800-259-5626
Phone: 225-219-1012
Fax: 225-208-1496
Website: www.osfa.la.gov
E-mail: CustServ@la.gov.

Maine

Finance Authority of Maine (FAME)
5 Community Dr.
P.O. Box 949
Augusta, ME 04332-0949
Toll-Free: 800-228-3734
Phone: 207-623-3263
Fax: 207-623-0095
TTY: 207-626-2717
Website: www.famemaine.com
E-mail: Education@FAMEmaine.com

Maryland

Maryland Higher Education Commission (MHEC)
6 N. Liberty St.
Baltimore, MD 21201
Toll-Free: 800-974-0203
Phone: 410-767-3300
Fax: 410-260-3200
Toll-Free TTY: 800-735-2258
Website: www.mhec.maryland.gov

Massachusetts

Massachusetts Department of Higher Education (MDHE)

Office of Student Financial Assistance
454 Bdwy., Ste. 200
Revere, MA 02151
Phone: 617-391-6070
Fax: 617-727-0667
Website: www.mass.edu
E-mail: osfa@osfa.mass.edu

Michigan

Student Financial Services Bureau (SFSB)

P.O. Box 30047
Lansing, MI 48909-7962
Toll-Free: 888-447-2687 (888-4-GRANTS)
Website: www.michigan.gov/mistudentaid
E-mail: mistudentaid@michigan.gov

Minnesota

Minnesota Office of Higher Education

1450 Energy Park Dr., Ste. 350
St. Paul, MN 55108-5227
Toll-Free: 800-657-3866
Phone: 651-642-0567
Fax: 651-642-0675
Toll-Free TTY: 800-627-3529
Website: www.ohe.state.mn.us

Mississippi

Mississippi Office of Student Financial Aid

3825 Ridgewood Rd.
Jackson, MS 39211-6453
Toll-Free: 800-327-2980
Phone: 601-432-6997
Website: www.mississippi.edu/riseupms/financialaid-state.php
E-mail: sfa@mississippi.edu

Missouri

Missouri Department of Higher Education (MDHE)
205 Jefferson St.
P.O. Box 1469
Jefferson City, MO 65102-1469
Toll-Free: 800-473-6757
Phone: 573-751-2361
Fax: 573-751-6635
Website: www.dhe.mo.gov
E-mail: info@dhe.mo.gov

Montana

Montana Guaranteed Student Loan Program (MGSLP)
2500 Bdwy.
Helena, MT 59601
Website: www.mgslp.org

Nebraska

Nebraska Coordinating Commission for Postsecondary Education (NCCPE)
140 N. Eighth St., Ste. 300
Lincoln, NE 68508
Phone: 402-471-2847
Fax: 402-471-2886
Website: www.ccpe.nebraska.gov

Nevada

Office of the State Treasurer
101 N. Carson St., Ste. 4
Carson City, NV 89701
Toll-Free: 888-477-2667
Phone: 775-684-5600
Fax: 775-684-5781
Website: www.nevadatreasurer.gov

New Hampshire

New Hampshire Postsecondary Education Commission

101 Pleasant St.
Concord, NH 03301-3494
Phone: 603-271-3494
Website: www.education.nh.gov

New Jersey

New Jersey Higher Education Student Assistance Authority (HESAA)

P.O. Box 540
Trenton, NJ 08625-0540
Toll-Free: 800-792-8670
Website: www.hesaa.org
E-mail: Client_Services@hesaa.org

New Mexico

New Mexico Higher Education Department (NMHED)

2044 Galisteo St., Ste. 4
Santa Fe, NM 87505-2100
Toll-Free: 800-279-9777
Phone: 505-476-8400
Fax: 505-476-8453
Website: www.hed.state.nm.us

New York

New York State Higher Education Services Corporation (HESC)

99 Washington Ave.
Albany, NY 12255
Toll-Free: 888-697-4372 (888-NYSHESC)
Phone: 518-473-1574
Website: www.hesc.ny.gov

North Carolina

College Foundation of North Carolina (CFNC)

P.O. Box 41966
Raleigh, NC 27629-1966
Toll-Free: 866-866-2362 (866-866-CFNC)
Fax: 919-821-3139
Website: www.cfnc.org
E-mail: programinformation@CFNC.org

North Dakota

North Dakota University System (NDUS)

600 E. Blvd. Ave., Dept. 215
10th Fl. State Capitol
Bismarck, ND 58505-0230
Phone: 701-328-2960
Fax: 701-328-2961
Website: www.ndus.nodak.edu
E-mail: ndus.office@ndus.edu

Ohio

Ohio Board of Regents

25 S. Front St.
Columbus, OH 43215
Toll-Free: 888-833-1133 (for information specifically about Ohio programs)
Phone: 614-466-6000
Fax: 614-466-5866
Website: www.ohiohighered.org
E-mail: hotline@highered.ohio.gov

Oklahoma

Oklahoma State Regents for Higher Education (OSRHE)

655 Research Pkwy, Ste. 200
Oklahoma City, OK 73104
Toll-Free: 800-858-1840
Phone: 405-225-9100
Website: www.okhighered.org

Oregon

Oregon Student Assistance Commission (OSAC)

1500 Valley River Dr., Ste. 100
Eugene, OR 97401
Toll-Free: 800-452-8807
Phone: 541-687-7400
Fax: 541-687-7414
Toll-Free TTY: 800-735-2900
Website: www.oregonstudentaid.gov
E-mail: osac@hecc.oregon.gov

Pennsylvania

Pennsylvania Higher Education Assistance Agency (PHEAA)

The Office of Consumer Advocacy
1200 N. Seventh St.
Harrisburg, PA 17102
Toll-Free: 800-699-2908
Phone: 717-720-1628
Website: www.myfedloan.org

Rhode Island

Rhode Island Higher Education Assistance Authority (RIHEAA)

560 Jefferson Blvd., Ste. 100
Warwick, RI 02886-1304
Toll-Free: 800-922-9855
Phone: 401-736-1100
Fax: 401-732-3541
TDD: 401-734-9481
Website: www.riheaa.org
E-mail: info@riheaa.org

South Carolina

South Carolina Commission on Higher Education (CHE)

1122 Lady St., Ste. 300
Columbia, SC 29201
Phone: 803-737-2260
Fax: 803-737-2297
Website: www.che.sc.gov
E-mail: cbrown@che.sc.gov

South Dakota

South Dakota Board of Regents (SDBOR)

306 E. Capitol Ave., Ste. 200
Pierre, SD 57501
Phone: 605-773-3455
Fax: 605-773-5320
Website: www.sdbor.edu
E-mail: info@sdbor.edu

Tennessee

Tennessee Student Assistance Corporation (TSAC)

404 James Robertson Pkwy, Ste. 1900
Nashville, TN 37243
Toll-Free: 800-342-1663
Phone: 615-741-1346
Fax: 615-741-6101
Website: www.tn.gov
E-mail: TSAC.AidInfo@tn.gov

Texas

Texas Higher Education Coordinating Board (THECB)

Texas Financial Aid Information Center
1200 E. Anderson Ln.
Austin, TX 78752
Toll-Free: 800-242-3062
Phone: 512-427-6340
Website: www.thecb.state.tx.us

Utah

Utah Higher Education Assistance Authority (UHEAA)

60 S. 400 W.
Board of Regents Bldg. The Gateway
Salt Lake City, UT 84101-1284
Toll-Free: 877-336-7378
Phone: 801-321-7294
Fax: 801-366-8431
Website: www.uheaa.org

Vermont

Vermont Student Assistance Corporation (VSAC)

P.O. Box 2000
Winooski, VT 05404
Toll-Free: 800-642-3177
Website: www.vsac.org
E-mail: info@vsac.org

Virginia

State Council of Higher Education for Virginia (SCHEV)

101 N. 14th St.
James Monroe Bldg. 10th Fl.
Richmond, VA 23219
Phone: 804-225-2600
Fax: 804-225-2604
Website: www.schev.edu
E-mail: communications@schev.edu

Washington

Washington Student Achievement Council (WSAC)

917 Lakeridge Way
Olympia, WA 98502
Toll-Free: 888-535-0747
Phone: 360-753-7800
Website: www.wsac.wa.gov
E-mail: info@wsac.wa.gov

West Virginia

West Virginia Higher Education Policy Commission (WVHEPC)

1018 Kanawha Blvd. E., Ste. 700
Charleston, WV 25301
Phone: 304-558-2101
Website: www.wvhepc.edu

Wisconsin

Wisconsin Higher Educational Aids Board (HEAB)

131 W. Wilson St., Ste. 902
Madison, WI 53703
Phone: 608-267-2206
Fax: 608-267-2808
Website: www.heab.state.wi.us
E-mail: HEABmail@wisconsin.gov

Wyoming

Wyoming Department of Education (WDE)

2300 Capitol Ave.
Hathaway Bldg. Second Fl.
Cheyenne, WY 82002-2060
Phone: 307-777-7675
Fax: 307-777-6234
Website: www.edu.wyoming.gov

U.S. Territories

American Samoa

American Samoa Community College (ASCC)

P.O. Box 2609
Pago Pago, AS 96799
Phone: 684-699-9155
Fax: 684-699 6259
Website: www.amsamoa.edu
E-mail: info@amsamoa.edu

Commonwealth of the Northern Mariana Islands

Northern Marianas College Financial Aid Office
P.O. Box 501250
Saipan, MP 96950
Phone: 670-234-5498
Fax: 670-234-1270
Website: www.marianas.edu

Federated States of Micronesia

Federated States of Micronesia Department of Education (FSMED)
FSM National Government
P.O. Box PS 87, Palikir
Pohnpei, FM 96941
Phone: 691-320-2609
Fax: 691-320-5500
Website: www.fsmgov.org

Guam

University of Guam (UOG)
UOG Station
Mangilao, GU 96923
Phone: 671-735-2288
Website: www.uog.edu
E-mail: finaid@uguam.uog.edu

Puerto Rico

Puerto Rico Council on Higher Education (PRCHE)
P.O. Box 1900
San Juan, PR 00910-19900
Phone: 787-641-7100
Fax: 787-641-2573
Website: www.sheeo.org

Republic of Palau

Republic of Palau Ministry of Education (MOE)

Palau National Scholarship Board
P.O. Box 1608
Koror, Republic of Palau 96940
Phone: 680-488-3608
Fax: 680-488-3602
Website: www.pnsb.org
E-mail: pnsb@palaunet.com

Republic of the Marshall Islands

Marshall Islands Scholarship Grant and Loan Board (MISGLB)

P.O. Box 1436
Majuro, MH 96960
Phone: 692-625-5770
Fax: 692-625-7325
Website: www.rmischolarship.net
E-mail: misglb@ntamar.net

Virgin Islands

Government of the United States Virgin Islands (USVI)

Department of Education, Office of the Commissioner
1834 Kongens Gade
Saint Thomas, VI 00802
Phone: 340-774-0100
Fax: 340-779-7153
Website: www.vide.vi

Index

Index

Page numbers that appear in *Italics* refer to tables or illustrations. Page numbers that have a small 'n' after the page number refer to citation information shown as Notes. Page numbers that appear in **Bold** refer to information contained in boxes within the chapters.

A

ACA *see* Affordable Care Act
academic clubs, extracurricular activities 30
academic competitions, extracurricular activities 30
academic enrichment programs, academic planning 20
academic year
    FAFSA® application 139
    receiving aid 165
    standardized tests 33
    studying abroad 80
"Accepting Aid" (ED) 163n
accreditation
    choosing a college 67
    college 73
    financial aid 69
    transfer credits 73
ACT *see* American College Testing
admissions requirements, admission tests 35
advanced placement courses
    college preparations 25
    9th grade 20
Advancement Via Individual Determination (AVID), defined 28
Adventures In Education, website address 309
Affordable Care Act (ACA), lowering college costs 45
"Aid For Military Families" (ED) 299n

Alabama Commission on Higher Education (ACHE), contact 313
Alaska Commission on Postsecondary Education (ACPE), contact 313
amateurism, college athletes 267
American Association of Community Colleges (AACC), contact 310
American College Testing (ACT)
    contact 310
    defined 34
American Council on Education (ACE), contact 310
American Indian College Fund (AICF), contact 307
American Opportunity Tax Credit (AOTC)
    cost comparison 41
    described 225
    education credits 234
    qualified education expenses 229
    tax benefits 226
American Recovery and Reinvestment Act (ARRA), American Opportunity Tax Credit 225
American Samoa Community College (ASCC), contact 326
American Youth Leadership Program (AYLP), study abroad 81
AmeriCorps
    contact 307
    education awards, overview 281–6

AmeriCorps, *continued*
  Peace Corp transition payment 212
  qualifying employment 209
  see also Segal AmeriCorps Education Award
"An Introduction To 529 Plans" (SEC) 113n
"An Overview Of Federal Aid For Students"
  (Omnigraphics) 139n
AOTC *see* American Opportunity Tax Credit
Arizona Commission for Postsecondary Education
  (ACPE), contact 314
Arkansas Department of Higher Education (ADHE),
  contact 314
"Assessing Yourself And Your Future"
  (Omnigraphics) 3n
assessment tools, described 6
associate's degree program, subsidized loans 196
athletes
  college scholarship, overview 265–8
  extracurricular activities 30
"Athletic Scholarships" (DOS) 265n
"Avoiding Scholarship Scams" (Omnigraphics) 241n
award letter, accepting aid 163
awards
  colleges 10
  financial aid 151
  foreign language fellowships 82
  institutional aid 274
  service commitment 250
AYLP *see* American Youth Leadership Program

B

bachelor of arts (B.A.) degree
  described 10
  earning potential 40
  eligibility 249
bachelor of science (B.S.) degree
  described 10
  earning potential 40
  eligibility 249
BIE *see* Bureau of Indian Education
borrowers
  loan servicers 217
  low-interest loans 195
  Peace Corps services 295
  private education loans 277
  public service loan forgiveness 210
  responsibilities 198
  student loan forgiveness 201

BrokeScholar, website address 309
"Budgeting" (ED) 101n
Bureau of Indian Education (BIE), loan income
  students 182

C

California Student Aid Commission (CSAC), contact 314
campus visits, college prep 27
career clusters, described 53
career school
  aid 143
  checklist 18
  choosing college 75
  cost 44
  expense identification 106
  federal grant 168
  Federal Pell Grant 176
certificate
  accreditation 69
  distance learning schools 52
  financial aid 150
  military service 299
  two-year college 10
certificates of deposit (CDs), saving accounts 99
certification
  eligibility requirements 159
  Federal Pell Grants 175
  National Health Service Corps 257
  PSLF 212
  TEACH-Grant-eligible program 180
"Changing Lives The World Over" Peace Corps 287n
"Choose A College More Easily With The College
  Scorecard" (ED) 67n
"Choosing A College: Questions To Ask" (FTC) 67n
COA *see* cost of attendance
College Board
  contact 310
  website address 309
college costs
  cost comparison 40
  education award payments 285
  overview 43–7
  tabulated *43*
College Data, website address 309
college degrees
  earning **40**
  job opportunities 12
  postcollege earnings 78

college fairs, choosing college 21
College Foundation of North Carolina (CFNC),
    contact 322
college guides, defined 65
"College Preparation Checklist" (ED) 17n
college savings plans
        Coverdell saving accounts 121
        education credits 234
        financial aid eligibility 117
        section 529 plans 113
college selection, overview 67–78
college scorecard
        choosing college 72
        cost comparison 46
        graduation rate 76
college support team, defined 14
Colorado Commission on Higher Education
    (CCHE), contact 314
community college
        described 50
        eligibility 248
        federal grants **167**
        federal student loans 189
        standardized tests 34
community service
        college preparations 27
        Federal Work-Study 221
        NHSC scholarship 263
comparison shopping, described 111
Connecticut Department of Higher Education,
    contact 315
Corporation for National and Community Service
    (CNCS)
        publication
                Segal AmeriCorps Education Award 281n
co-signers, private education loan 278
cost of attendance (COA)
        choosing college 67
        expected financial contribution 153
        Federal Pell Grants 175
        federal student aid 140
        federal student loan funds 87
        financial aid calculation 151
        higher education expenses 124
        nursing scholarship 255
        qualified education expenses 228
        scholarship 239
Council for Opportunity in Education (COE),
    contact 310

Coverdell education savings accounts
        alternative savings options 130
        described 96
        overview 121–7
"Coverdell Education Savings Account" (IRS) 121n
credentials, college 72
credit balance refunds, monthly income 105
credit card
        budgeting 102
        federal student loans 193
        private or alternative education loans 277
        scholarship scam **243**
        tabulated *186*
credit check
        federal student loans **193**
        NURSE Corps Scholarship Program 251
credit unions, private education loans 277
critical shortage facilities, NURSE Corps Scholarship
    Program 247
CSO College Center, website address 309
custodial accounts
        described 97
        overview 129–31
"Custodial Accounts And Trusts"
    (Omnigraphics) 129n

D

default
        forbearance **207**
        loan, tabulated *71*
        loan repayment 74
        Peace Corps 298
        qualifying monthly payment 211
        student loan repayment 198
"Deferment And Forbearance" (ED) 203n
deferments
        federal student loans, overview 203–5
        subsidized and unsubsidized loans 197
degree
        four-year college 10
        graduation rate 76
        international schools 85
        online education 59
        scholarship or fellowship 231
Delaware Higher Education Commission (DHEC),
    contact 315
Dental Admission Test (DAT), described 36
Department of Education (ED) *see* U.S. Department
    of Education

Department of Labor (DOL) *see* U.S. Department of Labor
dependent student
    expected family contribution 155
    federal student loan 87
DETC *see* Distance Education and Training Council
diploma mills, defined 69
diploma school of nursing, defined 249
Direct Consolidation Loans, federal student loan 190
Direct Loans
    federal student loan 190
    Public Service Loan Forgiveness 294
    tabulated *204*
Direct PLUS Loans
    federal student loan 190
    international school 87
Direct Subsidized Loans
    federal student loan 189
    financial aid 151
Direct Unsubsidized Loans
    federal student loan 185
    international school 87
disbursements
    education award payments 285
    receiving aid 165
Distance Education and Training Council (DEAC), contact 310
distance learning, overview 57–60
DOL *see* U.S. Department of Labor
dual enrollment options, distance learning 59

E

economic hardship deferment, Peace Corps 295
ED *see* U.S. Department of Education
"Education Credits" (IRS) 225n
education IRA *see* Coverdell education savings accounts
"Education Programs" (VA) 299n
education tax credits, overview 225–34
educational expenses
    American Opportunity Tax Credit 225
    Coverdell education savings accounts 96, 121
    federal student aid 150, 189
    federal work study 221
    529 plan 114
    NHSC SP 258
    Roth IRA 98

EducationUSA
    publications
        athletic scholarships 265n
        college scholarship guide 265n
        standardized tests 33n
EFC *see* expected family contribution
"The EFC Formula, 2017–2018" (ED) 153n
elementary school
    college prep schools 27
    FWS program 223
    TEACH Grant Program 179
eligibility requirements
    AmeriCorps education award 283
    direct loan 191
    federal student aid 140
    federal work study 223
    529 plan 117
    Free Application for Federal Student Aid 149
    Health Service Corp scholarship 259
    loan forbearance 206
    NURSE Corps Scholarship Program 248
    Pell Grant 176
    qualifying monthly payments 212
    study abroad 85
    TEACH Grant 179
employment
    extracurricular activities 29
    federal student loans **193**
    Peace Corps 297
    Public Service Loan Forgiveness (PSLF) Program 209
    Stokes Scholarship Program 84
English as a Second Language (ESL), community college 50
enrollment contracts, described 71
entrance counseling
    described 197
    international school 88
    receiving aid 165
"Estimation And Calculation Of Aid" (Omnigraphics) 149n
expected family contribution (EFC)
    Federal Pell Grants 301
    federal student aid 140
    529 plan 117
    overview 153–61
extracurricular activities
    choosing a college 63
    college scorecard 75
    overview 29–32

F

FAFSA® *see Free Application for Federal Student Aid*
"FAFSA: Applying For Aid" (ED) 143n
"FAFSA Changes For 2017–18" (ED) 143n
family income
    college expense 95
    financial aid 150
FastAid, website address 309
FastWeb, website address 309
Federal Direct Consolidation Loans *see* Direct
   Consolidation Loans
Federal Direct Subsidized Loans
    Free Application for Federal Student Aid 196
    see also Direct Subsidized Loans
Federal Direct Unsubsidized Loans
    federal student loans 141
    Free Application for Federal Student Aid 196
    international school 87
    see also Direct Unsubsidized Loans
Federal Family Education Loan (FFEL) program
    deferment 203–7
    federal student loans 210
    loan servicer 216
    Public Service Loan Forgiveness (PSLF) 295
federal loans
    choosing a college 73
    federal aid for students 141
    federal student loans **193**
    military service and education benefits 301
    Public Service Loan Forgiveness (PSLF) **292**
    versus private loans, overview 185–7
Federal Pell Grant
    estimating your financial aid 151
    Expected Family Contribution (EFC) 153
    federal education grants **167**
    federal student aid *144*
    military service and education benefits 301
    overview 175–7
    student support services 271
    study abroad 87
"Federal Pell Grants" (ED) 175n
Federal PLUS loan, calculating financial aid 151
Federal Student Aid
    publications
        accepting aid 163n
        applying for aid 143n
        budgeting 101n
        changes in federal students aid 143n

Federal Student Aid
    publications, *continued*
        choosing a college 67n
        college preparation checklist 17n
        deferment and forbearance 203n
        EFC formula, 2017–2018 153n
        Federal Pell Grants 175n
        federal student loans 189n
        federal *versus* private loans 185n
        forgiveness, cancellation, and discharge 209n
        FSEOG 175n
        getting federal student loan 189n
        grants and scholarships 167n
        loan repayment 199n
        loan servicers 215n
        military service and education 299
        Peace Corps and federal loan
        repayment 287n
        postsecondary education option 9n
        preparing for college 17n
        receiving aid 163n
        scholarship information 237n
        study abroad 79n
        TEACH Grant program 179n
        understanding college costs 43n
        work-study jobs 221n
"Federal Student Aid TEACH Grant Program"
   (ED) 179n
federal student loans
    accepting aid 163
    deferment, overview 203–7
    entrance counseling 197
    federal aid for students, overview 139–42
    loan cancellation 209–14
    loan servicer 216
    order of best financial aid *164*
    overview 189–94
    private education loans 277
    repaying federal student loans, overview 199–201
    versus private loans 185
    see also student loans
"Federal Student Loans" (ED) 189n
Federal Supplemental Educational Opportunity
   Grants (FSEOG)
    calculating financial aid 151
    Expected Family Contribution (EFC) 153
    federal grants 167
    federal student aid 140
    overview 175–7

Federal Trade Commission (FTC)
  publication
    choosing a college 67n
"Federal TRIO Programs" (ED) 269n
"Federal Versus Private Loans" (ED) 185n
Federal Work-Study (FWS) Program
  college costs 45
  overview 221–3
"Federal Work-Study (FWS) Program" (ED) 221n
Federated States of Micronesia *see* Micronesia,
  Federated States of
Federated States of Micronesia Department of
  Education (FSMED), contact 327
fees
  budgeting tips 109
  calculating financial aid 151
  choosing a college 73
  college costs 44
  Coverdell education savings accounts 96
  education tax credits 228
  institutional education grants 273
  Peace Corps 298
  prepaid college tuition plans 97
  saving for college 91
  scholarship scam 242
  school costs and net price 67
  section 529 plan 115
FFEL program *see* Federal Family Education Loan
  (FFEL) program
Finance Authority of Maine (FAME), contact 318
financial aid
  accepting and receiving aid 163
  budgeting 105
  choosing a college 68
  deferment 205
  described 14
  education award payments 285
  estimating and calculating aid 149–52
  Expected Family Contribution (EFC) 153
  federal student loans 192
  finding scholarships 238
  postsecondary educational options 11
  section 529 plans 117
financial aid administrator (FAA)
  Expected Family Contribution (EFC) 153
  military service and education benefits 303
financial considerations, searching for a college 65
financial planning skills, Educational Opportunity
  Centers (EOC) 271

"Finding And Applying For Scholarships" (ED) 237n
529 college savings plans
  overview 113–9
  saving for college 96
  savings options 131
forbearance
  deferment 203
  federal and private student loans *186*
  loan payments 200
  overview 205–7
foreign study, government resources 80
"Forgiveness, Cancellation, And Discharge"
  (ED) 209n
"4 Things You Should Consider When Choosing A
  College" (ED) 67n
four-year college
  admissions tests 34
  comparing costs and benefits 40
  federal grants **167**
  postsecondary educational options 9
  saving for college 95
  traditional college options 49
fraud, scholarship scam 241
Free Application for Federal Student Aid (FAFSA®)
  accepting and receiving aid 165
  Expected Family Contribution (EFC) 153
  federal student aid 139
  federal student loans 192
  getting ready for college 22
  overview 143–7
  searching for college 65
  study abroad 85
  TEACH grant 179
FSA *see* federal student aid
"FSEOG (Grants)" (ED) 175n
FTC *see* Federal Trade Commission
FWS *see* Federal Work-Study Program

G

Gaining Early Awareness and Readiness for
  Undergraduate Programs (GEAR UP), college prep
  programs 27
GEAR UP *see* Gaining Early Awareness and
  Readiness for Undergraduate Programs
general educational development (GED) certificate,
  eligibility criteria 150
Georgia Student Finance Commission (GSFC),
  contact 316

GI Bill, military service education benefits 299
gift aid, scholarships 141
GoCollege, website address 309
Government of the United States Virgin Islands
   (USVI), contact 328
grace period
   borrower protections 279
   federal student aid 141
   loan 196
grade point average (GPA)
   college preparatory courses 25
   extracurricular activities 29
   scholarships 15
graduate degree, NURSE Corps Scholarship
   Program 249
graduation rate
   choosing a college 70
   college search 62
   described 76
   Student Support Services (SSS) 271
grants
   college savings 91
   college search 62
   described 140
   federal aid 139
   federal education grants 167
   federal TRIO Programs 270
   financial aid 15
   income taxes 115
   monthly income 105
   students with disabilities 269
"Grants And Scholarships" (ED) 167n
"Grants 101" (OMB) 167n
guidance counselors
   scholarship scam 243
   value of education 39

H

Health Professional Shortage Area (HPSA),
   scholarship program 257
Health Resources and Services Administration
   (HRSA)
   publications
      National Health Service Corps scholarship
      program 257n
      NURSE Corps scholarship program 247n
high-school guidance counselors, described 64

higher education
   affording 16
   benefits 40
   college prep school 27
   community college 51
   Coverdell education savings accounts 121
   federal aid 139
   529 Plan 118
   military service 299
   online education 58
highly qualified teacher, TEACH Grant 181
Horatio Alger Association of Distinguished
   Americans, contact 307
"How To Go To College" (ED) 49n
"How To Repay Your Loans" (ED) 199n
HPSA *see* Health Professional Shortage Area

I

Idaho State Board of Education (ISDE),
   contact 316
Illinois Student Assistance Commission (ISAC),
   contact 316
"Importance Of Extracurricular Activities"
   (Omnigraphics) 29n
independent student
   Expected Family Contribution 155
   federal student loan funds 87
Indiana Commission for Higher Education (CHE),
   contact 317
institutional grants
   college choosing 67
   high academic merit 274
   overview 273–5
interest rates
   custodial accounts 129
   private education loans 277
   savings accounts 99
   student loans 185
Internal Revenue Service (IRS)
   publications
      Coverdell education savings account 121n
      education credits 225n
international baccalaureate (IB), college prep
   curriculum 26
"International Education Programs Service"
   (ED) 79n
International English Language Testing System
   (IELTS), English language ability tests 34

international schools
    study abroad 85
    traditional college options 52
"International Schools" (ED) 79n
international students
    community college 51
    international school 86
    online education 59
    U.S. standardized tests 34
internships
    career experience 135
    extracurricular activities 30
    Harry S. Truman Scholarship Foundation 83
Iowa College Student Aid Commission, contact 317
Iraq and Afghanistan Service Grants (IASG)
    federal grants **167**
    Federal Pell Grant 176
    military families 300

J

job opportunities
    college education 11
    college preparation 17
junior college
    NURSE Corps scholarship program 248
    see also community college

K

Kansas Board of Regents, contact 317
Kennedy-Lugar Youth Exchange and Study Abroad (YES Abroad), defined 80
Kentucky Higher Education Assistance Authority (KHEAA), contact 317
K-12 students, U.S. government resources 80

L

languages
    college courses 13
    extracurricular activities 30
    statistics **31**
legal dependent, described **157**
letters of recommendation, National Health Service Corps Scholarship 262
Let's Get Ready!, contact 311

Lifetime Learning Credit
    defined 234
    education tax credits 225
    income exclusions 232
loan cancellations (discharge, forgiveness)
    overview 209–14
    Peace Corps 296
loan consolidation
    federal loan 190, 193
    loan payment 200
    loan servicer 215
loan forgiveness
    federal student aid 141
    federal student loans 201
    student loan benefits 291
    see also Public Service Loan Forgiveness
Loan Forgiveness Program *see* Public Service Loan Forgiveness (PSLF) Program
"Loan Servicers" (ED) 215n
loans
    accepting aid *164*
    federal student aid 140
    military families 300
    private loans 185
Louisiana Office of Student Financial Assistance (LOSFA), contact 318

M

Mapping Your Future, contact 311
Marshall Islands Scholarship Grant and Loan Board (MISGLB), contact 328
Maryland Higher Education Commission (MHEC), contact 318
Massachusetts Department of Higher Education (MDHE), contact 319
Massive Open Online Course (MOOC), overview 57–60
master's degree, four-year college 10
MBTI *see* Myers-Briggs Type Indicator
military service
    Federal Pell Grants 176
    loan deferment *205*
    overview 299–303
Minnesota Office of Higher Education, contact 319
Mississippi Office of Student Financial Aid, contact 319
Missouri Department of Higher Education (MDHE), contact 320

Montana Guaranteed Student Loan Program (MGSLP), contact 320

MOOC *see* Massive Open Online Course

mutual funds, 529 Plans 115

"My Future, My Way" (ED) 9n

Myers-Briggs Type Indicator (MBTI), described 6

N

National Association for College Admission Counseling (NACAC), contact 311

National Association for Equal Opportunity in Higher Education (NAFEO), contact 311

National Association of Student Financial Aid Administrators (NASFAA), contact 311

National Center for Education Statistics (NCES)
contact 312
publication
institutional education grants 273n

National Collegiate Athletic Association (NCAA)
athletes 265
contact 312
SAT/ACT test 267
scholarships 266

"National Health Service Corps Scholarship Program" (HRSA) 257n

National Merit Scholarship (NMSC), contact 308

National Security Language Initiative for Youth (NSLI-Y), described 81

NCAA *see* National Collegiate Athletic Association

Nebraska Coordinating Commission for Postsecondary Education (NCCPE), contact 320

New Hampshire Postsecondary Education Commission, contact 321

New Jersey Higher Education Student Assistance Authority (HESAA), contact 321

New Mexico Higher Education Department (NMHED), contact 321

New York State Higher Education Services Corporation (HESC), contact 321

NextStudent, website address 309

NHSC *see* National Health Service Corps

North Dakota University System (NDUS), contact 322

Northern Marianas College Financial Aid Office, contact 327

NSLI-Y *see* National Security Language Initiative for Youth

NURSE Corps Scholarship Program—Fiscal Year 2016 Application and Program Guidance" (BHW) 247n

Nursing Scholarship Program, overview 247–56

O

occupations
self-assessment **4**
technical schools 52

Office of Management and Budget (OMB)
publication
grants 167n

Office of Student Financial Assistance (OSFA), contact 315

Office of the State Superintendent of Education (OSSE), contact 315

Office of the State Treasurer, contact 320

Ohio Board of Regents, contact 322

Oklahoma State Regents for Higher Education (OSRHE), contact 322

Omnigraphics
publications
aid estimation 149n
assessing future 3n
avoiding scholarship scams 241n
college preparatory courses 25n
custodial accounts 129n
federal aid for students 139n
importance of extracurricular activities 29n
loans and entrance counseling 195n
online education 57n
private education loans 277n
save for college 91n, 95n
searching for a college 61n
value of education 39n
working during college 133n

"$121 Million Awarded In Grants To Help Improve Outcomes Of Individuals With Disabilities" (ED) 269n

online college search tools 64

online education, overview 57–60

"Online Education And MOOCs (Massive Open Online Course)" (Omnigraphics) 57n

Oregon Student Assistance Commission (OSAC), contact 323

overseas study *see* foreign study

P

parent loan for undergraduate students (PLUS) loan
consolidated PLUS loan 296
described 142
federal loans 185

parent loan for undergraduate students (PLUS) loan,
continued
    forbearance 206
    international school federal aid 87
    non-need-based aid 151
    see also Direct PLUS Loan; PLUS loan
part-time students, federal work-study 221
PCIP *see* pre-existing condition insurance plan
Peace Corps
    contact 308
    overview 287–98
    publication
        leadership experience 287n
"Peace Corps And Repayment Of Your Federal
  Student Loans" Peace Corps 287n
Pell Grants
    expected family contribution 153
    federal grants 41, **167**
    military service benefits 301
    overview 175–7
Pennsylvania Higher Education Assistance Agency
  (PHEAA), contact 323
Perkins Loans
    deferment conditions, tabulated *204*
    described 141
    expected family contribution 153
    federal student loans 185
    Peace Corps volunteer benefits 291, **293**
    Public Service Loan Forgiveness 210, 295
    repayment information contact 218
    tabulated *191*
Peterson's Financial Aid, website address 309
PLUS Loan *see* parent loan for undergraduate
  students loan
postbaccalaureate program
    Federal TRIO programs 270
    TEACH-Grant-eligible program 180
postcollege earnings
    college scorecard 75
    described 77
Post-9/11 GI Bill, Veteran education benefits 299
postsecondary education
    community colleges 50
    Coverdell education savings accounts
    eligibility 123
    federal work-study program 223
    options, overview 9–16
    Segal AmeriCorps Education Award 281
    talent search program 271

pre-existing condition insurance plan (PCIP),
  reducing college costs 45
prepaid tuition plans
    advantages/disadvantages 97
    described 113
    tabulated *114*
"Prepare For College" (ED) 17n
private education loans, overview 277–9
"Private Education Loans" (Omnigraphics) 277n
promissory note
    described 165
    master promissory note 192
PSLF Program *see* Public Service Loan Forgiveness
  Program
Public Service Loan Forgiveness (PSLF) Program
    described 209, 294
    eligible loans 210, 295
    non-qualifying employers 210
    Peace Corps Volunteer service **292**
Puerto Rico Council on Higher Education
  (PRCHE), contact 327

Q

qualified education expenses
    college savings 93
    Coverdell ESA, tabulated *122*, 231
    described 228, 232
    state qualified tuition programs 230
    tax benefits 92, 131
    tuition deductions 227
qualifying repayment plan
    described 212
    public service loan forgiveness 209, **292**
"Quick Guide" (DOS) 265n

R

"Reasons To Save For College" (Omnigraphics) 91n
"Receiving Aid" (ED) 163n
repayment plans
    choosing the right plan 199
    federal student loan benefits **193**
    federal student loans 186
    loan servicer 215
    Peace Corps deferment 293
    private loans 278
    public service loan forgiveness (PSLF)
    program 209

Republic of Palau Ministry of Education (MOE), contact 328
"Research Your Options" (DOS) 33n
Reserve Officer Training Corps (ROTC)
    described 15
    Project GO (Global Officers) scholarship 82
    scholarships 300
Rhode Island Higher Education Assistance Authority (RIHEAA), contact 323
ROTC *see* Reserve Officer Training Corps
Roth IRA, described 98

S

Sallie Mae Smart Option Loan, private education loans 277
Sallie Mae's Scholarship Search, website address 309
SAT *see* Scholastic Aptitude Tests
SAT Subject Tests
    college preparations 21
    described 34
Saving For College, contact 312
savings bonds
    college savings 99, 118
    UGMA custodial account 129
Scholarship America, contact 308
scholarships
    athletes 265
    avoiding scams, overview 241–5
    described 15
    education/research 82
    finding/applying, overview 237–9
    military service 302
    National Health Service Corps 257
    NURSE Corps Scholarship Program 247
    Project GO (Global Officers) 82
    Reserve Officer Training Corps 300
    scholarship search tool, website 21
    study abroad programs 80
    tabulated *163*
Scholarships.com, website address 309
Scholastic Aptitude Tests (SAT)
    athletics scholarships 267
    college preparations 21
    described 34
"Searching For A College" (Omnigraphics) 61n
Segal AmeriCorps Education Award, overview 281–6
"Segal AmeriCorps Education Award" (CNCS) 281n
self-help aid, described 15

Serve America Act, described 25
Servicemembers Civil Relief Act (SCRA), limited interest rate 301
service organizations
    employment certification form 213
    extracurricular activities 31
    military service financial aid 302
SLA *see* Student Lending Analytics
SLM Corporation (Sallie Mae Bank), contact 308
SMART scholarship, described 84
South Carolina Commission on Higher Education (CHE), contact 324
South Dakota Board of Regents (SDBOR), contact 324
SSS *see* student support services
Stafford Loans
    costs and benefits 41
    described 196
standard repayment plan
    federal student loans 199
    Peace Corps 298
standardized tests
    financial and academic checklist 19
    overview 33–6
State Council of Higher Education for Virginia (SCHEV), contact 325
state education agencies (SEA), accreditation 69
statistics
    institutional grants 275
    school evaluation *70*
    tuition costs **46**
    yearly earnings **40**
Strengths Quest, described 6
Strong Interest Inventory, described 6
student aid
    federal loans 73
    Free Application for Federal Student Aid 85
    postsecondary eligibility 123
    see also federal student loans; financial aid
Student Aid Report (SAR)
    Expected Family Contribution (EFC) 155
    Free Application for Federal Student Aid 22
Student Financial Services Bureau (SFSB), contact 319
student loans
    budget 102
    education tax 228
    mandatory forbearances 206
    Peace Corps volunteers **291**

student loans, *continued*
  repayment, overview 203–7
  subsidized and unsubsidized 197
  see also federal student loans
student support services (SSS), described 271
study abroad
  choosing a college 75
  financial aid 151
  overview 79–88
  see also foreign education system
subsidized loans
  overview 195–7
  requesting forbearance 207
  tabulated *164*
"Subsidized And Unsubsidized Loans And Entrance
  Counseling" (Omnigraphics) 195n
Supplemental Security Income (SSI), Expected
  Family Contribution 157

T

"Taking College Preparatory Courses"
  (Omnigraphics) 25n
talent search program, described 271
tax benefits
  Coverdell education savings accounts 96
  529 plan investment 114
  Internal Revenue Service 68
  saving for college 99, 226
tax information, Expected Family
  Contribution 154
TEACH Grant *see* Teacher Education Assistance for
  College and Higher Education (TEACH) grant
  program
Teacher Education Assistance for College and Higher
  Education (TEACH) grant program
  Expected Family Contribution 153
  overview 179–83
  value 140
teachers
  choosing online courses 59
  college support team 14
  educational decisions 9
  forgiveness program 194
  TEACH Grant 140
technical schools
  AmeriCorps Education Award 281
  described 52
  religious denominations 49

Tennessee Student Assistance Corporation (TSAC),
  contact 324
testing programs, military service 299
tests
  admission requirements 69
  applying to schools 18
  qualifying work-related education 229
  standardized test, overview 33–6
Texas Guaranteed Student Loan Corporation
  (TGSLC), contact 312
Texas Higher Education Coordinating Board
  (THECB), contact 324
"Things To Consider" (ED) 67n
Treasury Department *see* U.S. Department of the
  Treasury
TRIO programs
  college prep schools 27
  described 270
trusts
  contributions 125
  described 130
  savings accounts 99
tuition
  college costs 43
  cost of attendance 151
  deductions 227
  educational assistance benefits 233
  federal student aid 139
  federal work-study 222
  graduate school benefits 293
  grants/student loans 166
  institutional aid 273
  nursing scholarship program 247
  refund policies 71
  saving for college 91
  savings plans 230
  statistics **46**
  value of education 39
  working during college 133
two-year college *see* community college
"Types Of Schools" (ED) 49n

U

undergraduate program
  standardized tests 33
  TEACH-Grant-eligible program 180
  see also GEAR UP
"Understanding College Costs" (ED) 43n

Uniform Gift to Minors Act (UGMA)
    custodial accounts 97, 129
    529 Plan investment 118
Uniform Transfer to Minors Act (UTMA)
    custodial accounts 97, 129
    529 Plan investment 118
United Negro College Fund (UNCF), contact 308
university
    Coverdell ESA 123
    federal student loans 189
    sports scholarships 266
    standardized tests 33
University of Guam (UOG), contact 327
University of Hawaii System (UH), contact 316
U.S. Department of Education (ED)
    contact 312
    publications
        choosing a college 67n
        college funding for disadvantaged
        students 269n
        college schoolcard 67n
        Federal Work-Study (FWS) program 221n
        funding for disabled students 269n
        study abroad 79n
        traditional college option 49n
        types of schools 49n
U.S. Department of Homeland Security (DHS)
    publication
        community college 49n
U.S. Department of State (DOS)
    publication
        studying abroad 79n
U.S. Department of the Treasury, loan funds 88
U.S. Department of Veterans Affairs (VA)
    publication
        education programs 299n
"U.S. Government Resources" (DOS) 79n
U.S. Securities and Exchange Commission (SEC)
    publication
        section 529 plans 113n
Utah Higher Education Assistance Authority
    (UHEAA), contact 325

V

"The Value Of Education" (Omnigraphics) 39n
Vermont Student Assistance Corporation (VSAC),
    contact 325
veteran
    education benefits, overview 299–303
    independent student 155
vocational school, Coverdell ESA 123
volunteer opportunities, college preparations 30

W

Washington Student Achievement Council (WSAC),
    contact 325
"Ways To Save For College" (Omnigraphics) 95n
West Virginia Higher Education Policy Commission
    (WVHEPC), contact 326
"What Colleges Contribute" (NCES) 273n
"What Is Community College?" (DHS) 49n
"Why Get A Federal Student Loan?" (ED) 189n
Wisconsin Higher Educational Aids Board (HEAB),
    contact 326
work experience
    interview benefits 135
    NHSC SP scholarship 263
work flexibility, study options 70
work-study funds
    financial aid for students 139
    see also Federal Work-Study
"Work-Study Jobs" (ED) 221n
"Working During College" (Omnigraphics) 133n
Wyoming Department of Education (WDE),
    contact 326

Y

youth schooling
    EFC 156
    Federal TRIO Programs 270